SAILING YEARS

K ADLARD COLES

SAILING YEARS

An Autobiography

John de Graff Inc.
1981

John de Graff, Inc.
Clinton Corners, NY 12514

Library of Congress Catalog Card Number: 80-71019
ISBN: 0 8286 0089 9
Printed in Great Britain

CONTENTS

LIST OF DRAWINGS

LIST OF PLATES

ACKNOWLEDGEMENTS

First, I thank my wife Mamie for the help and encouragement she has given me in the preparation of this book and for her forbearance while I have been engaged so long in its writing.

I am grateful to Commander Erroll Bruce who read the book in draft and made many useful suggestions. My thanks are also due to Mrs Barbara Clark for her typewriting, for dealing with my barely legible handwriting, and for her patience in retyping chapters, sometimes several times over.

Much of the chapter on the Bay of Biscay cruise was first published in the *Yachting World* and some of the material in the book first appeared in *Motor Boat and Yachting*. Most of all I wrote for *The Yachtsman* but, under different ownership, sadly the magazine had to be discontinued a number of years ago.

All the photographs are the author's, with the exception of plate 27, by Bermuda News Bureau; and plates 26 and 37, by Beken of Cowes.

FOREWORD

I was born in 1901 but did not start sailing until 1920 when a highly experienced and hard-sailing friend taught me dinghy sailing in Chichester Harbour, almost regardless of weather conditions. In the cruising which followed I was self-taught, though aided by books. In 1923, inspired by Erskine Childer's *Riddle of the Sands*, I made my first long cruise to the Frisian Islands and the Baltic in *Annette*, a 6-ton gaff rigged sloop, with two other undergraduates, taking my Cambridge degree by proxy. Arrival in Germany coincided with the crash of the mark where we certainly had some exciting experiences, rather too exciting at times.

I was exceptionally fortunate the following year in persuading my wife Mamie to marry me and we had a sailing honeymoon in the West Solent; she proved a real sailing wife, game for anything and became a very good helmswoman. The year after our marriage I heard that Arthur Ransome's yacht *Racundra* was for sale at Riga. We instantly decided to buy her and the moment terms had been agreed we took passage to Riga in the Wilson liner *Kolpino*. Then followed our voyage from Latvia to England, mostly visiting small out of the way harbours and anchorages, meeting interesting people wherever we went. This was our best cruise and a strenuous one for the two of us in a heavy displacement yacht (or ship as I called her) with a very small sail area and made virtually without an engine.

Navigation in these early cruises was by dead reckoning using compass, Walker's log and taking soundings by lead and line. There were no guard rails or safety precautions whatsoever. Weather forecasts were rarely available but we always had a barometer.

Mamie and I continued cruising together for most of our lives, in the Gulf of Finland and the Åland Islands in 1931 and 1938 and to France at the end of World War II, at a time when as yet many of the lights had not been re-established. All our cruises have been made in a spirit of adventure to find what lies beyond the next headland or island or over the horizon.

It was not until after the war that I took up ocean racing. I already had considerable experience in dinghy and round-the-buoy racing but I had always thought that ocean racing provided an ultimate test of boats, crews, navigation and racing skill. I started in 1947 and much to my surprise was lucky enough to win the Class III Points

Championship in *Cohoe* during my first year at the game, particularly as once one has done well it is easier to get good crews in future. I usually raced for the Royal Naval Sailing Association and cruised under the burgee of the Royal Cruising Club.

In my series of small ocean racers named *Cohoe* and *Cohoe II, III* and *IV* our successes were mostly won with strong crews in bad weather, which gave me the practical experience on which my book *Heavy Weather Sailing* was later based. These included the first ever RORC Trans-Atlantic race in which small class boats were eligible, Fastnet races, a race to Ireland in which only three boats completed the course, and a number across the Bay of Biscay to Spain, which were always good fun.

Strange as it may sound, ocean racing was the utmost help with the survey work for my pilot books. After the Dinard Race for example some of the crew members might have enough time to remain for cruising, or more frequently Mamie would join at St Malo for a short holiday visiting harbours before sailing the boat back with me to the Hamble River. Much more important in this respect were the long distance events in the Bay of Biscay when the offshore racing season ended somewhere on the French coast. Sometimes one or two of my crews had time to remain, or friends came with me to cruise home visiting as many harbours and anchorages as possible, always searching for new places. Often Mamie joined at La Rochelle or Benodet and sometimes our son Ross or daughter Arnaud sailed with us on minor voyages of exploration, including many to the seventy harbours and anchorages described in the two volumes of *Biscay Harbours and Anchorages* and fifty-six in *North Brittany Pilot*. Those were happy years indeed.

Turning now to more mundane matters. Being dedicated to sailing I chose my profession as a Chartered Accountant partly because it offered the best scope for sailing. It was one of my few sensible decisions as it provided me with a living for my wife and family, besides enabling me to work within easy reach of my base on the Hamble River.

It was not until after World War II that I took up whole-time maritime publishing in a difficult period when a great many of the new publishers came to grief. At that time I owned *The Yachtsman* magazine and later founded *The Yachtsman's Annual*. The book publishing business grew steadily over the years and the scope was widened to include books on ships. Publishing is a fascinating occupation but, even in a small company, the cash flow is slow so that considerable capital is needed in relation to size; when more was required I sold one of my other interests.

The story of my publishing career is told in two chapters of this book and certainly it was a strange one. Finally at the retiring age of 65 I founded a new concern jointly with Commander Erroll Bruce (my competitor in many ocean races) which we named the Nautical Publishing Company. This brought me into the strange position of finding myself in competition (happily friendly) with the company which bears my name and is publisher of two of my most successful books, as well as the present one. I have thus been founder or joint founder of what are probably the two leading yachting book publishers: Adlard Coles Ltd (now owned by Granada Publishing) and the Nautical Publishing Company Ltd (now owned by Macmillan and of which after retirement I remained consultant and honorary President).

Mamie and I moved to Lymington when the Nautical Publishing Company was founded and I continued active cruising, revising my pilot books in a good friend's boat until 1976, when I swallowed the anchor and the sailing years came to their conclusion. Since then I have only been sailing on paper, writing books. I made a detailed independent investigation with my son Ross into the Fastnet Race of 1979 for a new edition of my book *Heavy Weather Sailing* and then completed the present book in 1981.

Most of my sailing has been done on rocky coasts which do not seem to change a lot except in their buoyage but, for various reasons, there have been many alterations in the spelling of place names in the Baltic. When writing of Latvia and Estonia I have maintained the German spelling used in 1923 by Arthur Ransome in *Racundra's First Cruise*; on the other parts of the Baltic such as Finland, I have followed the spelling on the charts which I used when I was there. Times of day are expressed as a.m. and p.m. before World War II and in the 24 hour system afterwards. Barometer readings are given in inches of mercury pre-war and in millibars post-war.

On the personal side I write of many sailing friends, some of whom have inevitably since died, but I prefer to write of them as I knew them in active life.

KAC
March 1981

CHAPTER ONE

EARLY RECOLLECTIONS

As this is to be an autobiography, I shall start by giving a somewhat sketchy outline of my early life and how I came to take up sailing.

My forenames are Kaines Adlard, so I have not any ordinary christian names. Kaines was the name of my godfather, probably a Channel Islander, as there are rocks in the island bearing that name which I came to know later. Adlard was the surname of my grandfather on my mother's side, who was something of an 'empire builder'. He sheep farmed in New Zealand, and in Burma he secured concessions from the Government for his help in opening up virgin country. After retiring to England he eventually went to a hill station in India where he died. The Adlard family is stated to have escaped from France during the Revolution. Another surname that I should add is that of Ross, which was my grandmother's maiden name and later the christian name of our son.

I lost my parents at an early age and, after my mother's death when I was six years old, I was brought up by my grandmother and her second husband who was my guardian. My grandfather, a former staff colonel of the 9th Bombay Native Infantry (whose father had been in India in the 'John Company') had died long before I was born. He had not served during the Indian Mutiny, but was present as a subaltern later when rebels were shot out of the guns. Like so many in the Indian Army of his time he was somewhat of a character. For a bet he had crossed a river where the natives consigned their dead so that it was infested by crocodiles, which somehow he used as stepping stones, though the details are gone after all these years.

When I first came as a small boy to my grandmother's, she owned Kilravock, a large high square Georgian house, with a lodge, stables, a walled-in fruit garden and a large field. The house was situated on a hill off Ross Road, overlooking South Norwood to the Surrey Hills. It was said to be the Pondicherry Lodge of Sir Conan Doyle's book *The Sign of Four*. I do not remember much of it now, except for my schoolroom on the ground floor and the huge billiard room at the top of the house where there were big glass chandeliers. As a small boy I used to rush about the garden, living in an imaginary world of chivalry, with a cardboard shield embellished by a crest; but I must have been rather a grubby Knight of the Round Table as my activities led me among rhododendrons impregnated with the soot of London from northerly winds.

I received a Victorian upbringing. Most of my grandmother's relatives and friends were army, but there were also connections with the navy. One such was Emmie Patton whose father, Admiral Patton, had been one of Nelson's captains at Trafalgar, and there were also two admirals in the family.

My grandmother and guardian were wonderfully kind and affectionate, but this was coupled with the discipline and firmness of their generation. For instance, one afternoon at an early age I was taken to see General Maclean, a cousin probably twice removed, at his London club. I liked him immensely and he gave me a model gun which shot wooden shells, and came to be used extensively by me in the battles between toy soldiers and red indians on my schoolroom floor. But when we returned home I received a telling-off for not addressing him as 'Sir', a lesson I have remembered and not to my disadvantage.

Such breaches of etiquette were few and far between, and my grandmother and guardian spared no effort to make me happy. My guardian often took me to the Crystal Palace where there were figures of wild looking savages, armed with spears or blow pipes, coming from different parts of the distant world, while in the grounds there were huge concrete prehistoric monsters. I was also taken to see places of interest in London, including the Tower, the Zoo and Madame Tussaud's. On Guy Fawkes night I went with him to the bonfires and fireworks, and when I grew older he took me for walks at night so that he could teach me to recognise the principal stars and planets in the sky above.

Later came my schooldays. From early days it had been my ambition to enter the navy, so my grandmother sent me to Selwyn House, Broadstairs, which was something of a prep school for the naval cadet school at Osborne. My cousin, Hector Maclean, about 2 years my senior, was in the same dormitory but sadly he lost his life in service at Kronstadt shortly after the end of the World War I. I must have been an imaginative boy as, after lights-out in the dormitory, I used to tell stories about life under the sea. While my stories may or may not have been good, my singing was so bad that I had to be expelled from the singing classes as I put the other boys out of tune. I was delighted with this at the time, but in my later cruising and ocean racing life the lack of a sense of rhythm was a handicap in Radio Direction Finding signals.

In the winter term I got into the first soccer team, in which I was the youngest member, and played at left half. At that time there were many preparatory schools at Broadstairs; St Peter's was the leading school but we only played their second eleven, although we had the honour of having the then Duke of Gloucester's son on the touchline. However, my success on the football field was short-lived as next term the school changed over to rugger.

Easter term was a bitterly cold one and it was colder still hanging around being instructed in the new game. I developed Bright's disease of which the outward symptom was swelling of the face and legs. I remember being carried downstairs on a stretcher by the headmaster, Mr Price, and another master. I think I must have been taken home to Kilravock, for I remember a very happy Easter with as many presents as I would have received at a normal Christmas. What, of course, I did not know at the time was that Dr Batty Shaw, a leading specialist, had given me only six months to live;

but I never felt like departing this life as Bright's is not painful. The ailment is not, of course, particularly dangerous nowadays and is treated by antibiotics.

My next recollection is of Weymouth where I was sent to live with an uncle, who was a doctor, and my aunt and cousins. I had a trained nurse and the treatment was being wrapped in hot packs of blankets soaked in very hot water which were then wrung out; these did not hurt provided no water was left in the blanket before its application. I remember best the house and surgery on the front, close to the Gloucester Hotel; from my room upstairs I looked over Weymouth Bay. I forget how long I was confined to bed and my room, but eventually my health improved and I was allowed downstairs and gradually to lead a more active existence. I later went to Weymouth College as a day boy with my cousins, where I won the school chess championship while still in the junior house. I was not allowed to play games, but as I grew stronger I made long bicycle rides in the holidays to Osmington and along the lovely coast of Dorset. In the summer of 1914 I saw and knew by sight all the big yachts which were racing in Weymouth Bay; I bought *The Yachtsman* for two pence each week, little knowing that one day I would be the proprietor of the magazine. Then came the war and all the activity, with the town crowded with sailors from the fleet and soldiers in training, but boys could still buy coconut candy at 4 ounces a penny! I learnt a lot from my cousins as we were all keen on ships, the navy and model making, while I owe a great deal to my uncle for his medical skill. But on the whole Weymouth had not been a happy period; the illness set my school work back for a couple of years and I lost any skill that I had in games for a great deal longer.

When I became stronger I returned home to my grandmother and guardian, and to a period of happy recuperation with the Reverend Dand and his wife at Brockham, near Dorking. I had long walks almost every day and frequent bicycle expeditions over a large part of Surrey. I may have inherited some cycling stamina from my father who had the odd distinction of being a half-blue for bicycle racing when at Cambridge, but at the expense of severe head injuries incurred in an accident when he was racing.

If I remember rightly, Kilravock had been requisitioned by the army during World War I, so my grandmother and guardian had moved to a top flat close to All Saints Church in Upper Norwood. Anyway, it was there that we were living when it was arranged that I should go to Clayesmore, then a private school at Northwood Park, near Winchester, where the country air was expected further to improve my health. The headmaster, Alex Devine, known to us as 'Lex' out of his earshot, was a Greek educationalist who aimed at a wider education than was available at most schools, and to encourage boys to think for themselves. Manual work was one activity featured in the curriculum, so we kept the grounds in order and did all kinds of unusual activities such as tree felling. Lex was very much a cosmopolitan, so there were foreign boys from countries such as Roumania, Serbia, Montenegro and Mexico, as well as two Siamese princes. He was a popular headmaster who always smoked cigars, the scent of which gave us a timely warning that he was on the prowl. Most young schoolmasters were away in the war so at that time the work standard was not very high. In years to come Clayesmore became a public school and is well established at Iwerne Minster; it has been much enlarged and includes the Bower House for girls. It still retains a wider variety of interests and activities than most schools, following in the tradition of Alex Devine its founder.

What with the compulsory pre-breakfast dive into the swimming pool at Clayesmore which in winter had a thin film of ice on the water, and life at home with my grandmother, starting with the usual morning cold baths and exercises, I had quite a good training for ocean racing. Incidentally, Sir Francis Chichester likewise did regular morning exercises even afloat if possible.

I came to know Francis well (we were contemporaries, having both been born in September of the same year) when he and Blondie Hasler pioneered the first single-handed Transatlantic Race. Francis was a tremendous and outspoken character. In common with others I admired his sheer guts in voyages made in the face of grave and often painful illness.

He was game to the last; indeed, I received a postcard from him from the Royal Naval Hospital, Plymouth, in July 1972, suggesting 'If I get out of this I hope we can arrange a lunch à deux to celebrate your "gold".' He was referring to the Gold Medal of the Royal Institute of Navigation which, to my surprise and appreciation was awarded to me for 1971. Francis, as a great navigator both by sea and by air, had received the award himself some years earlier.

Returning now to minor matters in my youth during World War I, I remember bicycling out of morbid curiosity over large parts of the suburbs to find the damage left after Zeppelin raids. I also searched for health food shops where nut butter could be bought for the household, as fats were in short supply; my grandmother and guardian were vegetarians. An additional item in my home education was Pelmanism, as my grandmother had noticed that I was an unobservant boy. It was a useful course and I could do with a double dose of it today. Indoors, I had many interests in ships, postage stamps, chess and other games with my guardian (of which I shall say more anon) and model making. I spent many happy weeks in building a working model of a steam yacht some three feet long, powered by a reciprocating marine steam engine. The maiden voyage took place on a small shallow lake in a park; unfortunately something went wrong in the middle of the passage across, so I took off my shoes and socks and rolled up my trousers to wade in to the rescue, treading with my bare feet on numbers of dead worms, but the salvage operation was successful. I wrote an article about the construction of the model; this was accepted by *Junior Mechanics* and the fee of one pound four shillings provided my first literary emolument. It was soon followed by an article in *Chums* on *Waterline Model Ships* for which I was paid the princely (for a boy) sum of £2, equivalent to about £30 or more in modern money.

During summer holidays I occasionally stayed with relatives or school friends. I especially enjoyed visits to an aunt and uncle who lived at Bournemouth, and also had a bungalow at Sandbanks where I knew plenty of other children. From the bungalow one could look seaward across the Hook Sands to Old Harry Rocks. I remember in particular being confined to the house by a gale with rain pelting against the windows and rough seas breaking on the sands. It is always spell-binding to watch waves in onshore winds, but they are better on fairly steep shores off which they break and surge in angry lines, before retreating with the roar of the shingle sucked back until the next breaker arrives to repeat the process.

Sometimes my grandmother arranged for me to go to the seaside to stay with residents who took in boys and girls as paying guests when their parents were away, usually in India. These were quite happy establishments where I occupied my time by hiring boats, fishing and swimming, occasionally quite long distances as, for example, across Babbacombe Bay for a bet.

After the conclusion of hostilities, I had to think about the future. There was no longer any prospect of getting into the navy and the only alternative seemed to lie in engineering. I had been accepted for Cambridge University by Clare College, but there were no vacancies until 1920 as preference was rightly given to those returning from the war. So I had a year to fill and it was decided that I should go to the Crystal Palace School of Practical Engineering for the first year of the two-year course. The three terms were taken in draughtsmanship, pattern making and the machine room. I did reasonably well and left with the usual three diplomas; what was more significant for my future was that I met another student named Basil Rowe who was to introduce me to sailing.

CHAPTER TWO

LEARNING TO SAIL

It was at Cambridge that I learnt to sail. I spent part of the first summer vacation with Basil Rowe at Chidham on the west side of the Bosham channel in Chichester Harbour; there two ladies named the Misses Egan and their elderly father had a house where they took in paying guests in the summer. Basil Rowe and I hired a centre-board dinghy in which we sailed all over the harbour, taking sandwiches with us for lunch or tea. A favourite picnic place was Pilsey Island, which was little more than a deserted hump of sands at high water, but with a wide expanse to the south-west at low tide. With a light-draught dinghy we were able to sail behind Stocker's Sands as well as up all the channels and minor creeks. Basil was a first-rate instructor, who sailed every day regardless of weather and gave me the best possible initiation.

With the experience gained from him, I arranged a fortnight's single-handed sailing at Plymouth where I hired a dinghy. On another occasion I went to Brixham where, after making enquiries, I was lucky enough to get an introduction to Skipper Batho, owner of the large Brixham trawler *Carina* and regarded as one of the best skippers of his day. I sailed with him to the fishing grounds off the Scillies. Trawlers in those days had no auxiliary power other than a steam donkey engine to work the nets. Making a living from fishing was not easy, as there were so many wrecks left at the bottom after the war on which the trawls often became fouled. Skipper Batho allowed me to take as full a part in the work as my inexperience allowed and, when ashore, I stayed with him and his wife and son.

During the term time I got no sailing as I took up rowing to which I was a complete newcomer, whereas most of the best oars came from rowing schools such as Eton, Shrewsbury or Radley. Happily, my health had completely recovered by then and I succeeded in getting a place in the first Lent boat in my final year. We made four bumps and the members of the crew won their oars.

Coming now to the work side, which was less challenging than games, I was reading for the Mechanical Sciences tripos. At the end of the first year I took the qualifying examination, but only gained a third. At school I had been put in a special form for maths, but at University I found I was not up to the standard of men of higher ability from the big public schools, so I applied to my tutor who consented to a switching to an ordinary instead of an honours degree by taking Part I and Part II in engineering. I read economics in my final year at the time of John Maynard Keynes (later Lord Keynes). This was an easy subject for me, but no firsts were awarded in my year and I only took a second, plus voluntary subjects, one of which was unemployment, then, as now, a major economic problem.

I had a very happy three years at Clare, with no overburden of work such as might impair my sense of humour. Nowadays, the poor blighters have to work hard, as it is vitally necessary to aim at the highest possible degree in an intensely competitive world. However, I must mention one additional activity which did not exactly fit into the curriculum. I received a decidedly small allowance which, in addition to the term bills, had to cover expenses during the summer vacation, and unfortunately on one occasion I overspent this. My grandmother was firm about such matters as she wished me to learn to stand on my own feet financially, so I had to cast around for a temporary job, not easy in those times of unemployment. Interest in ships attracted me to an advertisement by the *Ship Compendium* for part-time advertisement salesmen, the pay being commission on results. The compendium was a kind of directory broken up into sections to cover almost every shipping requirement. I applied and was welcomed to the staff of salesmen. I lived independently at a cheap hotel and tramped around the City of London with a dummy of the compendium getting orders, while other undergraduates were enjoying sailing or other open air activities. I was tolerably successful as I genuinely believed in the value of the publication. The experience was invaluable to me later, because it gave me understanding and sympathy for 'reps' who face the rough and tumble in the front line of sales promotion.

When I attained the age of 21, I came into a modest sum of capital from my Adlard grandfather; enough to make me lazy, said an adviser, but not enough to buy a share in a business, which I did not want to do anyway. In the meantime, my grandmother had already lent me enough to buy a small yacht to start cruising. As already explained, she disapproved of me overspending my income, but buying a boat was another matter and she gave me every encouragement particularly in making the long cruises which were to follow.

My purchases were modest, first a double-ender named *Jessica* followed by *Lapwing*, an elderly 22ft cutter. I sailed these boats in Chichester Harbour, the Solent and as far as Poole. About a year or two later I acquired my first really good small yacht. She was *Annette* and I bought her from H L P Jolly, a friend of mine who was a civilian officer at the Ordnance Office at Southampton. By then I had made my sailing headquarters at Bursledon on the Hamble River. In the matter of cruising I was self-taught, most of my sailing being single handed and aided by books such as Francis B Cooke's *Single Handed Sailing*. Sailing by myself was a quick way of learning because, for example, I found if I dropped the anchor with 30 fathoms of chain in deep water in the English Channel, I had to pull it up again by myself and hence did not repeat the exercise too often.

Meanwhile, I had to think about my future. As my intention was to sail, I thought the best bet would be to become a solicitor somewhere near the Solent, but my grandmother felt sure I would never stick to what she called dusty tomes and offices. I think she hoped I would be able to enter the Sappers, for which my engineering degree provided a qualification. With their famous yacht *Ilex*, this regiment ranked high

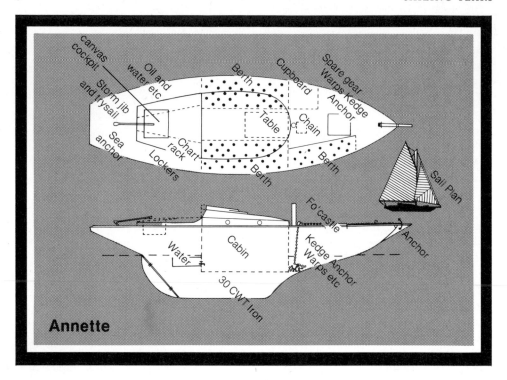

1. *Annette.*

LOA	26ft 6ins	Beam	9ft 2ins
LWL	19ft 2ins	Draught	4ft
Tons TM	6·7	Tons net	3·5

among the founders of the Royal Ocean Racing Club, and the tradition has been maintained to the present day as I was to discover in my ocean racing years, when I had the honour and pleasure of receiving the hospitality of the Royal Engineer Yacht Club at many of their annual dinners at Chatham. But I was not to know this at the time that I was thinking about my future occupation, so I consulted the very efficient Cambridge University appointments board. They recommended chartered accountancy, which they described as being a profession with a future, and which seemed to me just right, provided I was to enter articles and practise after qualification in a Solent seaport. I must have been one of the first to have chosen my profession to suit my sailing.

I am anticipating events. During my last term at Cambridge reading economics, I had plenty of time to plan and prepare for my first long distance cruise, for which I intended to take four months vacation before putting my nose to an office desk. My imagination had been fired by reading such books as the *Riddle of the Sands* and the *Falcon on the Baltic*. Places with strange names lent a sort of romantic attraction: 'Schiermonnikoog,' 'Memmert,' 'Als Sund.' Descriptions of the Frisian Islands with their windswept wastes of sand added to the allurement, and I saw, in imagination, the bleak German coast and the limpid waters of the Danish fiords.

The first things I had to obtain and familiarise myself with were charts of the North and Baltic seas, and also to learn a bit about navigation from a book on the subject. I was a member of the Cruising Association and had a copy of the club's invaluable handbook, then a small volume compared with what it is now. A good deal of advice was forthcoming from older cruising men of whom there were plenty at Bursledon. Some gave a measure of discouragement as they thought *Annette* was unsuitable since she was not of conventional cruising design; they were also aware of my comparative inexperience. The most helpful was the famous American yachtsman, Commander Paul Hammond, who had brought his lovely boat to Bursledon at the conclusion of an ocean race. He it was who advised me not to cross from Dover to France and follow up the coast and so across the mouths of the Schelde, but instead sail straight from Dover to Ymuiden in Holland, a distance of about 140 miles. Little did I then anticipate that one day I was to have the honour of receiving the Hammond Cup awarded annually by the Royal Naval Sailing Association.

I will now give a brief description of *Annette*, which had been built at Le Havre only three years before I owned her. Her planking was of softwood with iron fastenings and her construction condemned by everybody but, believe it or not, her present owner called at the Boat Show stand in 1978 and left a message for me that she had been renamed *Annette du Normandy* and was still afloat in good condition. Not bad for a boat originally costing £180, after a life of nearly 60 years. So much for the pundits of the time! As will be seen in the plan she had fairly long overhangs, being 26ft 6ins LOA and 19ft 2ins LWL, and had been designed for local racing in Le Havre estuary. The iron keel weighed 1½ tons, so she must have had a good ballast ratio. Sloop rigged, with roller reefing to mainsail and foresail, she carried an inordinate spread of canvas with a boom extending 3ft beyond her counter; but the feature of the design was the immense beam of no less than 9ft 2ins on a waterline of 19ft. She had 5ft 9ins headroom aft in the cabin, which had two berths with a table in the middle, and was roomy and comfortable, except when it was soaking wet. Forward there was a cot to starboard and stowage for warps and gear on the port side. As to equipment, there were no 'mod cons'. There was no doghouse or pramhood to protect the helmsman and no stanchions, lifelines or safety harness. In fact, there were no safety precautions of any kind; all the helmsman could do in rough weather was to hang on with one hand to a backstay or cleat. Equipment was meagre in the absence of winches, radio and all electronics. Navigation was entirely by dead reckoning (compass, Excelsior Log and lead and line for sounding) aided by the signposts of the sea in the shape of light vessels. However, we did not miss things that we never knew.

Undoubtedly a testing time lay before *Annette*, so I did my best to adapt her for the voyage. All the alterations were supervised by Moody's of Bursledon of which Mr Herbert and Mr Alfred Moody were then the heads. Both were great characters but, for some reason or other, Herbert Moody nearly always had a twinkle in his eye when dealing with me. The first thing was to cut two feet off the gaff and boom, the next to alter the big open cockpit, which was not self-draining. Mr Moody decided that it would be best to deck this right over above the coamings, except for a little canvas bucket in which the helmsman could put his feet. Entrance could only be effected by means of the forehatch or by lowering oneself down a small hatch aft into the cabin.

This led to amusing scenes when heavyweight visitors sometimes got stuck halfway with legs waving madly about in the cabin and arms in mid-air violently gesticulating for assistance. Tillings of Southampton made a set of new sails of lightly tanned flax (including a storm jib), and also arranged for the compass to be swung; there was no deviation as *Annette* had no engine, the most common cause of it. The 8ft pram dinghy was carried lashed down resting between the cabin top and the lee rail.

CHAPTER THREE

ANNETTE IN THE FRISIAN ISLANDS

I must now introduce my companions in the adventure who are most important, as even a good boat will get into trouble if she lacks an able crew.

We were all undergraduates at the start of the venture, although I took my degree by proxy before it ended. 'Buster', as we called him, was several years older than me. He had lost an eye and suffered leg injuries during World War I so was hampered in quick movements on the foredeck, but this disability did not prevent him steering and he took over the unpleasant job of cooking as well; he was also a tower of strength ashore. The other member of the crew was L W Dunsterville, who had some previous experience of sailing and was our interpreter as he could speak a little German. As it turned out, I was singularly fortunate in my crew as both were determined to make a success of the cruise and both were almost immune from seasickness.

On June 18th 1923, *Annette* was ready for sea and at 4.15 in the afternoon our voyage began, when we reached down Southampton Water with wind abeam to fetch Dover after some delay caused by a north-easterly blow between Beachy Head and Dungeness; the passage provided a useful shake-down enabling us to get to know the boat and each other. After breakfast ashore at Dover, I sent a reply-paid telegram to the Meteorological Office for a weather report; the answer arrived at 3 p.m. 'Moderate NW wind, mainly fine, but mist locally', so at 8 p.m. *Annette* glided out between the piers of Dover's east entrance with boom squared out before a light westerly wind. That was the real start of the voyage.

We were soon past the South Goodwin light-vessel and with a fair tide under us made the East Goodwin just before 10 p.m. The lights of Cape Grisnez, Calais and Dunkerque showed up in the distance and when we lit our new side lights we felt we were really at sea. The traffic up and down the Channel was thick, and after the Goodwins one or two steamers passed so close as to cause us considerable anxiety. The first light-vessel on the course was the Sandettié and the next one was the Noord Hinder, which we slowly passed at noon the following day, fanned on by a gentle westerly breeze in blazing sunshine. By 4 p.m. the glass had fallen two-tenths of an inch and the wind was freshening. During the night we put a two roll reef in the mainsail and made splendid progress, arriving off the Maas light-vessel at 2.30 next

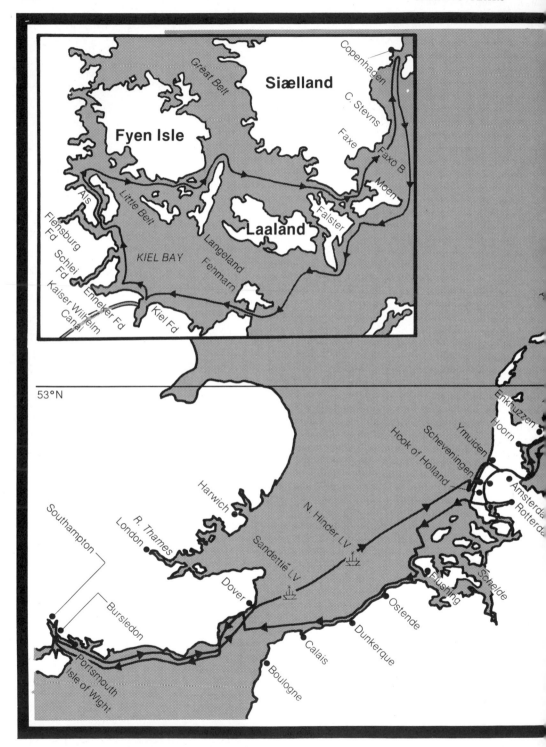

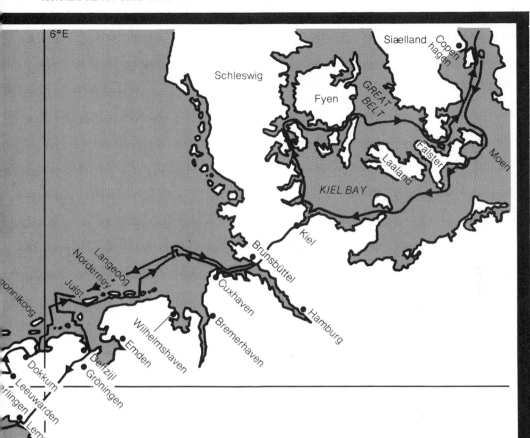

2. *North Sea–Denmark*. The cruise of *Annette* from Bursledon to Copenhagen and return, 1923

morning. By then it was blowing half a gale; we had to reef right down and a dirty sea was getting up.

Land ho! It was 7 a.m. and there it lay, a low grey streak on the starboard bow. As the yacht sailed nearer, occasional spires and towers appeared and I consulted the *North Sea Pilot* in a vain endeavour to identify the coast. We were bound for Ymuiden so we held our course and presently closed with a town off which we hailed a fishing vessel and gleaned the useful information that our navigation was correct for the town was Scheveningen. Ymuiden was about 25 miles to the north-north-east, and we did not fancy beating that distance against wind and tide, all the more so as the north wind was very cold, so we rounded and ran off south along the low coast for the Hook of Holland. The visibility was very poor in the rain, but the long breakwaters of the Hook proved easy to identify and at 10.30 a.m. we entered the harbour and brought up alongside a motor boat at Bergenshaven on the north side of the River Maas. Two friendly Dutchmen took our warps and gave us gin and cigars, which allowed us a rosier view of life and of our first arrival foreign.

From the Hook we sailed to Ymuiden and thence through the North Sea Canal to Amsterdam, where I engaged a pilot and, after negotiating the big locks, we entered the Zuider Zee. There we never tired of looking at the gaily decorated barges, very spick and span, very clean and polished, with curtains and flower-pots in the windows of the cabins. But what made us rub our eyes was a barge carrying an immense haystack amidships, the ends of which hung over each side of the hull. The haystack was as high as our mast, and completely obstructed the view from aft, so that a staging had been rigged on the stern for the helmsman to see over the top.

Having crossed the Zuider Zee (much of which has been reclaimed since then) we passed through the locks at Harlingen, and then through the canals of northern Friesland which follow the coastline a few miles inland. The North Sea was re-entered through the locks at Dokkum Siel which led to the tidal estuary of the Lauwer's Zee where, not understanding the Dutch method of marking the channel, we promptly ran

1. Barge on the Zuider Zee carrying an immense haystack amidships, with the ends hanging over each side of the hull.

aground on the top of a mud bank on an ebb tide. We went below for a cup of tea. Afterwards Dunsterville and I set out in the dinghy with chart, sounding line and binoculars to survey the channel and to find out the system of marking it. At low water Dunsterville and I jumped into the dinghy again and proceeded to dig a channel with the sculls and bucket through the soft mud leading to the deeper water when the tide rose. When all was done the boat and dinghy were both plastered with mud and so were our hands, feet and clothes. At about 11 p.m. she floated and after anchoring in the middle of the channel we retired to our bunks.

The wind remained west so, on the following morning, we got away at 8 a.m. and quickly reached down the channel. The channels were marked, on one side only, by withies with a bush at the top. When corners in the channel arrived, the last withie on one side had its top bush tied together to show that the withies would in future be on the other side of the channel. Having discovered this, we easily managed the navigation of these muddy waters—see chart page 17.

A long island appeared before us, low on the horizon. It was highest on the west where there was a tower and two beacons, and it gradually tapered away to sea level at the east.

It was Schiermonnikoog—a low upheaval of sand dunes some five miles long, which was really much nearer than it appeared, as the visibility was poor. The weather was fine, and it was very nearly high tide; just the time, in fact, for navigation behind the island, so we decided to take a short cut across the sands. We gybed and ran along a fairly well marked channel, leaving a row of withies on our port hand. It was none too easy to see these at high tide, since only the tops of the little bushes remained above water. Having come to the end of the withies, it was time to set a compass course and feel our way with lead and line across the sands. This we managed satisfactorily by constantly taking soundings, finding depths of water never less than five feet, which gave us a margin of safety of one foot. We then followed close along the south-eastern side of Schiermonnikoog until, after running aground twice, we got into a deep channel that appeared to lead to the open sea.

By that time the wind had fallen almost to a calm and the white sands, dazzling in the sun, looked very tempting. Down went the anchor and in a short time the dinghy was ready alongside. In the course of the day we had seen whiskered faces of seals suddenly appearing in the sea and staring at us. A few hard strokes with the sculls and we were ashore; having pulled the dinghy a short way up on the firm sand we set about exploring.

Schiermonnikoog is inhabited only at its western end; to the east, where we landed, it is a waste of sand dunes and sandy shores strewn with jetsam thrown up by the sea. As we walked along the shore we came close to an upturned barrel, behind which I thought I saw something move. I was not mistaken and, as I ran forward, it moved again. We had found a young seal, a friendly little fellow with beady eyes and long whiskers. The afternoon crept by whilst we bathed, lay in the sun, or played with the seal in a very juvenile way; it seemed hungry but refused the temptations of condensed milk and sardines. We remained in our anchorage under the lee of the land all night.

On the following day there was a lovely sunny morning but little wind, so we did not weigh anchor until mid-day when it freshened. We had to find a seegat (channel)

2. Author and baby seal at Schiermonnikoog.

3. *The Frisian Islands*. In the wake of the *Dulcibella*, *Annette* threaded the Frisians on her way to and from Copenhagen.

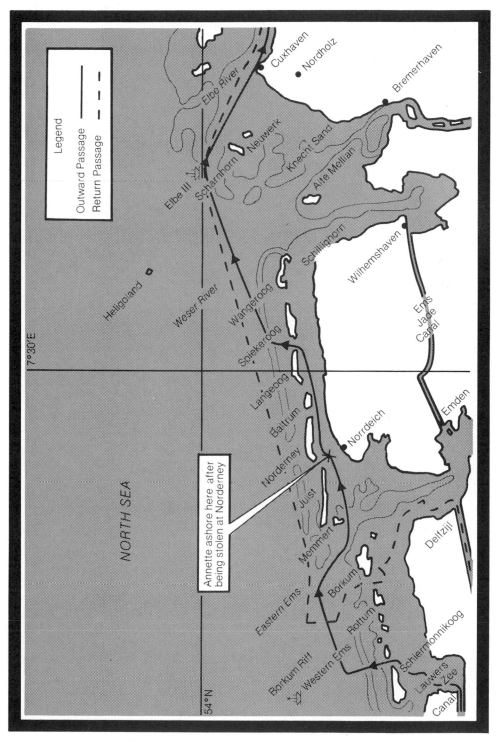

leading between the island and sandbanks further east, and between shoals to the open North Sea. The positions of the sands are always shifting, especially after gales, and the channel was narrow and unbuoyed. Charts, particularly small-scale ones, are, of course, useless for this kind of navigation, and one relies entirely on taking soundings and on the look of the water.

We could see where the channel lay approximately and, as it was a headwind, we lay on each tack until we sounded five feet – in practice not as easy as it might appear, for the channel was winding and the strong tide was not constant in direction, being deflected by shoals. Moreover, Schiermonnikoog was so extraordinarily low that, when a quarter-mile away, it was out of sight as the visibility was again poor. Happily, the lead began continually to record a fathom, neither more nor less, so we knew we were on the bar, but *Annette* was well out to sea before we sounded five fathoms.

The Frisian Islands, off which we were sailing, are like a string of long, mostly narrow beads strung five or more miles off the Dutch and German mainland. On their north side there are wide sands and shoal water extending far to seaward. Between the islands lie seegats, like the one we had just sailed through. The whole area between the islands and the mainland dries out at low water, exposing miles of sand and mud, except for the channels marked by withies. These are shallow at the watersheds, as described in *The Riddle of the Sands*, where the tide divides, ebbing to the west on one side and east on the other and running in the opposite direction during the flood.

Schiermonnikoog, which we had just left, is the most easterly of the Dutch islands – with the exception of a few sandbanks like Simon's Sand and the small oval island of Rottum, which is little more than a big sandbank. East of Rottum is Borkum, the first of the German islands, followed by Juist, Norderney, Baltrum, Langeoog, Spiekeroog and Wangeroog. Beyond Wangeroog lie the estuaries of the Jade, Weser and Elbe. These deep channels, leading respectively to Wilhelmshaven, Bremerhaven and Hamburg, are used by big ships and are well buoyed.

It was 1.30 p.m. by the time we reached deep water off Schiermonnikoog, and we were able to come on the port tack and set a course to the eastward. During the afternoon we passed to seaward of Rottum and Borkum and then picked up the outer buoys of the Eastern Ems. It was getting late by then so we freed our sheets and followed the well-marked deep channel between Borkum and Juist, until we passed Memmert, where we altered course and followed a shallow channel in the sands between the islands and the German mainland; it led eastward behind Juist until it became so dark that we could not see the buoys and had to let go the anchor.

Memmert is the island on which part of the plot of *The Riddle of the Sands* was centred. It is just a flat pancake of sand dunes, and we could not see any sign of habitation. Our anchorage was a lonely one. To the north-west was Memmert; three miles away to the north was Juist; the mainland, which here receded to the south, was about eight miles distant. At low water we were sheltered by the sandbanks, which dried out on either side of the channel, but when these were covered the yacht was in an exposed position.

We carried on next day behind Juist with little wind, but a hot tide. The channel, which is narrow and shallows progressively, soon became very involved. It was marked by withies on the north side, but we found these were sometimes difficult to spot, and not always in the right position. Twice we ran aground, so it was not until 2 p.m. that we covered the eight miles and let go anchor off the south-west corner of Norderney, under the lee of the island. I could appreciate the task which had faced Davies when he navigated the dinghy on a falling tide over the same ground, as he and Carruthers set out in the fog to solve Erskine Childers' riddle. It was proof positive that the Irishman had certainly been minutely over the ground.

café. Apparently there was no longer any urgency, and still less to contact the thieves or cut off their escape.

At 11.30 all was ready. The party was prepared for the fray and excitement was intense as we prepared to embark on the fast motor-boat. Our striking force consisted of the chief of police, a sergeant and two young constables, all armed with big revolvers. Next in command now appeared to be the pianist of the cabaret, who strutted about in a brightly coloured sweater. He, and of course, the Porpoise in his bright blue jumper made a colourful picture.

I wondered why we needed so many men to handle the motor-boat, but when we arrived at the quayside to embark I found out. The 'motor-boat' proved to be an old – very old – fishing vessel with antiquated sails and no trace whatever of a motor. It was a distinct setback after the romances spun about there being no chance of *Annette* escaping from the craft at the disposal of the police.

The fishing boat cast off and the police ordered us below, explaining that the thieves might recognise us. The others remained on deck, on the astonishing assumption that the thieves would see nothing odd in their appearance. We had about six miles to sail before coming to close quarters, but within a quarter of a mile of the harbour the fishing boat ran hard aground. The Porpoise explained it would have been all right if we had started half an hour earlier.

The big dinghy was pulled alongside and into it jumped the police, the Porpoise and the pianist. Before we realised what was happening they cast off and rowed away in the direction of Norddeich, leaving us and a couple of fishermen on the fishing boat.

The rest of the morning we spent drying out on the sands. There was neither water nor food on board, and the sun blazed down mercilessly on the hard hot deck where we tried to make up for lost sleep.

At 2.30 p.m. the tide had risen sufficiently to allow the fishing boat to sail back into harbour. Her total share in operations had been a quarter of a mile sail out of the harbour and a quarter of a mile back again. We spent the afternoon making various arrangements and fixing up at an hotel. We had, of course, only the clothes we stood up in, plus £2 and the Porpoise's million marks.

Late in the evening we received news that *Annette* had been recovered, and we walked down to the harbour where a crowd had gathered. After waiting a while, we saw *Annette* and presently she came alongside the wharf with a resounding crash. I elbowed my way through the crowd and went aboard.

The cabin was crowded with people. Everybody was talking at once, and high above the din I heard the Porpoise's voice raised in loud lament. He had been the first to board *Annette*, and had soiled his bright blue jumper. I gathered that the boat had been found deserted, and that the thieves had already made their escape over the sands at low water.

In the boat herself blankets, bread, papers, cups, clothes lay in confusion on the floorboards, all soaked through. The salvage party had drunk everything on board and eaten most of the provisions. I did not grudge them that, but I did object to the filthy mess they had made. However, the ship was safe and, wonder of wonders, my cash had not been found, although in the most obvious place of the lot!

Next day, we all met at the office of the chief of police. He fixed salvage at £16, to be paid to the skipper of the fishing boat. This in Germany was then equivalent in purchasing power to about £50 in England. During the interview it came out that the police thought the Porpoise to be my friend and representative. It appeared he had taken a place in the dinghy which should have been mine. The last I heard was that the fisherman was trying to make a claim against the Porpoise for trespassing on his ship! In retrospect I feel rather sorry for him as, after all, he had got things moving and lent me a million marks.

The thieves–two of them–left in their haste a lot of propaganda papers of the Militarist party, a hat, a German flag and eagle, a dagger and a book of addresses. They stole some clothes and my two cameras.

It appeared that, when *Annette* ran aground, the thieves waited until low water and then waded over the flats to the shore in full view of the land. One of them was wearing an English suit (Dunsterville's), and carrying on his back a large kitbag full of booty. Apparently they strolled like that through the little town of Norddeich, where the police were supposed to be on the look-out for them, and waited at the station for the next train. The papers they left identified them as being members of the powerful Ludendorff party. It was obvious that the motive was escape from the island rather than theft, and may be if they had been caught and arrested there might have been reprisals; certainly the police had made no great effort to stop them. We wondered who were the culprits and whether they were from the hostile ex-officers' café where we may accidentally have stepped into a hornet's nest of political intrigue. I have no recollection of the name of Hitler being spoken when *Annette* was at Norderney, as it was some 10 years before he came to power. I did not then know that General Ludendorff and Hitler had taken part in the unsuccessful Nazi rising at Munich in 1923, the very year when we were in German waters.

The days that followed were not exactly happy. We were pestered with officialdom and, to add to our troubles, a heatwave arrived from America and the temperature was overwhelming by day and by night. The harbour at Norderney was two miles from the front, where we had booked into an hotel, so two or three times a day I had to toil down a long dusty road. Everything in the boat had to be turned out and the inventory carefully checked, clothes washed, and the cabin dried and cleaned up. A new fore-hatch had to be made, as the thieves had heaved the original one overboard, just to add injury to insult.

Altogether it was an exceedingly trying time, and we got heartily sick of the business. Buster was the best of us in dealing with people and officials but, as I was skipper, most of the fuss fell on my shoulders; half Norderney seemed to want to see me for something or other connected with the police, the hotel, or the fitting out of *Annette*. We were, of course, quite at the mercy of the police, who not only held our money and our passports, but could at any time have tied us up in red tape and detained our ship.

The curious thing was that everybody in Norderney seemed to know how much money we had, and also how much we expected from England! When the cash eventually did arrive, we first heard of it from the hotel proprietor and not from the post office. Presently a postman arrived with a large bag and started counting out millions of marks. The manager had to swear to our identity and sign the receipt for the money on our behalf; this business took place in the private office, but soon the hotel buzzed with the news.

On July 15th we were free to leave, as we had recovered our money and papers which had been seized by the police. We were delighted with the prospect of getting clear of Norderney, though a sharp fall in the barometer indicated that the spell of fine weather was ending. We got under way in the afternoon. There was a light south-west wind and a strong tide which carried *Annette* round the western end of Norderney into the seegat leading to the bar, which is about a mile offshore. We experienced difficulty in keeping to the channel as the visibility was poor and was rapidly getting worse. About half a mile from the shore we heard the dull growl of breaking water and sounded bottom in one and a half fathoms. The sky was thickening and the shore out of sight. Suddenly, I saw breakers ahead, showing white through the haze, not only on the bow but to port and starboard as well. We seemed almost hemmed in, so I put *Annette* about and ran back, setting a compass course for the west end of the island. Then the fog came—thick. It was eerie work feeling our way back to Norderney. We were glad when we sighted one of the tall red spar buoys used in Germany, and the lead showed that we were in deeper water, and gladder still when a gap in the fog revealed the hotels of Norderney.

That night there was a heavy thunderstorm which broke up the weather completely. We were really lucky to be in harbour, and almost felt cheerful again as we listened to the wind in the rigging, the rumble of thunder, and felt the rain trickling down our necks through some of the numerous leaks round the edge of the cabin top.

Next day the high wind prevailed and it was too rough to put to sea outside the islands but, as the wind was north-west, we determined to continue sailing in *Riddle of the Sands* fashion behind the islands. Having cast off just before high water, we made splendid progress, scudding along under trysail and reefed jib. The channel was not difficult to follow and we passed south of Norderney and Baltrum, but the seas across the exposed seegats between the islands were steep and breaking, especially just west of Langeoog, where the boat at times was almost unmanageable. However, in the early afternoon, *Annette* arrived safely in a channel at the back of Langeoog, where we anchored. The position was somewhat exposed so we waited for low water and the protection of the dried-out sands, before Dunsterville and I set out on a foraging expedition to the island. It proved very difficult as in some parts we had to cross soft mud where there was a possibility of quicksands. We eventually got near the landing-stage and found our way to a little village where we bought provisions of a rather poor quality. The expedition took up the whole afternoon and we did not get back to *Annette* until sunset.

The next day, July 17th, we got under way at 10.30 a.m. and ran on behind Langeoog towards Spiekeroog. Navigation was similar to the previous day running along the inside channel, but it was much easier as the sea had moderated.

East of Langeoog, the wind died away and *Annette* was becalmed for a while, until a south-westerly breeze got up. This gave us a free wind out into the North Sea, through the wide seegat between Langeoog and Spiekeroog. Once outside, the boat headed eastwards, offshore of Spiekeroog and Wangeroog, the most easterly of the Frisian islands, where course was altered to the north-east to clear the vast areas of sand and shoals which in places extend over ten miles seaward, and lie between the deep estuaries of the Jade, Weser and the Elbe, where the *Dulcibella* was so nearly lured to her doom by Dollmann.

The distance from there to Elbe I lightship, the outer lightship, is about twenty miles; it was fortunate that the wind freshened when *Annette* passed the Jade whistle buoy, so that she sailed fast. The land lay to starboard, low and thus far out of sight, but navigation was quite easy as there were the outer fairway buoys of the big rivers by which to check our position. It was pleasant sailing, marred only by an accidental gybe.

The Elbe I lightship is far out at sea, as the sands here extend to their maximum distance from the German coast, ending in the Robben Flat and the Scharnhorn Reef. Three miles south-east of the former lay the West Hohenhorn Sand, which was the scene of the stranding of the *Dulcibella* so vividly and realistically described in *The Riddle of the Sands*. The first edition of Erskine Childer's famous book had been published only 20 years before we followed in these waters, and I did not observe any changes since he described them. The sands and channels remained just as lonely and unspoilt as in his time.

We duly sighted the lightship but, as the ebb had started, it took us a long time to run up the river. I say 'river' but to all appearances at high water it is open sea. The wind veered to west-north-west and steadily freshened.

The effect of wind against the ebb tide made quite a sea in the Elbe and our progress was so slow that it was dark long before we got to Cuxhaven where we let go anchor north of the town, as we did not like to try to find our way into the harbour and berth at night.

CHAPTER FIVE

CUXHAVEN TO COPENHAGEN

Next morning we weighed anchor off Cuxhaven on the first of the flood and made rapid progress up the river with the help of the strong tide and freshening wind. Although reefed we were really carrying too much sail, and a sudden squall brought things to a head, for we were near the edge of the channel and had to gybe, breaking the boom in doing so. Fortunately, we were able to edge across the river Elbe to Brunsbüt-tel under foresail alone, where we passed through the locks into the Kiel Canal. After an uneventful passage through the canal and, after clearing the locks at Holtenau, we sailed across Kiel Fiord to Heikendorf, a small cove on the east side. It was here that we found H L P Jolly, the old friend from whom I had bought *Annette*, who was fitting out his lovely 15-ton yawl *Ingrid* which had been built at the local boat yard. Having made *Annette* snug for the night, we joined Jolly and *Ingrid*'s crew and walked up the hill to a little inn overlooking the fiord, where we made a happy party of six for dinner.

We spent four days at Heikendorf whilst we had the necessary repairs done. A new boom was made, a new pump fitted, and I also ordered a new mast to be made, for which we would call on our return passage; the existing one was too light for the punishment it received in bad weather.

For some while the wound in Buster's leg had been giving him trouble, and it was not improved by the constant wetness of the cabin and the cramped conditions under which we were living. On talking it over, we agreed it would be better for him to return direct to England in *Ingrid*. Dunsterville was a strong and most able mate, so *Annette* could be handled by the two of us, though the work would be harder and we should miss Buster's good and uncomplaining company. We all had a farewell dinner at the inn, but we learnt later on our return to England that the passage in *Ingrid* proved to be a very short-handed one. The fitting out of the new boat at Heikendorf took far longer than anticipated and, when they eventually made Heligoland, they were weather-bound during severe gales of which we got a full share in the better sheltered waters of the Baltic. Holiday time ran out and, of the crew to man *Ingrid*, only Jolly and Buster were left to sail her to England, which they managed successfully when the weather improved.

Dunsterville and I got *Annette* under way from Heikendorf at 10.15 a.m. on

Tuesday, July 24th. We were bound for Copenhagen, a distance of about 250 miles, allowing for the roundabout way, cruising north along the coast of Jutland, and then across the Little and Great Belts and up the east coast of Sjælland. See chart pages 12–13. It was blowing a full gale and an experienced local yachtsman said the weather was unfit for sailing and we would soon be back in harbour. However, the wind was westerly and thus offshore, so that we should have some protection from the land. We shortened sail to trysail and reefed foresail, for which we soon had to substitute the storm jib. Even so, not only was the lee deck continually awash, but at times the boat was heeled so far that the cabin scuttles were under water, which was a lot for such a beamy vessel.

As soon as we got outside the shelter of Kiel Fiord we had to cross over some banks, and ran into a really dangerous breaking sea. I had imagined that this part of the Baltic would be comparatively smooth, as it was partly sheltered by the Schleswig and Jutland mainland and by islands, but I soon learned otherwise. The Baltic is comparatively fresh water and when it blows hard the waves are short, steep and confused. That day was one of the worst we experienced throughout the cruise, and I was in definite fear of damage forward as *Annette* slammed heavily into the cross seas, blinding us with spray. Things were so bad that we had to alter course and beat for shelter into Enneker Fiord. When, at length, we got under the lee of the land we found, in spite of constant pumping, that there was so much water in the cabin that the kettle floated like a toy duck in a bath. Everything had shifted – even the lamp on gimbals had overturned.

How different it all was in the fiord! Our anchorage was a delightful spot, with clean transparent water protected by low ragged cliffs, with a few houses in the background almost hidden amongst the trees.

Next day we ran down Enneker Fiord under trysail and storm jib. Although the wind was still of gale force, we were protected from the west by the mainland as we sailed north. Our progress with a beam wind and relatively calm water was splendid, and we averaged seven knots between the Schlei Fiord (which figures so much in the early part of *The Riddle of the Sands*) and Falshoft Head. By 1.15 p.m. however the wind had shifted to north-west by west, which was a headwind across the open entrance of Flensborg Fiord, which here is about ten miles wide. Once again we were thrashing to windward against the sea, and progress was so slow that we had enough of it by the time we made Sonderborg at 5 o'clock. We were very pleased with this, our first impression of a Danish town. Sonderborg nestles under the high ground at the edge of the sound which separates the Schleswig mainland from the island of Alsen and is spanned by a picturesque bridge. It faces across the water to the famous heights of Dybbol, which in 1864 the Danes gallantly defended against the onslaught of the victorious Prussians.

The following day it was fine but still blowing hard, and we started at 9.30. We blew our foghorns as a signal for the bridge across the sound to open, and then sailed out under reefed trysail and storm jib. The narrow channel of Als Sund is one of the most beautiful of the Danish sounds; it is bordered with reeds and hemmed in on each side by high ground and woods. After sailing along five miles in this glorious scenery, the charm of which was enhanced by the bright sunny morning, we anchored and spent the afternoon ashore under the pine trees. In the evening we were able to get under way again, but almost immediately ran aground.

For six hours we worked hard trying to get *Annette* off the sands and, whilst shifting ballast and heaving on the anchor chain, a thunderstorm passed, drenching us with rain and making things appear even more gloomy, for it was a wild sunset heavy with cloud, and even under the lee of the land the wind moaned with each strengthening gust. In the general excitement at nightfall the dinghy got adrift, and the wind rapidly carried her out into the fiord. Every moment blew her farther away, so I had to swim after her, and in my hurry got rather entangled with the long seaweed which grows to the surface. Fortunately, the water was not as cold as the night air and, after recovering the boat and dressing again, I felt all the better for the plunge. We continued work until midnight when, just as we were about to give up hope, we succeeded in heaving her off the sands, inch by inch, using brute force (we had laid the anchor a long distance off, and to the end of the warp we set up a six-part tackle; then we had both heaved for all we were worth).

We found in the Baltic that the wind often seems to moderate from about 4 to 9 o'clock, both morning and evening so, as it was blowing hard as ever the next day, I decided to wait until it might be expected to moderate a little. Accordingly, we started at 4.30 p.m. against a headwind which, on that particular day, did not drop until later. Backwards and forwards we tacked across Als Fiord, in cold driving spray. There was not a great sea, but the waves were steep and tumbled aboard, stopping our way. It took us five hours to make good ten miles, and we were wet through and miserably cold before we had sailed ten minutes. We had plenty of time, far too much in fact, to appreciate the scenery in which we were sailing; fields ripe with corn, dark woods running down to the low straggly cliffs and the little, homely Danish cottages. We anchored at 9.30 p.m. close to the shore under some trees.

I am told that summer in Denmark is usually fine, but we had nothing of the sort on our passage to Copenhagen. The weather was always squally and the wind usually extreme (a calm or a gale) and bitterly cold. Looking through the log I see numerous notes such as 'Hard squalls from NW.' 'Full gale of wind.' 'Rain and light E wind prevented further progress.' In spite of these conditions we both much enjoyed this part of the cruise. After our troubles in Germany we felt free in Denmark and were, moreover, in wonderful cruising waters, where the sea is so broken up by islands that, however bad the weather, it is usually possible to sail somewhere. We took full advantage of this.

Our passage took us across the Little Belt and eastward between Fyen and the little islands of Lyo and Avernake to Svendborg. The Sound provides a popular small boat anchorage, but it was blowing hard and raining so we only remained there for the night and the following morning when we went ashore to buy provisions. We left in the afternoon, when the wind had moderated a little. Time was getting short so we pressed on for Copenhagen as quickly as possible, passing to the north of Langeland where we anchored for a night and then sailed on south of Omoe. Over shallows the water was transparent, and it was exciting work watching the bed of the sea sometimes getting nearer and nearer, then sometimes farther and farther. There is no tide within the Baltic, but the wind can tend to bank up the water on the shores towards which it is blowing and reduce it elsewhere. Hence at times there can be strong currents in narrow channels and uncertainties about their depth.

Our most exciting passage was through the Ulvsund, which was so complicated with shoals that we had been advised to take a pilot. We reduced canvas in order to sail slowly and felt our way with the lead. The sound is in fact a sheltered strait which separates Sjælland from the islands of Laaland, Falster and Moen, which lie to the south. The luxuriant shores, and the little islands between which fishing boats and yachts wind their way, make the scene very beautiful on a fine day; but navigation was intricate as the sea bed is irregular and the channel was not then very clearly marked. The first part was not so difficult as there were plenty of beacons, but the last half had only a few leading marks and, as it was dusk, we could not see them until we were close up. I shortened sail and gave the helm to Dunsterville, and *Annette* drifted slowly forward whilst I stood forward watching the water. We sailed on our course wherever possible, but when I saw we were about to run aground I shouted and Dunsterville luffed until it was possible to carry on again. In this way we found a passage through the sands and boulders, and let go anchor at 9 p.m. under a lighthouse.

Next day, July 31st, was a great occasion for us as we arrived at Copenhagen. We left our anchorage at 4 a.m. and the wind was southerly so it was fair but, unfortunately, it was also light; so it was not until 2 p.m. that we found a temporary mooring outside the yacht harbour at Denmark's capital city.

3. *Annette* at Copenhagen alongside the gaff cutter *Tarpon II* from Finland. The picture shows our cockpit decked over except for a small canvas-covered foot well; also shown is the small hatchway.

It was raining in torrents, but calm, as we towed *Annette* with the dinghy into the yacht basin. This was small and completely protected from the roll set up by passing steamers in the outer harbour. Yachts berthed alongside each other, stem to a mooring and stern to the quay, where one could step ashore.

We remained at Copenhagen for five days and thoroughly enjoyed our visit. Both the Royal Danish Yacht Club and the Amateur Sailing Club extended their hospitality to us, and we had all our meals ashore at the clubs. We also visited the Tivoli, the famous amusement park so well-known to all tourists.

Copenhagen is a beautiful city, clean and clear-cut under the northern sky. Built on the edge of the Sound facing Sweden, it is a maritime town, but without any of the dirt and slums which are so often associated with great ports. We should have liked to stay there longer, but time was pressing and I was kept busy answering our mail and getting *Annette* ready for a rough passage homeward bound against the prevailing winds. I had the trysail cut down in size and wrote to Heikendorf saying I should shortly be putting in for them to step the new mast I had ordered.

We made our departure from Copenhagen on Sunday, August 5th, getting under way at noon. Starting in light winds we continued an enjoyable and interesting cruise in Danish waters which took us three and a half days to our former anchorage in the cove at Heikendorf in Kiel Fiord which we entered at midnight on August 8th. From the peace of Denmark we had arrived back in Germany at the time of the extreme crisis with the collapse of the mark.

Early next morning we were warped under the shipbuilder's crane, and our mast was lifted out. When it was carried ashore it was found that the new mast they had made for us was a foot short, so a delay of three days was incurred whilst they made another new one. Fortunately we had plenty to occupy our time, including passages to Kiel by the Fiord ferries.

The shops in Kiel were still open but nobody could buy anything. However, in the afternoon we had the help of a German ex-officer, Herr Schloe, who had returned from *Ingrid* when she was gale-bound at Heligoland. He could speak English fluently and managed to get a note changed for us through the friend of a friend of a friend in a bank. The printers had resumed work! As a result of this our shopping was a great success as prices were low and Schloe did all the bargaining for us. His help was also invaluable later when the day came to enter the Kiel Canal, where he saw to it that the charge for entering the huge locks was no more than sixpence at the correct rate of exchange.

CHAPTER SIX

RETURN FROM THE BALTIC

On August 12th, Sunday, our new mast had been stepped and we were ready to leave the Baltic. We sailed across Kiel Fiord to Holtenau locks at the east end of Kiel Canal. In the roads outside a considerable number of ships were lying, as there was a strike of pilots in the canal, and they were not allowed through without one on board, in addition to the pilot on the tug if being towed.

As a privilege to a foreign yacht, the Sluismaster gave us permission to go through the canal with the first convoy when, and if, it started. As no tugs were operating, we presently towed *Annette* by the dinghy through the huge locks and brought up alongside some barges berthed on the starboard hand. It was thought that the strike would be over next day when the convoy was due to start at 6 a.m. The morning arrived, but no tug, as the strike was still going on; a general strike throughout Germany threatened and the whole country seemed to be on the verge of revolution.

Happily, news came in the afternoon that the strike was settled. It was good news and true as it turned out. So at 6 a.m. on Tuesday we were awakened by the barge *Claus* getting ready and soon after that we were marshalled up, eight barges, two by two, and three small yachts tailing on astern. The passage through the canal was eventful as many pilots were still on strike, so by special concession a number of steamers were allowed through without pilots. Evidently something went wrong, as our convoy had to tie up in a siding while some twenty steamers of various nationalities bellowed at each other with their sirens. There were also other delays, but we eventually got into Brunsbüttel Locks at 8.30 p.m. I shall never forget the feeling of relief when *Annette* slid slowly out between the great slimy lock walls to the freedom of tidal waters.

Next morning we made sail at 7 a.m. There was very little wind but with the help of the strong tide we reached Cuxhaven. Bad weather delayed us for four days with very unsettled weather and two gales, one of which was severe.

We had almost given up hope of ever getting *Annette* back to England, when to our great delight August 20th brought with it fine weather. The barometer had risen to 30·3 and a nice breeze was blowing west-north-west. We got away at 7 a.m. with the first of the ebb to carry us down the Elbe, and to start with our progress was good, as there was a nice whole-sail breeze—although it was a headwind. However, it gradually fell off, and at about midday it gave place to a dead calm and the tide turned against us. We were near Elbe III, the inner lightship, and a big swell was running after the previous day's gale; but even that eased in the course of the day and enabled us to anchor out of the channel and slightly sheltered by the sands.

At 5 p.m. the flood tide had slackened and light airs helped us to get under way and drift north-west over the corner of the Scharnhorn, as part of the outlying sands was adequately covered.

In this way, with the tide gradually helping us along more and more, we slowly drifted until we were off the Elbe I, the outer lightship, at 9 p.m. The various lights could be seen very clearly to help our navigation; Roter Sand, Elbe I and the intensely powerful light of Heligoland in the distance. The wind had gradually backed to the south and freshened. I set a course for the Weser Lightship, which lies thirteen miles to the south-west, and gave the first watch of two hours to Dunsterville. Progress was splendid and at midnight we passed the light-vessel.

The good weather did not seem likely to last long, as the glass was falling again, whilst the wind freshened and temporarily veered slightly. *Annette* sailed fast to the west through the night, and when dawn came it revealed nothing but a desolate mass of broken grey waves with no land in sight. We sailed on close-hauled and reefed in the hard breeze. At 9 a.m. we spoke to a fishing boat whose crew understood English and they pointed out the direction of Norderney. Two hours later we made landfall and saw in the distance the houses on the island of Juist. The wind was south-south-west and blew hard, so it took us much of the day tacking for Rottum. See page 17.

This is a small, sandy, oval shaped island situated at the well-marked entrance of the Western Ems; it is the most easterly of the Dutch Frisian Islands facing the German island of Borkum. It was 6.30 p.m. when we worked into a pocket of adequately deep water on the east side of Rottum where we dropped the hook. The position was by no means secure, but I was influenced in my choice of anchorage by *The Riddle of the Sands*. In this book Davies explains how he used to anchor *Dulcibella* under the lee of any sands, reckoning that even when covered at high water they served as a kind of breakwater. I overlooked that the *Dulcibella* was an ex-lifeboat, and a centre-boarder of shallow draught equipped for the purpose with exceptionally heavy ground tackle.

Although we had only been 36 hours at sea we were very tired on arrival at Rottum. Had we known it we were soon to be more tired still, for at 4 o'clock the next morning we were awakened by the violent motion. It was blowing a westerly gale, and a severe gale at that. It was high water and we were plunging violently, with the tops of the waves breaking solid over the bows and streaming aft, where they came trickling into the cabin. The wind was screaming in the rigging and *Annette* was snubbing badly at her chain. The immediate and urgent necessity was to give her more chain, and I miserably donned oilskins preparing for a wetting. As I went on deck, two steep seas struck us and I clung to a runner for support.

Crash! Crash! and *Annette*'s bow suddenly paid off. I knew our cable (five-sixteenths inch and almost new) had parted, and we were being driven straight for the middle grounds only a quarter of a mile astern. It was useless setting sail, as there was no time to bend on the trysail and the roller mainsail required hoisting before it could be reefed. Moreover, it was questionable whether canvas would stand up to such weather.

It took some minutes getting the second anchor ready. I hurriedly bent on to it a new warp–thin, but good–and heaved it overboard. It held for a moment, but I knew eventually it must break. Dunsterville came on deck and the two of us managed to heave in a little and bend another warp to the end, making a total of 40 fathoms. Our weight in the bow made the seas break heavily aboard, and there was weight in the spray that drove over our heads. Dunsterville then volunteered to put a binding on the warp to prevent it fraying on the bobstay. He had to hang over the bows which, pinned down by his weight, simply cut through the waves instead of lifting, so that he was often under solid water and in danger of being swept off his precarious perch. When we came aft *Annette* rode more easily, and we remained in this unenviable position for four or five hours with the sea breaking on the sands now close astern–and only a two-inch warp between us and a watery grave on the middle ground. It was coir rope, which is not strong, but probably its great elasticity and its long length, coupled with the fact that it was brand new, saved it from breaking.

We were very wet and had nothing dry left on board to change into, and for some reason we were off our food. Altogether, we felt very depressed–at times cruising is anything but romantic.

When the ebb tide had run out we got under way for Delfzyl on the mainland to the south. We hoisted a reefed trysail and a corner of the jib, and under this we sailed splendidly with the strong beam wind. With the help of the young flood we must have made good eight knots over the bottom. The channel was well buoyed and protected from the west by sands which had by then dried out.

When in sight of Delfzyl we inadvertently passed a middle ground buoy on the wrong side and put *Annette* into the Emden channel, so that we had to beat back against wind and tide. We were in sheltered water but there was still a steep sea and a terrific wind, with spray up to the cross-trees as she threshed to windward. Suddenly the peak halyard lashing to the trysail halyard parted and the sail fell with a run. We soon lost all the ground we had gained as it took me some minutes bending the sail to the throat halyard and resetting it. Once again we slashed our way back to the wretched buoy that marked the division of the channel, and just as we were there we heard a tearing noise, and the reefed trysail split in two! I tried to get her into the right channel but the sail blew to ribbons and down we went, straight for the middle ground sands.

We worked feverishly to get some canvas up in time. The mainsail was in tyers and the peak halyard right up aloft. Dunsterville took his knife and cut the trysail adrift and cut the mainsail tyers, whilst I swarmed up the mast to recover the halyard.

By the time things were in order we had drifted right across the middle grounds–by sheer luck we had not touched. We hoisted the peak of the mainsail and reefed it as best we could; the sail was new and made of heavy flax. It stood up to the gale, and within an hour we were lying safely to our kedge anchor off Delfzyl.

During the night a succession of thunderstorms passed, bringing with them hard squalls of wind and pelting rain. Our original plan had been to make a bold bid for it and get across to England, but the next morning the fresh westerly headwind continued and things looked so unpromising that we decided to go through Holland again by canal.

Having arrived at this decision, we sailed round into the harbour at Delfzyl and tied up alongside a barge; her two seamen spoke English fluently and we were very glad of their help. One of them accompanied me to the Customs, bought provisions and procured us a new anchor of about 30 pounds weight for a modest price. The seamen also arranged for *Annette* to be towed in company with barges to the Zuider Zee for three pounds and helped us through the locks.

At daybreak we tied up to a large barge, as instructed, and then the barge and yacht were towed by a motor tug along an uninteresting canal for the 20 miles to Groningen, which proved to be something of a Clapham Junction of canals, although a picturesque one. Here we were cast off and we warped *Annette* through the locks and along a canal to *Ems II*, a powerful steam tug which was to tow us to Lemmer in the Zuider Zee. We set off at 6.30 p.m. the same day behind eight big brightly coloured barges, and the tow took three days, tying up each night alongside the canal bank. Every day it blew hard from the west with strong winds and rain, so we were glad of our decision to use the canals as progress outside would have been impossible. On Sunday no towing was done, but the following day the route took us through the Friesland Meres which are pretty and somewhat akin to the Norfolk Broads.

On August 29th we passed through the *Sluis* at Lemmer, where a storm cone was hoisted, into the Zuider Zee, and we set sail once more. Needless to say there was a headwind, so we decided to make for Enkhuisen on the western shore on one tack and then south to Hoorn on the next. The wind was light and variable so we were not off Enkhuisen until the afternoon. Later the wind fell and backed to the south-east accompanied by a sharp fall in the barometer. The weather looked threatening and, sure enough, it was blowing a gale before we arrived at Hoorn, which we eventually made at 6 p.m. running in under bare pole. During the night there was an exceptionally severe gale which continued all the next day. We were told later that things had been so bad in the North Sea that a German steamer had gone down near Ymuiden (only 25 statute miles SW of Hoorn) in deep water simply through the stress of weather, with the loss of forty hands.

The weather continuing bad, we spent the next day ashore. Hoorn was termed the 'Queen of the Zuider Zee' and, with its old houses and its spires, is very picturesque but so also is Enkhuisen, which looks lovely when it is approached from the sea. Leaving Hoorn at 4 a.m. the following morning we managed to get to Amsterdam by 2 o'clock in the afternoon despite a light and variable wind which continually headed us. We suddenly remembered that it was Jubilee Day; Queen Wilhelmina of Holland herself was evidently present when we passed the Royal Netherlands Yacht Club as flags were flying, bands were playing and the club crowded with people. Two big gigs lay alongside the entrance with oars raised at the salute. It made a brilliant scene under the August sun.

After passing Amsterdam we continued sailing in the North Sea Canal for Ymuiden. This, as usual, was full of shipping and, as there was a headwind, we had to tack across the canal in the path of the shipping. Near Zaandam Bridge I made a silly mistake. I tried to cross the bows of a tug with only 100 yards between us; the wind was light and at the critical moment the wind died on us, so it was difficult to get *Annette* onto the other tack. The tug missed colliding with us but it was a closer shave with the cargo ship she was towing. I was only just in time to pull the dinghy in to avoid it being struck. From almost end-on the ship's bows looked like a wall of steel rushing at us.

We continued beating westwards in the canal until 9 p.m. we brought up 5 miles short of Ymuiden. When we arrived there next day we found our mail and we bought provisions; by noon the wind had freshened from west by south, which meant a headwind along the coast outside, so I decided to go through the canal to Haarlem and thence to Rotterdam and down the Maas to the Hook of Holland. So we ran back along North Sea Canal and found the canal to Haarlem, arriving too late for the bridges spanning the canal to open as it was Sunday. Haarlem is a beautiful town and on the morrow we continued in the canals, sailing when we could or towing *Annette* by the dinghy when we had light headwinds. We obtained tows when possible. The best of these was when we managed to arrange a pluck from a big motor milk barge with an English-speaking skipper from Delft to Rotterdam for four guilders, which was well under a pound. The skipper was in a hurry and it was soon dark. It was exciting steering *Annette* in the black night, as she tried to sheer wildly about at a good 7 knots in the tug's wake. At headlong speed we raced past factories, streets and houses. I tried to divide my attention between avoiding other ships (not always easy to see) and looking at the shore, where Jubilee celebrations were still in progress. A great gas works loomed up to starboard, with an orange-tinted fountain playing in the fore-ground. Fireworks were being let off, and the banks were crowded with cheering, singing people. We passed a bridge, over which trams were passing, barely slowing at all and only at the last moment did the bridge fling open its span to let us through.

On we went, and then we were whipped along a quiet part, where the canal was flanked on one side by the backs of houses and by a hedge on the other. We were now approaching Rotterdam, and our bewildering rush was at an end. We were ignominiously cast off, as a big bridge would not open to our high mast, but the motor barge could get under it as she had neither mast nor funnel. We were near the *Sluis*, the skipper explained, and would be able to proceed early on the morrow. In this he was unduly optimistic as we were soon to learn next day. The canal by which we had entered Rotterdam is very rarely used by ships with fixed masts. The canal and bridge is usually opened only at certain hours when two or more ships with high masts are waiting. It was only out of courtesy to a British yacht that the bridge was opened for the diminutive *Annette*, holding up all the road traffic on a principal thoroughfare.

With our usual luck, we met a fresh south-west headwind by the time we sailed down the Maas on the ebb to the Hook of Holland. The bobstay tore the bolt out of the stem shortly before we tied up in our old berth in the harbour. We might have lost the bowsprit too, but for it being a very short one. The Hook was one of the best harbours in Holland; it was clean and quiet—a great relief after the canals.

It was not until Thursday, September 6th, that at last we really did get to sea; it was 6.30 a.m., with a nice north-west wind. The swell was still in evidence but, no sooner were we clear of the moles, than *Annette* was almost becalmed and the wind backed. However, we kept on tacking all day and throughout the night until at dawn we were off the Schouwen light-vessel, having made good only some 25 miles despite the wind having freshened. In the morning we had to reef and set a course to what I think must have been the West Banjaard buoy, because we experienced a vile sea as we felt our way with lead and line over the shoal to the south of it (by strange coincidence while rewriting this I have just found the long-lost large scale Blueblack Chart of 1921 which I was using at the time). We then set a course across the mouth of the East Schelde for Walcheren, the most westerly of the Dutch islands, but on passage the new bolt I had fitted to the bobstay broke loose, so we had to close reef to avoid risk on the lee shore. However, all went well and we cleared Walcheren safely and squared off to Flushing where we passed through the locks into the inner harbour. After a good meal ashore we put our clothes out to dry and turned in early, hoping to start again at midnight. I think we must have overslept as we did not get away until early next morning on the ebb, when to our delight we found the wind had gone round to the east. It was very light but the tide carried us past Zeebrugge and enabled us to creep into Ostende by 10 a.m. This is an attractive spot on a fine September day and we were tempted to stay there a while. But weather is a moody thing, and if scorned when fair it is apt to repay the offender with gales and rain. So, after washing and shaving and another good meal at a restaurant ashore, we sailed away with the tide at 3.30 p.m. and after passing Dunkerque we worked out seawards over the shoals. We sailed through the night and at 5 a.m. found ourselves becalmed off Dover in the sun of a perfect day. When eventually we arrived in the harbour the Customs visited us and gave us 'practique'. The cruise back to Southampton was made in a leisurely way without any incidents and we finished the voyage with a fair wind, arriving at 10 a.m. on September 16th, some three months after our departure.

4. *Annette* with cockpit restored after return from the Baltic.

The voyage was ended. I calculated at the time that *Annette* had sailed about 2,000 miles, but I expect this included the periods when we had been under tow in the Dutch canals and the Kiel Canal.

It had been a hard voyage, and at times a wet one owing to the exceptionally bad weather; but we had enjoyed it. We had sailed 'foreign' in strange waters, visiting countries new to us, meeting interesting people and widening our experience by almost a surfeit of adventures during a critical summer in the history of Germany.

Above all, aided by a good ration of beginners' luck, we had accomplished what we had set out to do.

CHAPTER SEVEN

A SAILING WIFE

This short chapter starts with wedding bells and also explains how I came to reconcile my profession with my sailing as planned.

I had first met my future wife, Mamie, when she came with her parents, Sir Robert Clegg KCIE and Lady Clegg, who had taken the flat below us in Upper Norwood for six months in 1919 on their return from India after World War I. When their tenancy of the flat was over they moved to the Isle of Man, then to Jersey and finally back to the Isle of Man where, during the war years, Mamie had lived an outdoor life during her school holidays and had become something of a tomboy.

After our first meeting at the Norwood flat, I had kept in touch, but it was not until she went to the Slade School of Art and lived in London during term-time, that I was able to visit her often. Even so, it seemed to me a long time before she agreed to marry me and we went to the Army and Navy Stores (of which my grandmother had been a founder member) to buy an engagement ring.

Mamie's parents gave their consent to the engagement but, not surprisingly, recommended deferring marriage until I had qualified in my profession. However, I could not wait as long as two years for fear of her changing her mind in the meantime. Hence, we married in April 1924 at the then exceptionally early age of 22 years. The wedding took place at St Paul's Church, Brentford, where the Rev. R B Dand (with whom I had stayed at Brockham) was then vicar; he and Mrs Dand made all the arrangements and were kindness itself. The wedding was very happy and informal as neither Mamie nor I wanted a large one. Only Mamie's parents and her former headmistress (who had connived at our romance), my grandmother and guardian and a few close friends were present. After the ceremony we ran hand-in-hand like children from the church to the vicarage, where there was a small reception.

It was proposed to spend our honeymoon at the Pier Hotel (since renamed the George Hotel) at Yarmouth in the Isle of Wight, and to sail over in *Annette*. We had taken a flat at Southampton but, as it had not as yet been furnished, Mamie had to bring all her worldly possessions with her in a heavy trunk. *Annette* was lying off the Royal pier at Southampton and I brought her alongside the steps. The deck over the cockpit, built for the Baltic cruise, had been removed so there appeared to be plenty of room. Assisted by the taxi driver and the pier master, we managed to get the trunk into the cockpit without dropping it on our toes or into the sea. But it proved too big to get below into the cabin. Happily it left just enough room in the cockpit for steering but, as the weather was fine, we put into Newtown, my favourite harbour in the Solent, where we enjoyed the tranquility of the river threading its way through marshes tenanted by countless sea birds. As we had few provisions we went next day by dinghy to the quay by the old saltings in Shalfleet Lake and followed the path along the creek to the village where there was a shop. Another delightful walk was up the coastal path leading to Upper Hamstead, passing a profusion of primroses and violets on the way. There was only one other yacht on the river and she was not in commission, but we made acquaintance with the Misses Gibson, known to all visiting yachtsmen at the time, who often passed *Annette* in their West Wight Scow sailing dinghies. After two days we sailed on to Yarmouth, where the trunk was duly transferred to the hotel.

When we completed our holiday, we set up house in the Southampton flat which was a pleasant one, but we did not stay there long and moved to a bungalow at Hamble facing Luke's Upper Yard, which is now Port Hamble.

As originally planned, I had taken articles with a Chartered Accountant 'near a Solent seaport', namely at Southampton, about a year before we married. For graduates the period under articles was then three years, so the training for the profession was fairly strenuous; one worked a 5½-day week in the office and did the preparation for examinations in 'spare time' at home by means of a correspondence course with

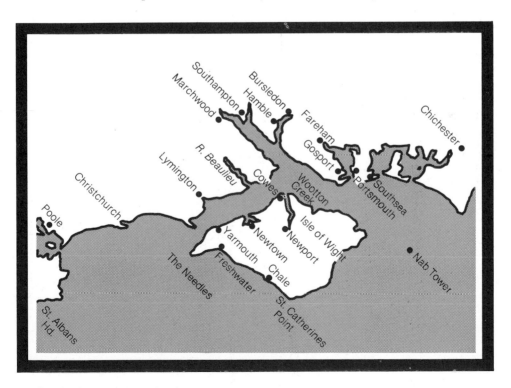

4. *The Isle of Wight.* The author's home waters.

Foulkes Lynch Ltd. Three weeks' extra leave was granted for preparation (not for sailing) before examinations. I found the first half of my period under articles rather tedious at times as it was mainly clerical work, but the second half was much better. The effort and swotting for examinations proved well worthwhile for, after qualifying, I liked the profession in a provincial town, finding it very interesting as its scope was so varied. The work ranges from the birth of a business, throughout its life and sometimes, alas, being called in at its demise. It is a human occupation as, perhaps unfortunately, money (including taxation) affects the lives of so many people in so many different ways.

I myself was in practice for some fifteen years and, even when I retired and took up magazine and book publishing, it was my previous experience in accountancy and knowledge of taxation that enabled me to avoid some of the pitfalls into which so many of the 'new' publishers fell when they started after the war.

Returning to my narrative, I took and passed the Intermediate Examination in 1925, after which my wife and I set out on the long cruise described in the next chapters.

5. A sailing wife with her large trunk.

CHAPTER EIGHT

ARRIVAL AT RIGA

It was in 1925 that H L P Jolly, the friend from whom I had bought *Annette*, pointed out an advertisement in the magazine *Yachting Monthly* by Arthur Ransome offering for sale his ketch *Racundra*, then laid up at Riga in Latvia. To buy her and sail her to England offered the chance of a lifetime: a really wonderful cruise for the most part in waters unknown other than to local yachtsmen.

I wrote to Arthur Ransome immediately, but it was not until we had nearly given up hope that, one day early in July, an envelope arrived bearing a stamp that immediately drew our attention. It was from Ransome in Latvia explaining that he had only just received my letter, which had pursued him from various addresses while he had been away. His letter enclosed the particulars I had requested. Terms were quickly settled and, to avoid confusion with Ransome's *Racundra's First Cruise*, I agreed not to mention the name *Racundra* in my own proposed book on the cruise from Riga to England with my wife. In compliance with this arrangement, I called my own book *Close Hauled*, now over 50 years out of print, and for *Racundra* I adopted the temporary pseudonym of *Annette II*, a somewhat ridiculous name for a heavy displacement yacht designed and built in the Baltic. Strangely enough, the true identity of *Annette II* was not generally known until 30 years later, when the distinguished American author, the late Alfred Loomis, made the discovery by comparing the photographs in the two books and reporting his findings in the US magazine *Yachting*, since when the secret was a secret no longer. Curiously enough, while writing this chapter and searching for photographs, I discovered Ransome's letters to me. Reading them now, I am amazed at the infinite pains he took in advising me on every detail for the fitting-out of *Racundra*, together with personal introductions to all that could help us on arrival at Riga. Ransome, then a powerful man of about 40 years of age, was correspondent for the *Manchester Guardian* and probably had more experience of Russia at the time of the revolution and of neighbouring countries than any then living Englishman. He was one of the most remarkable men I have had the privilege of meeting. His life story is given in his *Autobiography with a Prologue and Epilogue* by Rupert Hart-Davis, published by Jonathan Cape.

After buying *Racundra* my wife and I hastened to book a cabin in the freighter *Kolpino*, which gave us an uneventful but enjoyable six day voyage entering Riga on

July 22nd, after calls at Danzig and Libau on the way. After arrival, it was not long before we were lodged in a 'taximeter' with luggage piled high over our legs, which dashed along the cobbled streets, overtaking a number of the national vehicle of the time, the drosky. These were low one-horse open cabs, and the only objection to them was that the drivers seized every opportunity to whip or worry their horses.

On arrival at the Petrograd Hotel, which Ransome had recommended as the best in Riga, we were met by the head porter, a man of such striking appearance that we labelled him unhesitatingly as 'The Archduke'. He conducted us to a magnificent suite of rooms on the first floor, but we indicated that the price was too high. Disappointedly he beckoned us up another flight of stairs, where he offered us a slightly smaller set of rooms. These were cheap enough, but as we would be working on the yacht during the day, we asked whether he had not simply a large room. Passively he conducted us to a very nice large room at six lats a day. Now, as twenty-five lats corresponded to an English pound, this amounted roughly to five shillings—half-a-crown each per day for the best hotel in Riga. We accepted and even now remember a remarkable dinner there when the waiter persuaded us to have salmon, fresh-caught in the Dvina River, then boiled and afterwards fried. It imparted a most inviting smell as the knife cut through the bright bread crumbs and exposed the delicate pink colour of the fish itself.

The hotel was built when the Balt Germans were the greatest power in the city. The rooms were high and the furniture massive; even the doors were of flat, thick, solid timber, which were closed by great hand-made keys that clattered in the locks and echoed down the dark passages. Large fireplaces enclosed in brick, looking like miniature furnaces, were built up in each room, and they reminded us that Riga is under snow for half the year. Facing the window of our room was the 'Schloss', a large cream-coloured building, built originally by a semi-religious, semi-adventurous order of German colonists in the year 1230, but later captured and rebuilt by the Swedes. There was an air of romance about Riga which is one of the most historic cities of Northern Europe, and has seen many nations and many wars. From the narrow main streets one suddenly turns into even narrower cobbled side streets where old, almost decaying houses face each other. There was a smell about the whole place, strange, not unpleasant, and peculiar to Riga. When we were there the three powers which counted most were the Balt Germans who made Riga and the wealth of the city, the Letts who were the natives of the country and took advantage of the Treaty of Versailles to declare their independence, and the Russians whose influence was never far away with their army only separated by a nominal boundary. Sadly, the freedom of the Letts was not to last many years because the Russians reoccupied the country during World War II.

Our first requirement at Riga was to visit a bank to get some Latvian money, of which there were two currencies, roubles and lats. This done, we hailed a drosky to take us to the Riga Yacht Club in the Sportverein Kaiserwald, which was an extensive park, split up by wide shady avenues, situated about 10 miles from the city. After delays due to language difficulties, we arrived safely near our destination. Ahead of us lay a streak of blue which we guessed must be the Stintsee. It looked like a lake with reeds at its edges, but was connected to the River Dvina by a narrow channel called the

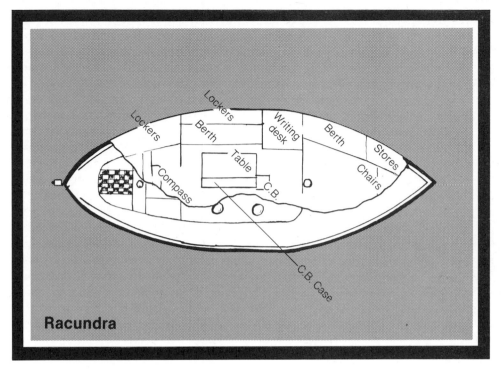

Racundra

5. *Racundra.*
    LOA   29ft 7ins   Beam   11ft 4ins
    LWL   28ft 9ins   Draught   3ft 9ins/7ft 9ins

Muhlgraben. A young German, who spoke English fluently, directed us to the yacht club where *Racundra* was laid up in a shed, so it was with considerable excitement that we hastened forward to make our first acquaintance with the ship of which we had heard so much, and which was to carry us to England.

From the description of her in *Racundra's First Cruise* she was quite unmistakable: bluff-bowed, beamy, strongly-built and with a typical Scandinavian pointed stern. She looked what she was, a powerful little ship which had been designed by Otto Eggers for long distance cruising. Her dimensions were 29ft 7ins in overall length, tremendous beam of 11ft 4ins with a draught of 3ft 9ins, or 7ft 9ins with centre-board down, and she had an iron keel of $3\frac{1}{2}$ tons. Her ground tackle was exceptionally good, consisting of a 70lbs bower anchor with 45 fathoms of $\frac{7}{16}$in chain and a second anchor of 50lbs with a shorter length of lighter chain. The barrel of the capstan was smooth and slippery, so it could not be used for chain although it was all right with rope aided by several turns. My method of weighing the heavy anchor and chain was to sit on the deck with my feet against the samson post. Then, as a former rowing man, I used my highly developed back muscles, leaving my arms merely as links between my body and my hands that gripped the chain. Finally, when the anchor came in sight of the stemhead, the last length of chain and the anchor had to be lifted aboard by brute force.

Auxiliary power was provided by a 5 h.p. hot bulb paraffin engine. This was small for her displacement and, in the absence of cartridges, had to be started by means of a blowlamp. Ransome had had no trouble with it during the previous year.

A ladder was brought for us and we climbed up to *Racundra*'s deck and down a few steps, past large cupboards and lockers, then through a small opening into the cabin. Cabin, perhaps, is not the right word; for the pride of *Racundra* should rather be termed a room. It was possible to walk about, stretch one's arms, to dress and to think without restraint. In short, she was everything Ransome said she was, while many improvements and much new equipment had been added since he wrote his book.

We saw Captain Sehmel, to whom we had been given an introduction by Arthur Ransome, the following day. He was to be responsible for the fitting-out. 'The Ancient', as Ransome called him in his account, was a little white-bearded old man whose fragile appearance belied his strength. He had been a seaman in the famous tea clipper *Thermopylae* and had raced in her against the *Cutty Sark*. He had also served in British ships and, as Ransome told me in one of his letters, his English was copious though ornamented with seaman's swear words of whose meaning he was quite unaware. He was an able rigger, very attached to *Racundra*, very loyal to Arthur Ransome with whom he had sailed, and very honest with me.

The days passed quickly. *Racundra* was launched from the Riga Yacht Club's slip; her mast was stepped and she was towed round to the little harbour, where she lay close to the shore under the loving care of the Ancient who completed the rigging and

6. Stores and *Racundra*'s gear were delivered by cart and villainous looking (but honest) messengers.

fitting-out. We spent much of the last two days provisioning and seeing the authorities about the papers and stamping of our passports before departure. They were very co-operative and quick. Finally, we bade farewell to the hotel before starting out for the Stintsee in a taximeter which bulged with the pile of luggage and stores. The ship's gear had been sent down the previous day under the supervision of three ruffianly looking, but honest, messengers of the Riga Express Company.

All the time since leaving England the weather had been tropically hot but, as I had come to expect now that comfort had been left behind, the first spots of rain fell, and no sooner than we were in the ship than a deluge started. *Racundra* had been laid up in a shed during the winter, so that her seams offered little opposition to the elements until she 'took up'. The water trickled through in gentle streams as we unpacked and, but for the size of the cabin, it would have been a miserable business. As it was we were able to choose dry corners. Thus we spent the first hours on our new ship, and when dusk came we lit the table lamp and the cabin seemed warm and cheerful. To save washing-up we had dinner at the Riga Yacht Club, at the same time paying the bill for the launching of *Racundra* and thanking them for their hospitality during our stay.

In a moment of wisdom I had engaged the services of an engineer, but he did not turn up so that was another 24 hours lost. He arrived the day following and worked from 7 a.m. until 5 p.m. by which time the engine had come to life, but the ship smelt of oil and the companion way was black with dirt.

At 6.30 p.m. the Ancient arrived. The sails were set and we got under way to the cheers of his wife and children. The Ancient piloted us from the Stintsee through a narrow reed-bound channel into the deep canal-like fairway of the Muhlgraben, with wharves on either side. The sky ahead to the west was tinged with pink, and soon against that peaceful background there rose the gaunt spectacle of a great roofless building, once the largest shipbuilding yard in Riga, which had been burnt down during the recent war so that nothing but the walls remained. It was dark before we got to the Dvina River, but the moon was up to silver the water and guide us. Helped by the current it did not take long before we took a turn to port and anchored for the night in the Winter Harbour on the west side of the entrance to the Dvina River.

CHAPTER NINE

LATVIA TO DENMARK IN *RACUNDRA*

On Wednesday July 31st 1925, our voyage began. This was late for starting in the far Baltic as the best time of the year there is spring, when the days are long and fair easterly winds are frequent.

   After a quick breakfast, we bade farewell to Sehmel, rowing him ashore in the dinghy, and we were then truly on our own. The Ancient stood watching as I swigged the boat to the foredeck, turned it over and lashed it down. The mizzen was then hoisted and the staysail made ready. Two minutes of hard work and up came the

7. The start of the cruise in the Stint Zee at Riga. Sehmel's wife and children looking on.

anchor (probably only the 50lb kedge) black with mud; the headsail filled, and Mamie steered *Racundra* from the winter harbour entrance into the Dvina River. The Ancient remained there waving his arm until he was nearly out of sight and the ship, with all sail set, was carried by the strong current out past the pier heads and to sea.

You can imagine what fun it was starting off in a little ship new to us to sail in strange waters until we should reach Copenhagen, the half-way mark on our voyage; see chart on pages 52–3. However, the lap that lay immediately ahead of us across the Gulf of Riga to its north-westerly corner at Dome Ness, a distance of little over 60 miles, and I set a course at 9.30 a.m. to pick up the coast near a point named Messargotsem about half-way. The wind was variable in force and direction; one moment it would be a gentle breeze from south-west with the ship scarcely moving, but the next a dark blue cloud, like a great mushroom, might be seen approaching. The breeze would strengthen to a squall, until dispersed by heavy rain, leaving the ship sailing as slowly as before. At 7.30 p.m. a calm settled down and the sun appeared for the first time.

The engine? Yes, what an excellent chance for testing its ability. I removed the companion steps that veiled its oily glory and started a blowlamp that for a considerable time refused to blow; but at length a steady roar broke the silence of a perfect evening. After ten minutes I turned on the paraffin, the water and the lubricating oil, and gave the flywheel a couple of half turns to which the 'smelly monster', as we called it, immediately responded with an outburst of furious din. Then the engine stopped as suddenly as it had started; and we gratefully packed it away. The engine always obeyed its master's (Ransome's) voice but was reluctant to listen to anybody else. Its performance during our whole cruise was to total about six miles, despite having it repaired in so many ports that henceforth I abbreviate 'repairs to smelly monster' to 'RSM'. Thus our voyage was continued virtually under sail alone, mostly against headwinds in a ship with very small sail area, designed for seagoing power and ability rather than close-winded performance.

Progress continued to be slow, and when at last Messargotsem Point was identified it lay some miles to starboard instead of on the port beam, thus revealing considerable compass error. Ransome had the compass swung at Helsingfors during his first cruise in *Racundra* and magnets had been put in to correct the deviation. I ought not to have accepted the Ancient's assurances that the compass was in order, as Ransome had warned me in one of his letters that, although Sehmel was a first-rate rigger and seaman, he knew nothing about navigation. I think the magnets must have been removed when the yacht was laid up. On a north-westerly course the deviation appeared to be about 20 degrees, but there was nothing to be done until we should arrive at a port where the compass could be swung again. In the meantime I would have to make my own estimates of the error.

It was not until 1.30 a.m. the following morning that we anchored about two miles south-east of Messargotsem Point. We breakfasted and made sail again at nine. The wind was westerly and the weather similar to that of the previous day: calms, squalls and thunder. During the afternoon many of the mushroom storms passed, darkening the sky, and in the evening several waterspouts forming dark funnel-shaped pillars of water from sky to sea passed to the north causing us some unnecessary anxiety. We did not reach Dome Ness, the north-westerly extremity of the Gulf of Riga, until 1.30 a.m.

next day (Sunday) August 3rd, when we anchored, only to be awoken two hours later by some fisher lads who had come to present us with a bucket of sprats in return for the liberal amount of vodka they had consumed the previous evening while they were instructing us in the art of fishing. They had actually hooked one—a long, powerful, silvery form threshed the water; then it disappeared, taking with it hook, line and sinker.

From Dome Ness a sandbank extends north-east for a few miles, and at the end of this spit stood a lighthouse. The breeze was so light that it took us three hours to bring this abeam. A schooner of rakish appearance was lying at anchor there, provisioning the occupants of the lonely islet. We slipped slowly past here, and rounded the corner before altering course to follow south-west along the mainland coast; and a nice little breeze sprang up from the east giving us a fair wind. The day passed quietly as the ship progressed steadily but slowly. Sometimes there were mirages. Far distant woods became discernible before the nearer coast, giving the impression of islands floating as it were in mist. The coastline along which we were passing was rather beautiful. The sea was edged with sand dunes backed with scrub which protected the vast dark forests that formed the background. It was a wild vicinity with scarcely a sign of habitation; a veritable refuge for the wolves and woodcutters that gripped the imagination in days of childhood.

During the day the wind backed until it steadied a little west of north, and the glass fell a tenth. By ten o'clock that night we were clear of the land and entered the Baltic now heading across for the Swedish island of Gotland, some hundred miles to the west. During the night the wind freshened and, when the glow of dawn lightened the sky, half a gale was blowing and *Racundra* was enjoying the weather that she was designed for. We hove-to for breakfast and then sailed on all day. It was exhilarating work with a rattling breeze in the sails, and spray flying at each plunge of the ship as she strained forward on her course. Land lay far below the horizon, and we were happy, for the day was very beautiful. Clouds raced across the sky, and sometimes black squalls, purpling the sea and bringing deluges of rain, would appear in the distance and swiftly pass over. Then the sun would break through and a rift of blue would appear between the dark clouds above; and the colour of the sea would deepen, save where the breaking waves flecked it with long white seething scars. It was deep water there—some 90 fathoms— the deepest in that part of the Baltic.

We had a grand passage and when, towards the fall of evening, distant land rose against the clouds on the horizon, we experienced a feeling of utter happiness. Our exact position, however, could not be determined owing to the inaccuracy of the compass and, since there are reefs, rocks and shoals off the coast of Gotland, the question was of more than casual interest. From the lie of the land compared with the chart we were a little south of Ostergarns on the NE side of the island; but as it turned out we need not have worried, for the wind fell and it was dark before we arrived close to the island, when the flash of a lighthouse confirmed that my navigation was correct, perhaps by good luck!

The glass had fallen another tenth and the moon glimmered pallid and damp through the enshrouding clouds. It was a certain warning and, as might have been expected, a gale was blowing before midnight. We hove-to under the lee of the land under short canvas and turned in. Next morning as it was blowing a north-westerly gale, we reached south-west and put into a little harbour marked on the chart as Lugarn where, with the help of a pilot, we lay alongside a quay.

We had a meal, washed and changed our clothes before setting out on a provisioning expedition under the guidance of a civil engineer who was on holiday from Stockholm. He spoke English perfectly and did everything he could to help us. The village itself was not particularly pretty, as it consisted merely of a few fishing huts and pensions, but the visitors there, mostly from Stockholm like the civil engineer, were exceptionally friendly. At 7 o'clock in the evening we went to an hotel where dinner had been arranged for us. A little old lady bowed us into a private room and then disappeared into the kitchen, where her shrill voice could be heard in heated admonition of the servants. Presently a vast assortment of food was brought in on separate dishes: a sort of glorified *hors d'oeuvre* fortified by fried eggs. No sooner than we had dealt with this than the maid entered again and, with a shy but charmingly old-fashioned curtsey, placed a large course of chicken and vegetables before us. The little old lady hovered in the background, and when the chicken was finished and cleared away the maid returned and, after another curtsey, placed a final glory of raspberries and cream on the table.

It was about half way through this repast that a young man entered; walked straight up to me; clicked his heels; bowed, and introduced himself as 'Herr R----'. I was already getting used to foreign customs, and rose to the occasion with an almost perfect bow, but my canvas deck shoes could not be induced to click in a very convincing manner. After this introduction we divided our attention between raspberries, cream and our new friend, who was a medical student, also from Stockholm. He explained that the old lady had never before had English people in her hotel and we were dining in the room usually reserved for the Governor of Gotland. The coffee arrived – splendid coffee such as the Swedes and Danes excel in making – and with the coffee came cakes.

The civil engineer had joined us and after dinner we all went together to the pier. It was a perfect night with a brilliant moon playing on the water and lighting the quay, which widened at the seaward end into a circular jetty, where a couple of fiddlers were playing to a whirling, swinging ring of dancers. Herr R---- soon disappeared, explaining that in Sweden there are two women to every man so it would be unfair to them not to join in. The dance was a country jig; a jolly rollicking rhythm which made the pier echo under the stamping feet. Presently he returned, and we boarded *Racundra* for a drink.

Singing seems to be quite a national custom in Sweden and Denmark where friends we made would burst into song with the least provocation. Herr R---- was no exception and, without any sign of embarrassment, gave us a number of sea shanties in Swedish and English.

We did not sail next day until the afternoon, but soon the wind fell light, so the ship reached along all through the night before coming to anchor next morning in a little bay called Slesviken, a distance of about 30 miles. The land hereabouts on the east side of Southern Gotland is very flat, and the most striking feature is the number of loose grey rocks, ranging from mere stones to huge boulders. These exist in just the same way below the sea, which deepens slowly so that the round shiny tops of rocks can be seen at some distance from the shore. There is no proper demarkation such as sand or cliffs separating land from sea.

Before continuing with the narrative, I think it may help if I explain the system (or lack of system) of watches. They were taken as convenient, usually three hours by me and two by Mamie or, to give more continuous sleep during long night passages, I took four hours and my wife three. Sometimes, if one of us was exceptionally tired, the other took an extra spell at the helm. Often we both had to be on deck for very long periods, and we did more night sailing than in any period of my cruising life.

All navigation and deck work to do with the sails, the anchors and the dinghy was my responsibility; and all cabin work, such as cooking and washing up, fell on Mamie, as well as her spells of steering and her help in identifying landmarks aided by her wonderfully good eyesight.

After these digressions I return to our anchorage at Slesviken. The next passage was to be to Karlskrona, the principal naval port of Sweden, distant about 125 miles by sea. We left Slesviken at 4 a.m., after a night of rolling fiendishly at anchor in the bay. We had a slow passage owing to the light weather and headwinds, which were not at all to *Racundra*'s liking. It took us two days and two nights to round the south of Gotland and cross the sea between Gotland and the island of Öland and to the Öland Rev lightship, which lay 12 miles SE of the southern tip of the island; a distance of only 80 miles made good. We passed the lightship at 8 a.m.; by then it was blowing hard and I replaced the staysail with the storm jib. In the early hours of the day the glass was falling and the wind had backed to SE; by eleven o'clock it had risen to a near gale. We decided to make for the shelter of Gronhogs Hamn, a small harbour marked on the chart only about 15 miles distant, situated on the west side of Öland under the lee of the island in a SE blow. But before we had run half the distance the wind shifted to south by west, putting the harbour on a lee instead of a weather shore. The sky looked very threatening and a big sea was running as there was a fetch of about 100 miles.

We lowered the mainsail and hove-to under mizzen and storm jib, prepared for the worst, while there was still room under our lee, for we were already almost embayed in the entrance of Kalmar Sund between the great expanse of Öland Rev to the east and iron-bound Swedish coast to the west. It was a dangerous position, as the seas were so large as to make sailing impossible because, being then unfamiliar with *Racundra*'s ability under such conditions, I had reduced sail far too much. We turned in to rest and await events.

At 5 p.m. the events arrived in the shape of some of the largest breaking seas I had seen up to then. The booms banged wildly about, shaking the ship from stem to stern. The motion was abominable. I took a sounding, but found plenty of water. The cause of the movement was merely the cessation of the gale, and at 7 p.m. the worst was over. A light, fair wind sprang up from the east, steadying the ship and enabling us to set more sail to lay a course crossing an area marked on the chart as having abnormal magnetic variation; there are many such in the Baltic. Extreme optimism followed deep pessimism, as *Racundra* gathered speed with the freshening breeze. We ate a little food and after more sail had been set, Mamie turned in for a well-earned sleep. Just after midnight (starting our fourth consecutive day at sea) we passed between the island of Utlänger and the reef on which Utklippan lighthouse flashed its warning. It was then that a storm, that had been playing round the horizon, approached to add to the impressiveness of the night. Thunder reverberated among the clouds, whilst flashes of lightning lit the ship with their vicious glare. The wind veered to the south, and at length it was Mamie's watch and I turned into the cabin for a spell, where it was bright and cheery. It rained hard but Mamie at the helm refused to mind.

Having found the flashing buoy south of Utlänger, I altered course to the west clear of the rocks to the north of Utklippan lighthouse. But as the compass could not be relied upon and there was an unlit, rocky shore to leeward with many outlying rocks, I had to allow ample margin for error, especially as it was a pitch black night. The margin of safety was, unfortunately, so ample that when at 2.30 a.m. we calculated that we were off Karlskrona, no leading lights were to be seen. We hove-to, to wait for dawn before approaching the land with its offlying rocks and reefs.

Our feelings cannot be described as anything but wretched, when we found ourselves forced to keep to sea at this early hour but, just as we were about to turn in, Mamie announced that she thought she could see a light. First hint of dawn enabled us to see sufficiently to warn us of dangers ahead, so we got under way again and ran towards the point where the light was suspected. The sky was gradually brightening and, just before it was too late, Mamie announced definitely that she could make out a flashing light ahead. At 4 a.m. we passed the buoys that mark the entrance to the channel leading to Karlskrona, and sailed on towards land. It was blowing half a gale and a large sea was still running. Away to starboard huge fountains of white spray reared towards the sky on some sunken rock. To port several spurts of white revealed the presence of other dangers. It was anxious work, but the anxiety was of short duration as, a few minutes after passing the buoys, a leading mark was sighted and we saw Karlskrona in the distance. Shoal after shoal we passed, each clearly marked by beacons and a cruel breaking sea. Then *Racundra* sailed between two breakwaters and into the calm beyond. At 7 a.m. I let go the big anchor and the chain roared out into the clear water. The passage was finished.

After 75 hours at sea, we felt distinctly tired. A liberal breakfast with porridge made matters better, but it was sleep that was most needed. Before we had rested an hour our peace was disturbed by the arrival alongside of a Customs launch. The two officials were decidedly suspicious. I had not shaved for three days and, in my torn and dirty clothes, did not look at all like a conventional yachtsman. Other little deficiencies, such as the absence of shoes and socks, evidently made a bad impression. Although our passports and papers were in order, the men remained decidedly suspicious, particularly as we had come from Riga which was reputed to be a smuggling centre and was also the capital of Latvia, a buffer state between Russia and the outside world. I think they may have taken my small red ensign for Russian at first; the same mistake was made when we first visited Tallinn in 1931. So they insisted upon towing us two miles to the yacht anchorage. Here the two Customs officials left us so that they might make a report to their authorities. I took the opportunity to shave, and we both had a wash and donned shore-going clothes.

After waiting a long time for the Customs, we decided to go ashore, despite the risk of getting locked up as we had not received permission to land. First we went to an

hotel to get a substantial meal and next to a bank to replenish our stock of Swedish money. Feeling rather like criminals, we decided it would be best to put in an appearance at the British Consulate. We received a most kindly reception from the Vice-Consul, who was Swedish but spoke English fluently. He immediately telephoned the Customs and learned that we were free of all formality; not even our passports required to be stamped. The Consul arranged for the engine to be repaired and our compass to be swung. His lady secretary spent all the next morning helping my wife to shop, and no trouble was too much for her.

We spent three days in Karlskrona, in lovely summer weather, during which we thoroughly provisioned the ship and an engineer performed RSM, so that on the last day we were able to proceed under auxiliary power with two compass adjusters to have the compass swung and corrected. The two technicians were most co-operative; in appearance and manner they seemed like petty or chief petty officers of naval training. Their only misgivings were respectfully shown later when *Racundra* was under engine which decided to work only backwards. Consequently, we and the compass adjusters had to proceed through the anchorage stern-first, much to the amusement of spectators, including those on a fine full-rigged ship in which Swedish youth was trained for the navy.

The observations revealed that the deviation in the compass was up to 24 degrees, with the maximum at about west and a minimum a little east of north; the work took

8. Compass adjusters at Karlskrona disclosed errors up to 24 degrees. The plank forward is not a bowsprit.

the whole morning, but it was a great relief to have a proper deviation table and to be able to lay courses accurately instead of by guesswork.

The following morning we set sail at 10 a.m., as the absence of tidal streams in the Baltic allowed us to start at whatever time it suited us. Instead of leaving Karlskrona by the principal (south) channel by which we had entered, we made our departure through the inner (west) passage. Despite headwinds this provided interesting sailing among the inner skerries, and in the late afternoon we found a delightful anchorage almost landlocked by rocks and skerries. Towards dusk we rowed ashore to a farm on a neighbouring wooded island, with a meadow running down to the sea; here we obtained fresh milk.

Next day we set sail early. The compass adjusters had warned us that the west entrance was complicated and so it proved, especially as we had only a small scale British Admiralty chart. However, once clear of the rocks *Racundra* met the swell of the open sea. We were bound for Skillinge—a little fishing village mentioned in the *Baltic Pilot*—where we arrived after 30 hours, tacking all the way against light head-winds, except during the night (a very dark one) when there was a strong wind which suited the ship and good progress was made.

On arrival at Skillinge we received a friendly reception. The village itself was rather dull but its population were mostly seafaring people who could speak English. We were held up there for two days owing to contrary and strong winds. Numbers of Baltic traders were likewise delayed and anchored off the harbour under shelter of the point awaiting better conditions. The last day at Skillinge was spent in RSM, in which we were privileged to have the work done by the Head of the Customs in Sweden, who happened to be spending his holiday from Stockholm in the village. He made a hobby of engines and kindly devoted a lot of his time to putting it right.

On August 19th the wind veered through north to north-east, and at midday we were ready for sea, well provisioned. It was a great surprise to us, for earlier it had been raining and blowing a gale. We decided to leave harbour under power and, without any hesitation, the 'smelly' roared away. Once safely at sea the engine stopped and, after many attempts to get it going again, I packed it away in its housing.

We were bound for Copenhagen, little over 70 miles by sea, but it was destined to be the slowest passage in a lifetime.

During the afternoon the wind gradually shifted to a headwind from the west so that by sunset we had logged only a few miles. It had been a warm sunny day and, as evening drew on, the sky became quite free of cloud and a thickness in the air heralded good weather. A calm fell, and *Racundra* rolled in what was left of the swell from the gale. Around us lay a fleet of schooners and other sailing ships with every stitch of canvas set to catch any breath of wind. Even the horizon was dotted with topsails of ships afar off to east and west, or following a line further seaward. Occasionally a 'thud-thud' would draw attention to a ship passing under power with her sails quivering from the breeze created by her own speed.

Night fell, and *Racundra* showed up as a dark mass of sail and spars aloft against the sky. On deck a yellow glow shone through the port-holes and from the steering well; the side lights burned brightly in their brackets. Occasionally I went on deck to see that nothing threatened our safety; but no sailing vessel moved fast enough to be a source of danger and no ship under power could approach without attracting our attention in the still silence of the night.

On the third day the calm remained as complete as ever; the sea was unruffled by even a hint of a ripple. A school of porpoises came to join the ship and frolicked around us for some hours, providing a welcome diversion. When the third night approached, two ships lay near us, mirrored in the sea, with their sails listless, waiting motionless for wind. *Racundra* had only made good thirty-three miles in three days and two nights, but at 9 o'clock that night a faint but perceptible air crept up and the sea was ruffled by tiny wavelets; by five o'clock the following morning (the fourth) the wind had strengthened from the east. This was fair as we were bound west as far as Falsterbo Point, where the coast of Sweden sweeps to the north to face Denmark. Separating the two countries was the famous Sound, the most important fairway in the Baltic. Off Falsterbo lay long fingers of sand marked by a lightship about eight miles off the land. Here all ships converged. Steamers and sailing ships passed constantly in northerly or southerly directions, and others swung past from the east, rapidly altering course to north as they rounded the lightship. *Racundra* was able to cut inside this owing to her light draught, leaving it close to port by midday. She seethed along rejoicing in the strengthening wind and by 6 o'clock we were off Copenhagen. Soon after, we picked up a mooring close to the tall spars of the Greenland whaler belonging to the Amateur Sail Club.

9. Baltic traders were still under sail in those days. Off the Swedish coast we were becalmed among them for three days, making good only 70 miles.

On arrival at a new harbour there is always much to be done, and I suppose it must have been about 8 o'clock when at last we werc able to row ashore. We landed at the steps of the yacht basin and walked along the Langelinie to the hospitable Royal Danish Yacht Club. The Secretary was kindness itself: he produced some large scale charts that we wanted to see, and sent a club steward out to get the beer and provisions we needed, as the shops were closing for the week-end; he also introduced us to some of the cruising members of the club. After having lived for some days on ship's stores, we looked forward to dinner, which we had upstairs in the famous dining room; it was round in shape and had a polished wood ceiling, divided into the points of the compass. The outer wall overlooking the Sound was made up of a number of large windows; it was night by then, and we sat at a table where we could look down on the Langelinie and over the harbour with its moving lights to the mysterious distance of the Sound. By then it was blowing hard, and even in the security of the large building we could hear the swish of the vicious little harbour waves and see the riding lamps dancing. Music from the restaurant below came faintly to our ears. To us, tired mariners as we were, it was something like heaven to be in such luxury.

We had a splendid dinner, but the sudden change from hardship to luxury was almost intoxicating and, when the time came to return to our ship, we found the utmost difficulty in walking straight across the room. The place seemed to be moving, and I sincerely trust that the members dining at other tables had observed that we had only drunk a glass of beer, a cup of coffee, and one solitary liqueur each. In my ocean racing years, later in life, I found this experience was not uncommon. At the end of a really hard race tired crews would reel about ashore until they had recovered their land-legs (but they had often taken something stronger than one liqueur).

Once in the open air the feeling of unsteadiness became even more pronounced, so that we rolled down the Langelinie arm-in-arm to the boat. The Secretary had sent their club boatman down with our purchases, and we embarked in the dinghy with provisions and water in the bows and Mamie in the stern. The dinghy was a stable one designed, I think, by Arthur Ransome himself, but when we had rowed out of the yacht basin into the choppy water of the more open harbour, there seemed some risk of sinking. Tugs and ferries were passing frequently and the bows of the dinghy were only just capable of rising to the bigger washes. It was blowing hard and the small yachts were pitching violently. I edged into the wind, always keeping close to some yacht or other when we saw a bad wash approaching. I had only a hundred yards to row through the anchorage, but in the difficult conditions it seemed to take a good quarter of an hour; we were glad when we had *Racundra*'s stout decks under our feet once more.

CHAPTER TEN

AMONG THE DANISH ISLANDS

During the night *Racundra* rolled and pitched on her mooring at Copenhagen and, as it was difficult to get much sleep, we were glad when morning came. It was still blowing hard, but the sky was sunny and we cast off at 10 a.m., northward bound through the Sound. The coast of Denmark, smiling in the sun, lay close to port and that of Sweden about 5 miles to starboard. At 1 p.m. the castle of Kronborg, the reputed grave of Hamlet, which guards the narrowest point of the Sound, lay on the port beam with the sun painting its walls and ramparts gold and lightening its green weathered copper turrets. We had a simple lunch and Gilbierg Head, the most northerly point of Sjælland, soon came abeam. Altering course to south-west, *Racundra* sped along the coast and as evening drew on she reached into Ise Fiord to the entrance of Hundested Harbour. The 50lb anchor roared out on its chain, followed by the bigger 70lb one, growling as the heavy chain rasped over its lead. With the aid of a decent fair wind *Racundra* had averaged about 6 knots.

On waking up next morning, August 24th, the wind was whistling in the rigging and it was raining hard. Instead of sailing we decided to move a cable east into the shelter of the harbour. I had the two anchors to raise. The fifty pounder was easy enough but weighing the big anchor and heavy chain, without an operable capstan, was a formidable task and on that occasion I had to enlist the help of my wife, whose slim weight just made the difference in breaking it out. We then moved under sail, in pouring rain, and laid alongside in complete security.

After changing into dry clothes we set out along the quay. Hundested was one of the principal ports for the herring industry and had a large fishing fleet. The sail area of these vessels was small and they were propelled by powerful engines; most of them were in harbour when we were there. We were delayed two days at Hundested for RSM. The engine had to be lifted out of the ship and sent off to the sty where other engines were under repair. In the afternoon we caught a train of miniature and antiquated appearance for Hellerod where we found our way to the castle, Frederiksborg Slot, which is one of the most historic in Denmark and is surrounded by moats and a lake. After an eventless return journey in an electric train, we stumped back along the dark quays to our ship before the clock had struck eleven.

On August 16th, the wind was fair from the north-east and moderate. By 3.30 in the afternoon the engine had been returned to its den under the companion steps, and was reported to be in a well-disciplined condition. No sooner than we were outside the harbour than the wind shifted to the north-west, which was almost a headwind. We were bound for Ballen on the Island of Samsö, distant only about 25 miles. During the night we sailed past the navigation hazards off Sjælland Point and Sejrö Island, at the extremities of which there are cruel reefs of rocks. We anchored off Sejrö on its west side at half past six the following morning and, after a quick but excellent breakfast, we turned in for a rest.

The island looked interesting and by 1 p.m. we were ready to explore it in the dinghy. Once ashore the landscape lost its wild appearance as viewed from seaward. Far from being barren, every inch of ground was cultivated or occupied by cows, horses, sheep, geese or hens. We came to a farmstead where a track led off towards the village. The sky was blue, there was not a breath of wind, and we found walking hot and thirsty work, so we turned back to *Racundra*. At three o'clock the engine was induced to raise its roar, and the ship slowly made her way across the sea between the islands of Sejrö and Samsö for the harbour of Ballen, a distance of only about 20 miles. Presently a light wind came from the south enabling us to set sail and dispense with the engine, which was a tactical error as without it we averaged only 3 knots.

The weather seemed to be changing and a grey mass of cloud blocked out the sky to the west. In the late evening the light of Hatter Barn shoal came abeam to the north and a low line of hills, that indicated the island of Samsö, lay but about eight miles ahead. I suppose it must have been about 10 o'clock that night when Mamie made out weak lights on the bow and called my attention to them. They were certainly houses, but might have belonged to any little group of homesteads. There were no red and green harbour lights that I could identify. I took a sounding of 2 fathoms so we knew we were close to the coast. Then came a deluge of thick rain which blotted out the lights immediately and the wind shifted to the west. It was a pitch black night with not a hint to differentiate between sky and sea.

We hove-to for a while on the starboard tack and then resumed our search for harbour lights. First we sailed about south-west peering into the murk and taking frequent soundings, without sighting anything, then we tacked (through 100 degrees or more) to the northward and soon found deeper water.

It was an hour or two later that the sound of breaking water became audible and I took another sounding.

It was one and half fathoms.

We at once bore away to the east, but the sea got no deeper. There was only one course of action open to us. I did not know on which side the dangers lay, but we had nine feet of water under us. Down went the foresail, and in a couple of minutes *Racundra* lay to her anchor by ten fathoms of scope.

It was midnight, and the rest of the night passed slowly. Sleep was impossible owing to the motion of the ship in a strong northerly current broadside to the wind. At last the indefinite light of approaching dawn revealed a totally unexpected picture. Close aboard on the south-west the gaunt pile of some rocky islet rose sheer from the sea and farther away on the other side there was an island. Nothing could be seen of the regular shore of Samsö. We had awoken in another world.

Before long the sail of some fishing or trading boat came into sight and, as she passed, I weighed anchor quickly. My wife took the helm to follow her while I kept soundings going by lead and line. The sea soon deepened and, as the sky grew light and the configuration of the coast cleared, an idea crossed my mind. We looked once more at the chart, but at a position some twelve miles north of Ballen; the coastline depicted agreed with that lying in front of us, and what made the matter certain was that the vessel ahead altered course, and then we saw two beacons which we found on the chart. During the night *Racundra* had found her own way through a narrow channel in intricate waters to the position where we had come to anchor at midnight.

Having ascertained our position, it was no great difficulty to sail back to Ballen. In the narrow channel there was a strong current running against us, and a sound of water breaking on rocks similar to that heard in the dark hours of the previous night. On arrival off Ballen we anchored and later in the day we sailed *Racundra* into the harbour and berthed alongside a quay built on rough boulders. The Harbour Master called to collect the small dues and a drink. The harbour lights proved to be one fixed (not flashing) light, which must have been the one Mamie sighted the previous night, and weak red and green lights at the end of the piers with a range of perhaps two miles in clear weather, but probably little more than a cable or two in the thick rain and murk. With the aid of a new large scale Admiralty chart I may now have found where we anchored. It was probably close north-east of Lindholm, which I described as a rocky islet rising sheer from the sea. If so, the channel through which we passed was the Lindholm Dyg, now marked by buoys, two of which have lights. It was the strong unknown current that helped to carry us so far to the northward.

Everybody in the village of Ballen was hospitable. When we went to the ship chandler's the elderly lady owner took us to her shady and pretty garden where she gave us pears and a selection for a salad. The farmer to whom we went for milk asked us into their private room for a talk. On our return to the ship we found that a 20-ton ketch named and spelt *Amfitrite* had arrived in the harbour. She was owned by a ship chandler from Aarhus who had a doctor and his family sailing with him, while forward two sea scouts comprised the crew. Both men were oldish and great characters, especially the jovial doctor. He was Swedish and, in his younger days, had served his time in the American navy in China. He had only recently qualified in medicine and had taken his degree later in life than almost anybody in Sweden. The best medicine he advised for all purposes was akvavit, a strong spirit which he offered us liberally.

We had breakfast in *Amfitrite* next morning and, with a fair southerly wind we sailed in company bound for Aarhus, about 30 miles to the north-west on the Jutland coast. Later in the day the wind shifted and freshened. *Amfitrite* stowed her mizzen, double-reefed her mainsail, set her storm jib and bore away for Ebeltoft. *Racundra* did not need reefing and both yachts made harbour by 4 p.m. Ebeltoft is one of the oldest towns in Denmark, and its out-of-the-way harbour was rarely visited by British yachts. It had a sea-wall over four hundred years old, built of layers of compressed seaweed, and an ancient court house, converted to a museum, with gruesome dungeons, where a witch had once been incarcerated before being burnt to death.

The doctor had to leave by train as he had an important engagement in Aarhus. Our ship chandler friend remained and helped us in every possible way. Up till then we had been using British Admiralty charts of very small scale and he gave us some large scale Danish charts, and his copy of the *Danske Havne-Lods*, which gave plans of every harbour. To my wife he presented a little gold brooch representing a Viking ship, declaring she had been unanimously elected a member of the 'Viking' club. Whatever this might be I thought she well deserved it.

The weather was threatening and it was getting late in the year, so our friend decided to lay up *Amfitrite* at Ebeltoft. Out of the kindness of his heart he implored us to lay up *Racundra* at Aarhus and go home by steamer but, of course, we had no such intention, having received similar advice so many times before.

Next morning the wind moderated and we fetched back to Ballen the same night, which was easy to enter in clear weather. The following morning we got under way early. There was soon half a gale of wind and the sea was very rough south of Samsö, but it did not take long to enter the Great Belt and get under the lee of the island of Fyen. The weather grew wilder but at dusk we were in sheltered water near Svendborg Sound. As night fell we sailed on through the narrow twisting sound, which was well marked by a series of leading lights. At about 9 p.m. we anchored under a lighthouse near a schooner.

It rained heavily in the night and it was blowing as hard as ever when we turned out at 6 a.m. next morning. We had to navigate through a narrow channel in a poorly marked area of shoal water and I had only a small scale chart of this particular part. When we came to Rudkoping, *Racundra* ran like a hare into the shelter of the harbour entering the eastern basin in the western harbour. This was smaller than we expected. In fact, it measured only about 80 metres on each side, and this was reduced by ships alongside quays, so there was little room for handling the long keeled *Racundra*, which was slow in stays.

Quick, helm up; and she ran along and passed a quay; then another quay came straight ahead and a dolphin to starboard. Close round this we sped, while every ounce of strength was thrown in getting the sheets home quickly. Lee-Ho! and she was close to another quay and off on the other tack. Then once more round the dolphin, close to a steamer, and with helm hard up she gathered speed. Hard down, and she luffed head to wind alongside a quay. Down came the jib. Down the peak. A line was taken by willing hands ashore and the ship was moored.

The sudden quiet after the wind and spray was almost stunning. We were soon visited by the Harbour Master and Customs. I went ashore to the ship chandlers where I had a new strop made for the peak halyards which had just broken, and bought a large scale Danish chart of the surrounding area. There I met the English speaking skipper from a neighbouring three-masted schooner. His ship was northward bound for timber, and then back to Cork.

At 3 p.m. we set sail again, this time under storm jib and mainsail leaving the mizzen furled, as by then it was blowing a full gale. A crowd had assembled on the quay to cheer us off. Mamie was at the helm and had to make two short tacks to clear the basin and harbour entrances. Once outside in the proper channel, she handed over the helm to me, as the ship was hard-mouthed in such wild conditions so that steering for long was beyond her physical strength. She became the 'pilot' and I the 'crew' until we had secured a good offing when I went forward to deal with a jib sheet that had parted. We also had trouble with the patent boom jaws which had come adrift, but I managed to slip the boom into its proper place when we tacked and put a wire strop to replace the broken fastening. Breakages such as these are liable to occur in gales, but one does not welcome them off a lee shore.

Our course took us only a few miles to a small island named Strynö where we sailed into the harbour after a short but exceedingly rough passage, getting a real dusting. We received an instant welcome by the skippers of other crafts gathered there waiting for a better turn in the weather. In my shirt sleeves and soaked to the skin, I was immediately conducted to the warm cabin of a neighbouring schooner, where we all shook hands and I sat down to a bottle of beer and a glass of akvavit; Mamie joined us after changing into dry clothes. We returned to *Racundra* at about 9.30 p.m. It was a wild night with the clouds racing across the moon. The barometer had fallen eight-tenths in forty-eight hours, of which four-tenths had been in the last twenty-four. We remained at Strynö for some days. A succession of gales of winter violence passed over the island and the barometer jumped up and down like a yo-yo.

The village in Strynö was a charming old-world spot, unknown to tourists. The old houses, with beams picked out in black against the white background and crowned with heavy thatch green with age, were clustered in haphazard fashion round an open space.

Fortunately, an end comes even to gales and we were able to make our departure on September 8th. A local character named Karl, who had helped us in many ways during our stay at Strynö, insisted on towing us out of the harbour in his open motor-boat with a 5 h.p. engine, to pilot us across tricky (then unmarked) piece of water with many shoals to Marstal. But he had not a clue about navigation or pilotage, so we had to cast off from the tow and set sail. We had the large-scale chart bought at Rudkoping and had no difficulty in the navigation from Marstal and then through a winding channel to the open sea. Aided by a freshening wind and occasional squalls bringing rain, *Racundra* sailed fast, but it was almost dark before we entered Kiel Fiord, and a very dark night by the time we arrived at Heikendorf, which I had known in *Annette* only two years previously.

Next morning, as the Customs had not come to examine us, we went to Kiel by a fiord ferry. Germany had changed a great deal since I was last there at the time of the crash in the mark. There had been a remarkable recovery; the shops were busy and the prices higher than in England. The people seemed prosperous and happier, although it was said that taxation was very heavy. Early on the second morning at Heikendorf an engineer from the shipyard came off for RSM, and in the afternoon the engine burst forth into a happy roar as we thundered our way across to Holtenau Locks. Next morning we were towed through the Kiel Canal to Brunsbüttel.

CHAPTER ELEVEN

RACUNDRA IN THE NORTH SEA

We were now in familiar waters and *Racundra* entered the River Elbe just before the flood tide had finished. It was perfect weather with a nice little breeze from the north. Our intention was to sail continuously until we made Ymuiden, before crossing the North Sea to Dover.

We sailed past Cuxhaven and then tacked down the Elbe with a fair tide passing Elbe lightships III, II and I. From there we could lay to the west with little alteration of course for two or three days and nights. The low line of the Frisian Islands with their treacherous offlying shoals would lie to the south, but our course would take us past a series of lightships some 10 miles out to sea. When night fell the Roter Sand and Wangeroog lights flashed to port, and to the north-east the light at Heligoland was very clear. During the first night we had an unpleasant incident.

The sky to the north was gradually becoming overcast by a mass of black cloud. Thunder muttered in the distance and the wind freshened. It continued to increase, and the heavy bank of clouds approached steadily, blotting out the stars. The waves began to break and the yacht heeled over and plunged forward into the night through the foaming water. I lowered the mizzen and prepared for trouble.

The squall then struck.

The wind screamed in the rigging and a flash of lightning lit the breaking waves from horizon to horizon.

Then came the rain in one huge burst. The sea hissed with its violence; hail came roaring on the deck and drove into my face; and every light of ship and lighthouse disappeared behind the veil of utter darkness.

It passed, and *Racundra* lay becalmed, rolling in a heavy swell with her decks covered with hailstones. She rolled and pitched and rolled again. The booms crashed madly to and fro; and somewhere in the distant cabin some loose bottles clinked in empty misery.

The side lights had been extinguished and a steamer was bearing down at us. Mamie slipped to the helm, whilst I went forward to relight the lamps; I replaced the starboard light and, with the port lamp in my hand, crept forward again on the rolling deck (there were, of course, no stanchions or life-lines in those days), reached the shrouds and began screwing it in place. A sudden lurch, fiercer than the rest, threw me off my balance and in a second cold water rushed up to meet me. One arm was crooked round a shroud and, as I fell, I managed to grasp it in my hand. For a moment I lay suspended half in the sea and then, as the boat lurched towards me, I climbed aboard again.

The lamp was out and the red and green lights of the steamer lay straight ahead as the yacht rolled helplessly in the waves. I rushed aft and had almost gained the companion-way when the boom struck me on the forehead and I found myself lying on the weather deck. Mamie shouted something and pushed an electric torch into my hands. In a moment I had recovered and got to the lee mizzen shrouds then, with my arms embracing these, I flashed the torch through the red glass of the lamp.

The steamer came on, and *Racundra* rolled lifelessly in the deep. The side light was smoky and the feeble rays of the cheap hand torch had not the strength to pierce the sooted glass. As a last resort I flashed the torch free at the oncoming ship, and shouted at Mamie to wave the riding lamp that lay ready in the steering well; but the moment it was raised I could see that it was too dirty to avail much, and the torch that I held was but a minute speck in the darkness.

On came the ship, now so close that her side lights looked far apart and high up.

On she came, and we prepared for the impact—two life buoys lay handy, lightly tied to the mizzen shrouds.

All was noise, but above all could be heard a sound of threshing water. Suddenly the port lamp of the steamer disappeared whilst a green light glimmered above us, and a great black hull lay across our bow.

At the last moment we had been seen and the ship had altered course and backed her engines. Possibly it was the light of the cabin lamp shining through the portholes that had saved us.

Shortly after this narrow escape from being run down, a nice wind came from the north and we continued on the westerly course. It was ordinary routine work, watch by watch: navigation and calculation of tidal streams; sail trimming in winds varying in direction and strength from fresh to calm; getting meals and washing up (without modern detergents); spells of sleep with one ear open always instantly ready to go on deck at call; cleaning lamps and the other innumerable minor duties of a ship at sea.

After sailing continuously for 48 hours the wind shifted, absolutely contrary to our course. We had made good 150 miles from Brunsbüttel and had arrived off the Dutch Terschelling lightship at 5 a.m. The prospect of beating slowly to windward for another 24 hours seemed most uninviting, so we decided to get behind the islands where, at the end of the day, we could get some sound sleep.

Accordingly we squared off for Terschelling Seegat, between the islands of Terschelling to the east and Vlieland to the west. The channel was clearly marked and we were soon in sheltered water behind Vlieland, taking a buoyed deep channel leading south-east between miles of sandbanks. Two handsome Terschelling pilot boats passed us under sail. It was peaceful and indeed beautiful, for the sun lit up the yellow banks and shone through the shallow water, lighting the pale shades of green and brown. Off the shoals, now bare, little trickles of water came pouring down in miniature cascades to joint the silent swift ebb tide.

After lunch we invoked the aid of the engine for an hour until the stern bearing became overheated. All the afternoon and evening we tacked on in a falling breeze along a winding little channel. Night crept on slowly, unnoticed except that buoys became more and more difficult to see, until the time came to anchor to avoid being set onto a sandbank. Our little world lay in a narrow channel of water surrounded by miles and miles of partially covered sandbanks and mussel beds. I hoisted a riding lamp forward and went below for the quick meal Mamie had prepared. We then turned in, and I fell asleep the moment my head touched the pillow.

Next morning there was more breeze and *Racundra* sailed at good speed. The narrow channel was soon left behind and, assisted by the ebb tide, we were swept south-west down the wide Texel Stroom along the sandy southern shore of Texel Island. It was a grand morning, and this part of the cruise had completed my nodding acquaintance of all the east and west Frisian Islands. Towards midday we came to the gat leading to the North Sea past Den Helder, the principal Dutch naval port, where we saw a warship and a submarine as we passed the town. It had taken about six hours to gain the North Sea, and it took another six hours sailing off the mainland coast of Holland before we reached Ymuiden at midnight.

After three days at sea, without touching at a port, provisions were getting low so we remained in harbour during the morning attending to this and refilling the water tank. We then made a premature start for England but after several hours of sailing there was a heavy squall and, thinking it heralded bad weather, we returned to Ymuiden in company with a fleet of fishing vessels from the Zuider Zee port of Urk, arriving back late the same night.

We remained at Ymuiden the next day where we were visited by a few acquaintances I had met there in 1923, including the Zuider Zee pilot.

At dawn, September 18th, with the lighthouse still flashing in the weak light of early morning, *Racundra* departed from Ymuiden bound for Dover. Close-hauled she lay a little south of west and, as the hands of the clock in the cabin marked the passing hours, the Dutch coast dwindled from a yellow sandy ribbon until the time came that it could be seen no more.

During the morning the wind backed to the south-east, which was not a propitious change, but it enabled us to lay a course to the south and in the evening we passed a few miles west of the Maas lightship. We ate a meal, and packed the crockery away. When night came the flashes from the lightship and the Hook of Holland pierced the darkness astern, and on the port bow the distant loom in the sky of flashes revealed the presence of the Schouwen lightship to the south-west. During the night the wind was light and the sea calm, but little progress was made against a foul tide. Often both of us had to be on deck, as *Racundra* passed through a fleet of fishing vessels and several steamers crossed our course. Two hurricane lights, one green and one red, had been purchased at Ymuiden to supplement the inefficient side lights and these, kept lighted and protected in the steering well, were shown as required when a ship passed close.

At dawn the following morning, September 19th, I relieved Mamie at the end of her spell at the helm. It was as usual cold and damp at that hour, but the wind had freshened so *Racundra* was making good progress and the prospect of getting to England was cheering. The morning passed and in every direction lay a waste of grey heaving sea. The glass was steadily falling tenth by tenth and the wind was hardening. We were off the mouths of the Schelde, and a trail of submerged sands bounded the

Dutch coast to the east. The possibility of making Flushing or Ostend crossed my mind but was dismissed as unpractical.

On we sailed for the North Hinder lightship. At about 2 p.m. I began to get anxious, as it ought to have been sighted by then, but presently the spidery red form of the vessel could be vaguely discerned ahead and in less than an hour we passed close to her. My calculations had been exact as regards course, but our speed had been over-estimated. The whole crew of the lightship turned out to see us, but I had no time even to wave a reply to their signals; a squall had struck us and I was busy reefing the mainsail.

By then it was blowing half a gale and the glass had fallen six tenths since morning. We were evidently in for a dusting. In readiness for the gale we carried a small jib, the reefed mainsail and the mizzen, but it may be wondered why I had not reefed more. The reason was that we were getting to know *Racundra*; she had immense stability and her sails were so small that in effect she was double-reefed even with all sail set, while her canvas was more evenly distributed over her length than in any yacht I had seen.

On sailed *Racundra* for the Sandettié lightship with the wind strengthening all the time. The sea was rough, but the waves were not notably high as their fetch from Belgium was only some 20 miles. Time passed and the glass continued to fall. By the evening it had dropped another two-tenths.

Half way to the Sandettié lightship the gale hit us. The sun had been low and fiercely yellow, while a great bank of purple cloud had gradually crawled across the sky from horizon to horizon. The sun became hidden but a wan light lit up the white-capped sea.

Suddenly the waves were obscured in whiteness and there was a sizzling noise. The ship staggered under the weight of the wind, which howled so that every spar and rope tautened under the fury of the first stroke of the gale. Steering was useless as the lee rail was under until I released the mainsheet. That eased her. I then sheeted the jib to windward and the mizzen hard in before sheeting the mainsail. *Racundra* lay hove-to on the port tack, heading away from the land and forereaching slowly to the safety of open water in mid-North Sea. I remained in the steering well for a while. I think the violent rain continued; certainly there was thunder and lightning, but it was the force of the wind that was so stunning. Later, seizing the opportunity between waves, I opened the hatch and slipped into the warm interior of the cabin.

Mamie had been busy with the hurricane lamps, white, green and red, which she had jammed on the cabin sole between the central table and a bunk. She had also prepared malted milk, and this, together with some dry biscuits, formed the evening meal. It was all we wanted as, although not sea-sick, we suffered from a feeling of nausea under such conditions.

At night a number of steamers occasionally passed near, and one or other of us had to go on deck to show lights. The scene was grand in the extreme. White crested waves came rushing on top of our hard-pressed ship; up lifted her bow to meet one, down it fell on the sloping mass of water into the trough; then up again it would lift to meet the next. There was tremendous noise from wind in the masts and rigging, but above all raged a continual 'thrumming'. Noise is a feature of gales, as I was to learn later in my ocean racing years. It was miserable below and we were very wet, for no oilskins could have resisted such conditions. We lay on our bunks and even that was difficult owing to the violent motion, as there were no canvas leeboards to hold us in; such equipment did not come into general use until much later.

I believe the sea was building up, for the motion became worse and worse. Two of the lamps got smashed, but it did not matter, as they flickered so much when exposed to the gale that they were unlikely to be seen anyway; moreover, we became worn out, so visits to the deck became fewer and fewer. We just lay in our bunks as best we could. The ceaseless hammering and shaking were tiring, but night went by steadily, neither slowly nor quickly until the moment arrived when the outline of the portholes started to become dimly discernible against the light of approaching day.

It was then that Mamie had one of her premonitions and summoned me to go on deck again. It was bitterly cold and a big sea had built up, but the force of the wind was not so great as it had been. To my surprise, reflected in the sky I saw the loom of several distant lights to the nor'west.

Suddenly on the starboard quarter a red flash came and went. A long interval and there it came again.

Unfamiliar as I was with the English side of the North Sea, I could not be misled by the two red flashes. On the face of the chart they could mean but one thing–the Galloper lightship.*

The wind, which had shifted from time to time during the night had veered south-south-west when I came on deck. I unlashed the tiller and sheeted the jib to leeward and eased off the main and mizzen sheets. *Racundra* began to sail fast to the north-west for the lightship. The seas in the middle of the North Sea had built up during the night. With a roar a big sea flung itself aboard, struck the dinghy and fell on the cabin top. A few minutes later another reared up and came crashing over the ship, breaking in solid mass over the companion cover, and struck me a heavy blow across the chest. Mamie joined me in the cockpit; all the night we had laid in our bunks as best we could, damp to the skin and, now in the bitter cold of dawn, the driving rain constantly penetrated our oilskins and chilled us to the bone. We were also hungry as cooking below had been impossible.

We had a few sips of whisky and Riga Balsam, a potent drink which we had bought in Latvia; it has rather an unpleasant bitter taste like medicine, but it has a high alcoholic content and it is warming. The edge of hunger was relieved by eating macaroons, bought at Ymuiden; these were wet as a sea arrived aboard at the exact moment the tin was opened.

When the Galloper lightship came abeam three or four miles to starboard, the sea was tremendous and very confused as we were passing over comparatively shallow water. I was steering as this was beyond the physical strength of Mamie; she sat with me in the cockpit trying to make out the distant lights. She kept cheerful, even when things were at their worst, and took her full share of any work that she could do and her good eyesight was a godsend.

An hour passed, but the other lights still remained out of sight and presently even their loom was no longer reflected in the lightening sky.

I had no previous experience of the east coast of England, nor had I any large scale

* *Note*: The light is no longer red.

charts. Rather than attempting to make the tricky entrance of Harwich, which was the nearest port, I eased the sheets and *Racundra* fled for Lowestoft, some fifty miles to the north. In the furious sea and wind the ship needed every ounce of strength to hold her on her course and, in the misery of the near dawn cold, the time seemed to pass very slowly. Mamie again tried to take a trick at the helm, but the effort was beyond her strength. Hours and hours seemed to go by; on sailed the ship, on and on and on.

Then suddenly Mamie saw something on the port bow. I knew it must be land and the end of our difficulties was in sight. Mamie went below and got a primus going to heat the cabin. The sea was steadily moderating, and presently she reappeared on deck with a tin of cold baked beans, which between us we devoured. She then took a watch, and I went below into the warm, peeled off my oilskins and slowly changed into dry clothes. This took an hour and, when I went on deck with dry clothes on my exterior

10. Journey's end. *Racundra* safely laid up at Southwold in 1925 after the North Sea gale.

and whisky in my interior, I felt a different man; but Mamie, who was also wet through, refused to change; not surprisingly, I think she must have been too tired to make the effort.

A low coast was abeam, and short brown seas replaced the confused breaking waves, we passed a black buoy, the sun appeared, but the minutes still seemed like hours. At last we saw a town on the port bow, and after consideration came to the conclusion that it must be Southwold. It came nearer and, through the glasses, we distinguished two long wooden piers. The *Cruising Association Handbook* gave a few notes which were far from encouraging, but on nearer approach we realised we had a leading wind up the reach between the piers. We sailed closer inshore, the entrance came near and we could see waves breaking on either side. I calculated that it was two hours after high water, but the sea did not look shallow in front of the harbour entrance. As Lowestoft lay twelve miles away, we decided to try to gain port at once, and sailed straight for the piers. I took two soundings with the lead; and *Racundra* foamed up the entrance and her anchor was dropped in the calm water of the harbour.

The voyage was at an end.

*   *   *

Not long after our arrival in port the Harbour Master's representative boarded us and helped to move *Racundra* to a position alongside a wooden staging. She was a shambles below deck as the water in the bilges had risen nearly to the cabin sole, and everything capable of moving had been thrown there during the gale, including a big unlidded tin of biscuits. After a meal and a sleep it began to rain again, so we decided to desert the soaking cabin of the ship and sleep ashore for the first time since the voyage began. The village of Walberswick was only a few hundred yards away on the west side of the harbour and we were recommended to put up at the Bell Inn. It was wonderful on arrival there to have tea in front of a blazing fire, listening to the rain dashing against the window without having to go on deck.

As time was getting short, and we were still some 200 miles from our home port of Southampton, we decided to lay *Racundra* up at Tom Martin's shipyard and to return home by train. We accordingly stayed two days at the Bell enjoying the comfort of being waited on, and watching the ship being hauled up and her gear stored. Walberswick was a charming unspoilt little village with moor and marsh-flats to the sea, the home of many varieties of sea birds.

We had felt worn-out on arrival, but we were both young and quickly recovered energy. Years later Mamie told me that for weeks after getting to port she had suffered from nightmares of huge seas. But happily this did not put her off long distance cruising. If I may be allowed to say so, I think her tolerance and endurance during the long voyage were remarkable.

So far as I am concerned the voyage had been the toughest of a lifetime. The low speed of *Racundra* in light and moderate winds made it necessary to sail day and night, even on short passages, and made her a sitting duck for bad weather if such should follow. On the other hand she was at her best under severe conditions owing to her stability. In the North Sea gale, for example, I referred to us sitting in the steering well. This was done without fear of danger and without any safety precautions whatever; in any of the ocean racers I owned later in life this could not have been done without risk of being catapulted over the side if there had been no life-lines or safety harness.

In retrospect, I would sum up the voyage as pure adventure in what to us was the unknown, never sure what was going to happen the next day. The hardships were forgotten, only the happy memories remained.

As to the gale, this was featured in the Sunday and Monday newspapers. The *Daily Mail* recorded it as the worst week-end of the year, with many vessels in distress around the coasts. I describe it in my book *Heavy Weather Sailing*, giving synoptic charts and lessons learned from the experience.

The disturbance was reported as developing off the north coast of Spain early on Saturday morning and travelling north-east across England at the rate of 40 to 45 knots, but the gale in the North Sea was caused by the development of a vigorous secondary depression. At Dungeness the wind was Force 8 and was sustained from 9 a.m. on Saturday evening until 5 p.m. on Sunday. At Calshot, Hampshire, and Spurn Head, Yorkshire, it attained Force 9. The frontal squalls when *Racundra* was hove-to could have been anything up to 50 knots or more.

CHAPTER TWELVE

FAMILY, WORK AND SAILING

After the voyage from Riga in 1925 we returned to Hamble and sold *Annette* in the winter. The following year *Racundra* was also sold and we moved from Hamble back to Southampton, where our daughter Arnaud was born. The same year my term under articles was completed and I sat for the Final Examination of the Institute of Chartered Accountants but failed at my first attempt. We always seemed to be moving and in August or September we took a cottage for six months at Chale, on a lovely part of the south coast of the Isle of Wight, with breezy coastal walks over the fields above the cliffs to Atherfield Ledge. It was at Chale that I swotted up for a second shot at the Final Examination, this time successfully. We then bought Bridge House at Wootton Creek on the north side of the island, where our son Ross was born in December 1928. Most of these places are marked on the chart in Chapter 7.

In the meantime I had set up in practice at 17 St Thomas' Square, Newport, with a branch office at Freshwater. The practice prospered reasonably well and I took into partnership a very able Scottish chartered accountant.

With a family, in common with most parents in a like position, we gave up the ownership of yachts for a number of years, but we had a sailing dinghy and also a nanny to help with the children, which nowadays few, living on a limited income, can afford. We were very happy in the Isle of Wight with our family and many friends.

Two years later I was advised to start in practice in Southampton where there was much greater scope. Mamie and I reluctantly came to the conclusion that, taking the long term view, the advice was sound, particularly as the time would come when substantial school bills had to be met. So we sold Bridge House and my share in the Newport practice, then moved to Compton, near Winchester, which was a splendid place for bringing up the family in country surroundings. I took an office at Southampton and bought a small practice from an unqualified accountant, which gave me a start, and opened branch offices in Alton and Farnham which I visited once a week. I soon had plenty of work and was fortunate in many ways. Three years later an eminent London firm opened an office in Southampton and I met the local partner. A merger was arranged and I became a partner in the Southampton subsidiary firm in 1932; a branch office at Portsmouth was opened a few years later by my partner Stanley Saunders.

Among other interests were books. I wrote financial ones under my name of K A Coles, coupled with my qualifications of MA, FCA; these were two on income tax, one on a specialised branch of accountancy and another a semi-paperback entitled *Safe Investment*, if I remember rightly. This was fairly bursting with prudence, which was not surprising as I wrote it when I was laid low with mumps and hence my outlook was on the pessimistic side. Nevertheless, I seem to remember that it sold an edition of 10,000 copies. For my sailing books I wrote under my name Adlard Coles or K Adlard Coles; these were more interesting and rewarding than my financial works.

Besides writing books in my spare time, a small family publishing company, Robert Ross & Co Ltd, was founded, the name being an amalgamation of the christian name of my father-in-law, and the maiden name of my grandmother (after whom our son Ross had been called). The early publications were not books but the indoor games which I had invented in my school days during World War I. The originals, which I played with my guardian during school holidays, must have been very crude but they provided all the essential principles. There was a yacht racing game whose board was in squares, and I think it was my guardian's suggestion that these should be tilted at 45 degrees to the north, by means of which the movements of the yachts could simulate tacking, reaching or running.

The published version was named *Ship-a-Hoy*, which was not a good name for a yacht racing game, but suitable for registration as a trademark. The number of squares which a yacht could move on the board depended on cards dealt numbered 1 to 8, or special wind cards such as 'calm', 'fresh breeze', 'strong wind' and 'gale'. The cards were beautifully designed by a friend of ours, the late Sir Alker Tripp, who at the time was an Assistant Commissioner at Scotland Yard; he was a cruising man and a first rate marine artist and sailing author. Blanketing competitors was one of the tactics of the game which was partly skill and partly luck. The race started on the Royal Yacht Squadron line, round the buoys and the Bramble Bank, but finished in Cowes Harbour. It was a pretty looking game, played with six brightly coloured metal yachts with white sails, which gave Mamie and me much pleasure when we played with our children, and later with our two grandsons and our grand-daughter with all of whom it was a positive favourite.

The other game which I invented was *Flotilla*, a game of naval tactics which I think must have been devised during school holidays when I was at Selwyn House, then hoping to go from there to Osborne and enter the navy.

To these games were added some invented by Mr Edmund Vale, the author of some fourteen books on the sea, topography and other subjects, who can best be described as a 'worker in ideas'. I shared his view that games were a creative art in a world of imagination. The one of which he was proudest was *Drake*, a board game of skill played with galleons and privateers on an imaginary chart. 'To have proper ships', as he put it in his autobiography *Straw into Gold* (Methuen), 'was one of the essentials of enjoyment in the game, though the sea, rocks, sandbanks and coral-reefs were all reduced to conventions on the board.' Edmund Vale was positively a genius in ideas and inventions, but we lost touch with him during World War II.

Mamie ran the business with great efficiency, doing the selling and organising pre-Christmas demonstrations at most of the leading London stores. I attended to the inventions and copyrights as well as being the financial director or rather the financial mis-director. The games were good and differed from others in the shops, so they were quite successful in a small way, with limited editions backed by limited expenditure on advertising in periodicals such as *The Listener*, *Punch* and the yachting journals. However, when the business developed and was expanded to include ordinary cheap games, it got out of hand and began to make substantial losses so further production had to be discontinued. Happily, the company had also published some books and henceforth its activities were confined to book publishing, which was more successful.

Another interest I had was in the magazine *The Yachtsman* which, as mentioned in Chapter one, I used to take in at tuppence a week when I was at school in Weymouth. It was the magazine in which, when I took up cruising, parts of my books were serialised; from time to time I had also contributed articles. About two years before World War II, I was asked by its printers whether I knew anybody who might like to buy it. As it happened I was a director of a small investment company for whom I vetted the financial side of every proposal submitted to it. I looked into the accounts of *The Yachtsman* which were not encouraging; if I remember rightly, the circulation was at an all-time low and so were the advertising rates, but I thought there might be an element of goodwill in the fact that it was the oldest established of the British yachting magazines. I put the proposition up to the directors of the investment company, who unanimously decided to buy the publication. It was thus that the Yachtsman Publishing Co Ltd came into being, and I was appointed a director and honorary editor.

I knew nothing about magazine production, but one of the directors was a retired printer and he explained the elementary principles. The first thing I did was to reduce the magazine from a weekly to a monthly; apart from the fact that no time was available to run a weekly, the alteration enabled the advertising allocations to the magazine to be concentrated in 12 issues instead of being divided over 52. As soon as possible Terence Stocken, an efficient commercial artist with experience in page lay-outs, was engaged part time; he also had the necessary knowledge of sailing. Later the Rolls House Publishing Co Ltd, who were distributors of a number of periodicals, were appointed to look after circulation. One of the directors was a chartered accountant and he gave me much time and advice on publishing, about which I had a lot to learn. Circulation and advertising revenue increased and the initial losses were greatly reduced although not entirely eliminated. However, the directors of the investment company, who were professional or business friends of mine, generously allowed me to buy the shares. Thus *The Yachtsman* surprisingly came under my control and editorship nearly a quarter of a century after I had first subscribed to it as a boy.

Besides work, I retained my sailing connections. I had been elected a member of the Royal Southern Yacht Club in 1923, on my return in *Annette* from the Baltic, and I served on all the committees: general, finance and sailing. The club house then faced the Royal Pier at Southampton; I lunched there whenever possible and years later was one of the committee instrumental in the move from Southampton to Hamble. I was also a sailing committee member of the Royal Southampton Yacht Club, so for many years I was nearly always present at Cowes Week. Both clubs started and controlled their regattas from the Royal Yacht Squadron, where the visiting race officers were guests for the day.

I also managed to get a generous ration of sailing. In 1931, when we were at Compton, Mamie and I had a happy month's cruising in the far Baltic, as we had a very trustworthy nursery governess to take care of Arnaud and Ross, besides many friends who would have helped temporarily in any emergency. A second cruise, mostly in the Gulf of Finland, was made in 1938, when the children were at their first small boarding school at Sherborne, which was owned by Edmund Vale's sister-in-law. Visits to Reval (Tallinn) and the Estonian coast in both these cruises were inspired by Arthur Ransome's book *Racundra's First Cruise*; to me he was a spell-binder.

Although I could not afford a boat of my own at that time, I was occasionally asked to skipper racing yachts in the absence of their owners. Somewhere about the mid-thirties, Charles A Nicholson and others including myself, founded the Centreboard Racing Club. This was centred at the Ship Inn at Cracknore Hard, at the top of Southampton Water. The dinghies were one-design 14-footers, clinker built and designed by Charles Nicholson's uncle, the famous C E Nicholson. The first six dinghies were built at Husband's Yard, followed by others from Camper & Nichol-sons. Mr Husband was a big friendly man, who lived nearby with his wife and family of thirteen boys and girls. He always treated the members of the club with a twinkle in his eye and the price he charged for the first six dinghies was £32, including a Ratsey mainsail and jib; no spinnaker was carried. Over the years Husband's shipyard has progressively grown to be a large one with seven family directors.

The Centreboard Racing Club was a remarkable institution and the members were mostly young local professional men and their wives. I owned the first (sail number 1) and was crewed by Mamie. Dinghy racing of this kind has the advantage of making the least demands on time and pocket. Combined with the Island Sailing Club dinghies of the same design, they formed the smallest Cowes Week class, racing every day of the week. A feature about the Centreboard Racing Club was the large proportion of its small membership who later became well-known in the sailing world, among whom in particular I should mention Owen Aisher.

In the years leading to World War II Mamie and I often sailed with Francis Usborne who, after the war, became secretary to the Yacht Racing Association soon to become the Royal Yachting Association, or RYA as it is so well known with an ever growing membership and an ever widening scope of activity. He owned a heavy displacement gaff cutter named *Curlew* and in 1937 commissioned Robert Clark to design him a really modern yacht. She was a 10-tonner named *Mystery II* and was built by A H Moody & Sons Ltd at Bursledon to a high specification. She attracted a great deal of attention as being one of the early examples of high performance cruising yachts, equally suitable for ocean racing. Francis Usborne was trusting enough to lend her to me for a cruise down West with other friends of his. Another friend of mine, John Boycott, a member of the Oxford and Cambridge Sailing Society, was good enough to lend me his delightful Tumlare *Zest* for the last year before the war. People were wonderfully generous when I was without a boat of my own.

In 1937 or 1938 we bought a house at Bursledon and for the first time in our lives we settled down, remaining there for over 30 years. At about the same time we bought an 8-foot dinghy for Arnaud and Ross. It was one of A H Moody's excellent standard yacht tenders, but I had a deep dagger plate and housing added. At that time most sailing dinghies were rigged with lugsails of one kind or another which gave a poor windward performance. Instead of this I devised a modern high aspect ratio rig with mainsail and a small jib so essential for good windward performance. The silver spruce mast was made in two pieces and scarfed with two metal straps, so that it could be stowed inside the boat when not sailing. She was called *Jenny*, named after a favourite hen. By accident I had happened on an almost perfect design for what was wanted; the boat was close-winded, responsive to the lightest airs and happy as a sandboy in fresh winds when other dinghies were reefed. Cosby Smallpeice, a friend of long standing, ordered a similar boat for his daughter.

Above all things, children like to be independent. Although *Jenny* could be sailed with two, Arnaud and Ross (who could both swim) usually preferred to sail single-handed, once they had learned the ropes, exploring the little tidal creeks in the upper Hamble River on their own.

CHAPTER THIRTEEN

GULF OF FINLAND AND SWEDEN

It was in 1931 that H L P Jolly suggested that it would do us good to have another cruise in the Baltic, and offered an introduction to Dr Mustelin, a friend of his who lived in Åbo (Turku), Finland. He owned *Sjöfröken*, a sister ship to Jolly's own yacht *Ingrid* which was being built in Germany at the time I was there in 1923 with *Annette*.

Arrangements for charter were quickly made on terms which were generous to us and a passage booked in the *Ilmatar*, a freighter due to dock at Helsingfors early on Monday morning, August 3rd. On arrival a taxi took us to the station, an imposing building built in light-coloured stone and surmounted by a high tower, which stood facing a large cobbled square, through which glided the bright-coloured trams so typical of the north. The train for Åbo did not leave until 2.50 p.m. and was drawn by an engine with a huge pot funnel, and fired by wood fuel. From the windows could be seen a constant succession of pine woods, sheets of water, reeds and hillocks with hard outcrops of granite rock. When we came to our destination we stayed at the 'Hamburger Bors' where Dr Mustelin, a big, warm-hearted man, met us. By hurrying through dinner there was still enough light for a visit to the Airisto Sailing Club anchorage, situated a few miles down river, and for a brief introduction to his Bermudan-rigged yawl *Sjöfröken* (meaning in English something akin to a mermaid).

Her particulars were Thames tonnage 15 tons, displacement 8·5 tons, LOA 33ft, LWL 29ft 5ins, beam 11ft 3ins, draught 6ft, and sail area 770 sq ft. She had an Andros 2-cylinder, 8 h.p. petrol engine, with 3-blade feathering Hyde propeller, and large capacity water tanks. Her anchors were 70lb and 40lb, and the compass was accurately swung and lit by electric battery. She had ordinary reefing gear with points, except for Wykeham-Martin roller reefing on the jib. The arrangements below were particularly good, as her owner was an experienced cruising man, who had given much time and thought to making her comfortable in every detail, and the cabin was really dry in any weather.

We had only two days in which to prepare and provision for the cruise starting on August 5th. Owing to a professional engagement, Dr Mustelin was unable to accompany us to the Airisto Club moorings so we were taken in the Club launch. The passage was enthralling among Finnish shipping, i.e. little white steamers plying to the outer isles, tramps and timber schooners alongside the wharves, motor-boats and yachts rejoicing in a stiff breeze and a sunny day. We also passed the new 'pocket battleships' under construction for the Finnish Navy and nearby lay four new submarines. After about half an hour, the launch drew alongside the white topsides and shining varnish of *Sjöfröken*. she soon presented an unusual spectacle; her decks loaded with old suitcases tied up by string, an enormous sail bag full of oilskins and old clothes, together with crates of stores, such as sausages of diverse brands (never judge a sausage by the colour of its skin), cases of beer, boxes of bottled milk, and all the necessaries for the cruise. We stowed it all below temporarily, but it was not until about 4 p.m. that the yacht was ready to start.

Sjöfröken lay facing a fresh north-westerly wind, with a steam yacht at moorings on her port bow and shallows under her stern. It was not an ideal position for getting under way with an unknown boat in strange waters. I had just set the mainsail and jib when, owing to our inability to understand each other, the Finnish paid hand suddenly cast her off from the mooring.

Thus, unexpectedly, we found ourselves under sail. I hurriedly backed the jib, and we made a short leg on the starboard tack towards the steam yacht. When we came about (rather dubiously, as we had little way on), we suddenly noticed a rowing boat under our lee bow. For a moment it was touch and go, but we just missed her and steered away into more open water. *Sjöfröken* was fast, the feel of her tiller was unfamiliar, and she seemed to be one mass of lines and tackles. Our sails were set shockingly, and there was neither time nor room to attempt experiments. I ran forward and hoisted the staysail, but in a second the sheets raced through the blocks— no knots had as yet been made in them. By the time we had dropped the staysail and eased the main sheet the other shore was near, and we just had time to come about, with sails flogging. We soon straightened things out, however, and set a course out into the open fiord. The wind then became free; as we cleared the land we felt its full force, and in the squalls the yacht lay down to it, as she tore forward to the south-west. We realised then that this was the fastest ship we had ever before handled together.

Confidence was soon regained and sailing was exhilarating in the keen air over the blue, white-flecked sea. To port stood the broken coastlines of the wooded inner islands, full of rocks and indentations, and to starboard lay innumerable skerries stretching away for a hundred miles.

That was our first sail in Finnish waters, and after about an hour and a half we stood into a channel between two high wooded islands. Course was altered slightly and we brought up under the lee of two little islets, both too small to be honoured with a name. Nothing better could be asked for than this our first anchorage. To the west lay a fringe of green reeds only a few yards distant, edging the islets, which were backed by the grey rock and green fir trees of a larger island. When the wind fell later there was an absolute peace in these sheltered waters. Silence, but for the splash of a rising fish, the lowing of a cow, and the occasional bark of a dog on a neighbouring farmstead. But we had not much time to appreciate the scenery. We had been busy the whole day, and although we had put away most of the gear and stores, much still remained to be done. Sails had to be stowed, lines coiled down on deck, and the riding-lamp lit. The cabin was in a state of confusion and our sea-going clothes were still unpacked. There was also the not unimportant matter of supper to be considered.

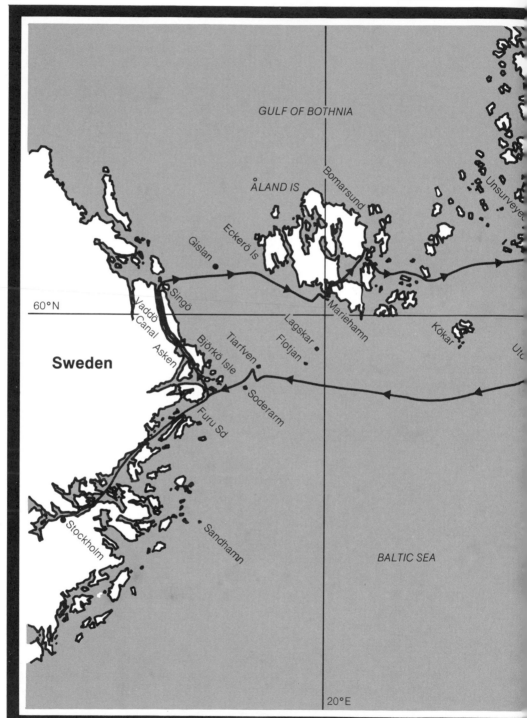

7. *The Baltic. Sjöfröken*'s cruise from Reval to Stockholm and return, via Finland.

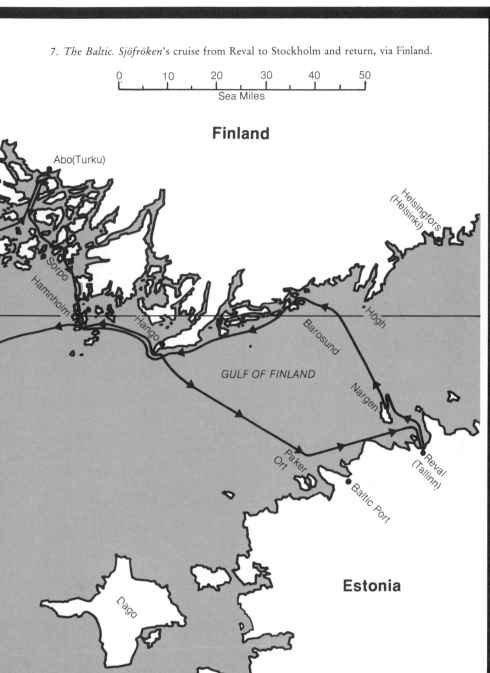

11. *Sjöfröken* anchored under the lee of an island in Barö Sound, Finland. Her high rig meant early reefing in a blow.

Next day we were up early and found a glorious sunny morning. There was time for a short swim in beautifully warm water before breakfast, and afterwards we pulled ashore in the dinghy, pushing through the reeds and tying up alongside the rocks.

At 11.30 we set sail following the track marked on the chart, and in the afternoon *Sjöfröken* came into the narrow Sound of Sorpo or Pargas, meaning 'Gate'. Here the channel was incredibly narrow in places, and the wind was fluky, owing to the trees. The route was well marked, but at times the tacks were so short that it was difficult to hold steerage way, although when coming about we could often almost go alongside the rocks themselves, as in most parts these were steep-to.

Sjöfröken then came to the wider but rock-strewn waters of Guldkrona Fiord and, just as it was getting dark, we altered course and made two short tacks into the wonderful natural harbour of Hamnholm, formed by an island with a breakwater of islets and rocks.

Next morning brought a change of weather, with half a gale of wind from south by east.

Breakfast was a very English meal, composed of 'three-minute' porridge boiled on a primus stove, eggs, bread of various colours and textures, and also marmalade, which we had brought out from England. Washing-up over, we rowed in the dinghy across the little bay, through a belt of reeds, and drew in by some rocks. The island was thickly wooded, and along the edge we found low shrubs, wild strawberries and

12. Looking west from Hamnholm. Trees, lichen-covered rocks and more islands.

blueberries. We struck west, climbing over lichen and heather covered rocks, trunks of fallen trees and occasional patches of soft moss, until we reached the summit of the island. To the west lay the sea, deep blue, white-capped. A schooner heavily laden with timber was running north-west, and in every direction as far as the eye could see lay islands—wooded islands and barren islands.

When back on the ship we found the south-easterly wind had freshened. A bed of reeds indicating shallow water was uncomfortably close under our stern, so I decided to shift our berth. We hoisted a reefed mainsail and the yawl fell off on the starboard tack, then luffed, and anchored in the centre of the bay. It was well that we moved, for the glass continued to fall, and during the night it blew a gale.

Next day it was blowing as hard as ever but, as the first part of the course lay in semi-sheltered waters, we decided to make a start in the afternoon. To get the anchor under such conditions was extremely difficult. Mamie took the helm and I slowly turned the capstan round, using my right hand only, because the left was needed to keep the chain taut as it came on deck and guide it to the chain locker below. At first all went well, and the chain came in slowly foot by foot over the starboard bow. Meanwhile, the boat sheered about as her high mainmast was stepped so far forward that she tended to fall off the wind. The moment the mainsail was hoisted she took charge, and drove up over her anchor. This dragged, and she did not answer her helm. I turned the capstan as fast as I could, but it was a long task using one hand only. By the time the anchor was brought to the stemhead *Sjöfröken* had crossed the narrow anchorage to the far side. Once again I rushed forward and let go the anchor. Too late! She held on, dragging it after her. I dropped sail with a run, the anchor gripped a little, but before *Sjöfröken* could swing head to wind, she hit a rock, drove to leeward, and brought up in a little bight between the rocks–fortunately quite unharmed. The holding ground was doubtful, so I ran off a warp and tied it to a tree. To make everything doubly sure in case of a shift of wind, I pulled off in the dinghy and dropped the kedge anchor astern.

Then we had tea, and talked things over. *Sjöfröken* had an engine, but I think I was right in not trying to use it in such restricted water before becoming familiar with it and handling the yacht under power (I was also remembering *Racundra*'s unreliable 'smelly monster'). My mistake was impatience in attempting to get under way in a gale in confined waters when we were so short-handed.

The wind continued all night. In the cabin we heard the beat of the rain on deck and the splashing of the water under the bows. Above all other sounds could be heard the incessant roar in the rigging and through the trees of the island.

The wind veered next morning to south-west and moderated a little. As this was fair for Hangö we prepared to get under way. There was precious little sea room, with a little rocky island only about 40 feet away from our stern, but it was managed successfully, *Sjöfröken* drew away on the port tack with double-reefed mainsail, staysail and storm jib. We made two short tacks and then steered out into the fiord, where we felt the full weight of the gale, necessitating a further shortening of sail. Still unfamiliar with this kind of navigation, we found the number of islands and the variety of channels confusing; nevertheless, they were well marked and, after putting into another anchorage for a night, we arrived at Hangö at 5 p.m. on the following day in bright sunshine.

Hangö is the principal port on the south-west corner of the mainland of Finland and

13. Typical lighthouse built on bare rock near Hangö in the outer skerries.

owes its importance to usually being ice-free even in severe winters. For the cruising man it provides a useful point of departure or arrival when crossing the Gulf of Finland, and for provisioning; in the summer it is a popular resort with good bathing. The town was not particularly interesting, and then consisted mainly of timber houses situated in a few streets, and dotted along the rocky coast or further inland amongst the trees. Although it was only the middle of August, the season had ended, but the large casino was open and provided us with an excellent dinner at a very low price.

Our next port of call was to be Reval (Tallinn) in Estonia. It was only about 50 miles ESE as the crow flies, or 70 miles on the course sailed. We started at noon on the next day, August 12th, which was again fine, but the wind, instead of being half a gale in force, was very light, though it remained south-westerly, fair for Estonia. However, before we could gain the open sea we should have to beat out of the narrow channel, so we decided to risk the engine. Dr Mustelin had shown me how this should be started and for half an hour I tried unsuccessfully to get it to go. Before putting back the engine casing, I gave the flywheel just one more push over compression and it started instantly.

The motor made up for lost time. *Sjöfröken* simply charged down the channel, her ensign streaming. When we left the channel we altered course south-east and soon switched off the engine. It was a perfect sunny day and, in the north, Hangö water tower and church stood out remarkably clearly, and away to the east stood Segelskär, a tower erected miles out to sea and surrounded by outlying dangers. The wind was falling and speed dropped away. By three in the afternoon there was not a breath of air. All day the Segelskär and Hangö landmarks remained in sight, the yacht rolling in the swell. I took the night watch but it was not until 11 p.m. that a slight air came from the north-west, so that all sail could be set and the ship steadied. The wind shifted and freshened from the west, and soon *Sjöfröken* was sailing fast.

It was a grand sail, with a strong, fair wind. Under such conditions, to be alone on deck piloting a ship across the Gulf of Finland was an experience I would not have missed for anything. The night was very dark. Occasionally the lights of passing ships came by, and towards dawn next morning I strained my eyes, looking for the light of the Paker Ort lighthouse which was to be our landfall on the Estonian coast. At 2 a.m. the loom could be seen over our bow, and not long afterwards the sky began to lighten; by 4 a.m. the lighthouse itself was silhouetted against the sky. Mamie then turned out and made her welcome and warming porridge before coming on watch. A course was set for Sourup Head, then about ENE 14 miles distant. This was passed at 6.30 a.m. and course was altered slightly to leave the Estonian island of Nargen to port. But the wind was falling again and so was the speed of *Sjöfröken*.

When at last the city of Reval was opened up to the south, it presented a wonderful picture from the sea. The old part of the town clustered on and around a hill, from which rose spires, towers, and turrets and the golden domes of the Russian Cathedral. Factory chimneys usually give a modern appearance to a place, but here they seemed to fit into the scene, and from their summits clouds of smoke slowly spread eastwards in the light wind, giving the city a dreamy, sleeping effect. As we came nearer we could distinguish the grey wall, the towers and the red roofs.

But with the falling wind it was to be a long time before we should actually get into port and find where the yacht club lay. At length on near arrival, the club motor boat was sent out to take us in tow; in a short time *Sjöfröken*'s bows were made fast to a buoy, and the stern was warped to the quay belonging to the club. It was 12 noon—exactly twenty-four hours since we had started from Hangö.

At the Estonian Yacht Club we were given a warm welcome, especially by the Vice-Commodore, and an Englishman who had spent most of his life in Russia until the Revolution. It was the practice of the club to hoist the flag of each country represented by a yacht in their anchorage and on that day there were three—Finnish, German, followed by the British on our arrival; it was the first time it had been hoisted for thirteen years, so we were told. In the afternoon we walked up to the town itself.

There can be no place that is more essentially a seaport than Reval. We walked towards the city, along the quays, through the docks, past cargo steamers, white-hulled passenger boats, and sturdy timber schooners being unloaded by picturesque peasant women. The docks themselves were kept clean by convict labour, and occasionally we came across a gang working under the supervision of armed warders. We continued our way in the direction of the bastions of the Domberg Fortress. The city has been conquered in turn by the Danes, the German Knights, the Swedes and the Russians, and there remained much about its appearance and character that was Russian. The club which had received us so hospitably had formerly been the old Imperial Yacht Club. Estonia became a free state in 1920, coming under the rule of its original population, the Esths. Its independence was sadly lost during World War II at the end of which, like Latvia, it returned to Russian rule and became a constituent republic of the USSR.

14. An old time photograph of Utö, showing lighthouse and anchorage, with gaff cutter and local craft all with vertically cut mainsails without battens.

What struck us as strangers most about Reval was the number of churches and towers. On the citadel there was the Dom Church standing in sharp contrast with the Byzantine architecture of the Russian Cathedral with its five gilded domes. In the lower city stood the churches of St Nicholas and St Olaf, which had a massive tower surmounted by a very high spire. And, as to old fortifications, the place seemed full of them. There were the Sea Gate, the Viru Gate, the Pikkjalg Gate, the Kik-in-de-Kok Tower, and many others whose names I have forgotten. The whole place seemed full of towers, ramparts, flights of stone steps, arches and narrow passages.

We spent the next day seeing to the countless small things which required attention, including refilling the water tanks, and buying provisions in the market. During the morning this presented a most animated appearance, with women in country costumes, peasants from all parts, policemen in uniforms of pale blue and dark blue, soldiers and people of every sort.

We bade farewell to our friends at the club on the Saturday afternoon. The launch towed *Sjöfröken* out to a mooring and we were able to get under way in ideal conditions, but the wind slowly died so we anchored under the lee of Nargen for the night. It looked a wonderful island, with its white sand dunes along the shore, backed by ruined fortifications and forest; we were not allowed to land as it was still fortified. On the following morning, Sunday, we set sail for our return to Finland, – the distance was only about 35 miles but the wind being light it was 8 p.m. when we brought up in a lovely anchorage in the entrance of Barö Sound, after navigating through the outer skerries.

We enjoyed sailing next morning in the Sound, much of which lies between thickly wooded islands. The weather was sunny, navigation easy and safe anchorages could always be found. But there was only a week left as we were due at Stockholm on August 24th, where our friend Francis Usborne was to join us. Sailing westwards we came off Hangö in the afternoon of the 19th, but we had to press on without stopping. By 10 p.m. it was dark and I navigated in the channel, which frequently changes its direction, by means of the little lighthouses, each having red, white (indicating the correct course) and green sectors. At midnight we brought up in an out of the way anchorage we found marked on the chart. Next day we started on navigation of a somewhat different kind as we wanted to visit Utö, a lonely outpost among the barren skerries lying on the way to Sweden. To reach this we had to sail through what I think is called the Vidskärsfjörd, which looks like a wide fiord but contains many dangerous rocks. The navigable track is narrow and its changes of direction are indicated by a series of pairs of leading marks which must be kept exactly in line. Hence it can be dangerous if caught out in bad visibility or in rain thick enough to blot out the marks.

It was almost dark before we found ourselves off the island of Utö. The anchorage lies between three almost barren skerries, and finding the entrance was rather difficult work. We noticed that a pilot launch had disappeared behind a rock a few hundred yards ahead of us, but when we came to the point where we lost sight of her, it was difficult to see where she could have gone. Our chart marked an island of reasonable size, but it showed that we also had to pass two tiny islets before steering in. We found the big island and the first little island, but when we came to look for the second we could only see quite a smallish flat rock. It seemed unbelievable that we should have to round that rock as it was only a few yards from another larger island; yet such proved to be the case. With our hearts in our mouths we steered in through this extraordinarily narrow entrance, finding when we were inside that the flat rock was much bigger than it had appeared.

Once within the harbour the boat was in sheltered water. After we had anchored, when night came, the lighthouse on Utö appeared flashing away close to the south, and the sky overhead was clear and covered with stars, which threw enough light on the water to set off, in sharp contrast, the dark forms of the rocks around us. There was silence, except for the constant sound of the surf on the iron-bound coast, and the occasional siren of a passing steamer calling for a pilot.

The weather remained fine, and next morning was bright and sunny. We had intended to make an early start, but this was delayed owing to an elderly fisherman coming alongside at 8 a.m. He was evidently a patriarch at Utö, and took us hospitably to the timber built cottage home of his married daughter where we were joined by her husband and brother-in-law who, I think, were also fishermen.

We weighed anchor at eleven o'clock bound for Stockholm, a distance of about 120 miles by sea—see chart pages 78–9. Before 9.15 that night the loom of the lights of the Swedish lighthouses could be discerned away in the west. There was no mistaking the flash each minute of the Soderarm Lighthouse, and the group flash of the Tjarven north-west of it, but many hours were to lapse before we should draw close to them. The wind fell, and once again we were inflicted with the abominable roll of the Baltic in which *Sjöfröken* barely held steerage way.

I was in theory to keep watch for the full night at the helm, from sunset to dawn. But at 2 a.m. a squall of wind and rain bore down on us and I had to call Mamie on deck to take the helm. In practice we were both to be on deck for most of the time until arrival at Stockholm. I began the slow and tedious operation of reefing down single-handed at night; even when the mainsail had been brought down on deck it was difficult to find the right reefing points in the dark in the absence of any deck light. It took me nearly half an hour, and by the time I had finished the squall had passed, and we lay pitching heavily in a steep swell. It was still raining but I did not shake the reef out, waiting to see what the weather held in store.

In this fashion I spent another two hours sitting at the helm feeling very damp and cursing the infernal swell. We were not far from the Swedish lighthouses but we decided to stand off and on. Towards dawn we ran in a little closer, but we were unable to identify any leading lights; it was raining hard at the time and the visibility was poor, so we kept at sea and waited for the dawn. It came on to blow very hard indeed; the wind had shifted to the east, so we were now off a rocky lee shore. It was bitterly cold and wet, but by 5 a.m. the sky was lighter and the waves could be seen. We hove-to while Mamie went below to make large cups of Horlick's malted milk. The problem that lay before us was not the entry between Söderarm and Tjärven lighthouses, which is easy providing one does not approach either too closely, especially the Söderarm which has off-lying dangers. The difficulties would come when we passed beyond the line of the two lighthouses into the comparatively narrow channel with unseen rocks on either hand.

In the approach we were somewhat helped through being overtaken by a white-hulled passenger ship that had picked up a pilot; but, although she led the way in between the lighthouses, she had rapidly out-distanced us before we reached the five miles of narrow channel. In the ordinary way, given clear daylight, there would have been no problems but when we came to it, running very fast before half a gale of wind in rough seas, navigation with only a small scale chart was tricky. We had, as strangers, to identify the slender spar buoys or beacons one by one as we sped past them in the wan light of early morning and the poor visibility of heavy rain. It was anxious work, even when aided by Mamie's keen eyesight, as a single error might have meant disaster. As *Sjöfröken* ran farther into the channel gaining shelter from the outer skerries, the seas began to moderate, and at 6 a.m. Mamie went below and made porridge. It was not long before we entered the well marked Furu Sound, one of the busiest fairways in Sweden. The islands on each side were populated, and houses stood on the shore facing the Sound. After we had made a proper meal and I had shaved, we felt fit to face anything, particularly as the wind moderated and the sun came out. We had not then realised that the distance to Stockholm, allowing for deviations between islands, was still over 50 miles.

Later on we found ourselves in company with several trading vessels, schooners and also one or two cutters, which we gradually overhauled. Freighters and passenger steamers frequently passed us. About noon, when off a small village named Noten and sailing along comfortably, we were intercepted by a very fast, bright-varnished speed launch. She came up under our lee, and before she had stopped a man had taken a flying jump aboard of us. He was a Customs officer and was extremely courteous; we told him our port of departure and where we were bound, and produced the ship's papers. As we belonged to a recognised yacht club there was very little formality beyond the declaration for alcohol, of which we had very little. In a few minutes the motor launch came racing back, slowed down to pick up our examiner, and then shot away, rapidly overtaking a schooner ahead of us.

In the afternoon we left the coast of the mainland and bore south between islands, passing the fortress of Vaxholm. An hour or so later Stockholm came into sight at the end of a fiord with high hills on either side, truly a magnificent approach to Sweden's capital. We sailed on, making little progress and finding ourselves gradually headed by the wind; we were also slowed by the wash of passing ships, ferries (which run almost as frequently as motor buses), motor yachts and launches. There is no speed limit and in the restricted channel the wash and cross wash between them defied description. At 5 p.m. I managed to start the engine and an hour later, after a search, we found the Royal Swedish Yacht Club. It lies on the northern side of the fiord with its entrance facing east. The club boatman obligingly came off in a launch to meet us and *Sjöfröken*'s bows were soon moored to a buoy; a gang-plank was placed between the stern and the quay so that we could step ashore whenever we liked. The club gave us every facility and made us temporary members.

It was 6 p.m. on August 21st when we actually brought up, and we were delighted to find that by Swedish time it was only 5 o'clock, which made it possible for our mail to be sent down from Thomas Cook & Sons before their office closed. It was an exciting moment when they arrived as we had been out of touch with the world since we left Reval.

Needless to say we went ashore as soon as possible, where we enjoyed dinner at a moderate price, although more than in Finland. We were up very late next morning and before we had finished breakfast we were hailed from the quay by a man in uniform and, when he boarded *Sjöfröken*, I suddenly realised that he was another Customs officer. Like the one in the launch he was exceedingly polite and obliging and when the formalities had been completed for the second time, the officer indicated with a benign smile that we were now free to go ashore when we liked.

After breakfast we went into the city again and visited the A/B Nordiska Companiet, which is the Harrods of the North. Mamie had a shampoo and a water wave (apparently preferable to a sea wave) and I had my hair cut, a quicker operation. We enjoyed our brief visit to Stockholm; it was fine sunny weather and we had plenty to do preparing *Sjöfröken* for the return passage to Åbo so we had little time for sightseeing. All the stores which we purchased were sent to the club, and there we were able to replenish our water tanks, and take in a supply of fuel. The club house at Stockholm was small, as in summer months most of the yachts are stationed at Sandhamn in the outer archipelago, but it was exceedingly well kept and comfortable; a great boon to us during our visit.

Francis Usborne was due to arrive in the early morning of August 24th, but his ship had been delayed and it was not until the afternoon that we met him. I think my last letter had made him somewhat apprehensive for he brought with him no less than thirteen half-pound slabs of chocolate and, when I casually mentioned that there was a shortage of blankets, we were off again immediately to the Nordiska Companiet.

CHAPTER FOURTEEN

ÅLAND ISLES AND ESTONIA

We departed from Stockholm at 10 a.m. next morning, bound for the Åland Islands and Åbo. There was a westerly following wind, but so light that, although we sailed all day, we only made good 20 miles. To make up lost time we made an early start the following day, finding a dramatic change in the weather; the wind had shifted and was blowing hard from the north-east. It was very cold and before mid-day we had arrayed ourselves in clothes sufficient for the Arctic, whence came the wind. We spent nearly two days in Furu Sound with the wind dead on the nose, most of the time beating against the short steep fresh water seas, close-reefed and making innumerable short tacks, for in some parts the fairway is very narrow. While getting under way from a temporary anchorage the kedge anchor was lost overboard and half a day was spent trying ineffectively to find a replacement. However, our last anchorage in Furu Sound was a pleasant one in a cove near the entrance, where we lay near a handsome little trading cutter, with bright-varnished topsides and loaded with a deck cargo of timber, waiting for better weather. We weighed anchor next morning and, with the engine going all out, it took us two hours to cover a few miles in a smother of sea, white with breakers, to get clear of Furu Sound. We then entered a fiord leading northward and were soon in sheltered water under the lee of a group of small islands and it was not long before we could bear away to find anchorage behind a small island named Asken on the west side of the fiord. There we were well protected from the wind and it seemed almost warm compared with the previous two days.

From Asken followed one of the happiest parts of our cruise. We decided to take a north-north-west passage for 25 miles in the shelter of the islands of Björkö and Väddö and then emerge into the Åland Sea through a narrow channel named Singösund.

After little over an hour's sailing we entered the main fiord but the wind headed us and was failing. Just at that time we noticed a large ketch proceeding under power, so I hailed her and her skipper kindly agreed to give us a tow. The weight of *Sjöfröken* seemed to make little difference to the *Diligence*, as the ketch was named, so she towed us steadily at a speed of about five knots. The fiord was a pretty one, the sun was shining, and we enjoyed having the leisure to watch the shores, with their rocks, houses and trees.

The channel gradually grew narrower, and later in the day we found ourselves

15. In tow of the trader *Diligence*. When her engine later broke down, we towed her laden with 50 tons of cement.

approaching that part of the fiord which is really a canal–the Väddö Canal. Here *Diligence* slowed up and proceeded with the utmost caution, for the channel was so narrow that little room was left on either side of her. Not long afterwards we suddenly heard a hail and learned that she was stopping alongside a landing stage as something had gone wrong with her engine. After accepting the kindness of her skipper, we felt we could not possibly desert him, so we offered him a tow. We were somewhat short of fuel, so the mate of the ketch set off with me along a country lane to a garage situated about a mile away, where we obtained a large can of it, for which the mate insisted upon paying. His knowledge of English was a bit rusty, though this quickly came back to him. As we walked he told me about *Diligence*. Her English name was accounted for as she had been a Lowestoft fishing vessel, which he and his brother (the skipper) had bought cheaply, and used for trading. She was ninety tons, and her cargo consisted of fifty tons of cement, so I could not help feeling that 140 tons would be rather a heavy load when we took her in tow.

On my return to *Sjöfröken* we had lunch, after which Francis started the engine, and we drew ahead until the end of the tow rope had been reached. There *Sjöfröken* came to a halt as she felt the weight of *Diligence*, but she gradually obtained steerage way, and presently we found that we could tow *Diligence* at about two knots while still in the sheltered canal, and at about one knot in the more open reaches.

We continued in this fashion for an hour or two through little lakes, and through stretches of narrow canal with trees on either side. Towards seven o'clock in the evening we entered the southern end of the fiord that opens into the canal from the north. We stopped there to cast off *Diligence*, for the channel was wide enough to enable her the next day to proceed under sail. We then continued on our way alone, after bidding a grateful good-bye to our friends in the ketch.

When *Sjöfröken* was freed of her load of 140 tons she moved at an astonishing speed through the water. In the late evening the wind had dropped, and in the still water she seemed to be making about seven knots. We were anxious to get away from the archipelago into the deep water of the Åland Sea before dark, but this proved to be impossible. The light failed whilst we were still amongst the islands, but in the wider reaches there was just enough to enable us to navigate, and the buoys loomed up out of the dusk as we drew close to them. The surface of the fiord was unruffled, and made a perfect mirror for land and sky.

Soon we altered course to round a small island and headed eastwards through Singösund to the open sea. This narrow sound started between the island of Singö and a small island named Fogdö. The *Baltic Pilot* states that the channel is 'very tortuous' and 'at times the current is strong and the buoys are dragged under water', but fortunately we did not find any current on this occasion. The reflection in the water of the dark woods made it impossible to see the buoys, except those which we passed very closely. The engine was throttled down and the yawl glided slowly forward. Before long the centre of the fiord was lit by the moon, which rose above a gap in the trees ahead, but most of the channel lay in darkness. As *Sjöfröken* drew nearer the gap between the islands, it looked as though she could hold on her course in the path of the moon into the Åland Sea. But a glance at the chart showed that this channel was strewn with rocks, and the real track lay in a narrow cut leading away to the south-east between a small islet and Fogdö. We altered course, and found ourselves once more in the shadow of the trees.

The next ten minutes before we made the open sea were wonderful. *Sjöfröken* was slipping down a narrow unbuoyed channel between the rocky shores of the two thickly wooded islands, so we depended on compass and sense of direction. As she drew further out, the moon came into sight again and a rocky point stood silhouetted before us. Altering course again we crept along close to the point, gradually feeling the surge of the open sea and hearing the sound of the waves breaking among the unmarked rocks close to starboard.

At 9 p.m. we were clear so we streamed the log; Mamie then went below to prepare dinner. The sea had gone down so much that only a slight swell was left; it remained a marvellous moonlight night, and to be at the helm was a joy. The course was due east across the Åland Sea to the island of Eckerö, where we proposed to find a temporary anchorage. Navigation was easy and Gislan Lighthouse, marking the south end of a group of skerries, was passed at midnight some seven miles west of Eckerö. After continuing on course for a while we decided to save time by sailing to the south-east towards Mariehamn, the principal port of the Ålands. Francis took a two hour watch which was followed by me but, before he had enjoyed half an hour's sleep, I had to call him back on deck again as I had sighted a light ahead. It proved to be a ship with her masthead light appearing in regular sequence in the waves.

The approach to Mariehamn from the west is difficult at night as, before joining the main channel from the south, one has to find and follow a devious track through nearly four miles of outlying skerries and rocks. We could not identify any leading lights, but we sighted a red light and ran further to the south before approaching any closer. It then turned white indicating what I thought must be the right approach. As we came nearer in half light towards dawn, we discovered the light came from a lighthouse or beacon standing on an outer island. I cannot now recollect what chart we were using, except that it was on small scale and this lighthouse (which we learnt afterwards was called the Kobbaklintarne) was not marked on it, so I assume it must have been an old one.

We started the engine and lowered sail, proceeding at the lowest possible speed. Francis went forward to keep a look out whilst I steered and navigated. We passed the lighthouse safely and then found ourselves in a perfect maze of rocks and skerries. It was quite certain that we were in the wrong channel, but we continued, relying, as in the days of old before lighthouses and buoys, on our own judgement and a sharp look out for danger. One can almost always tell from the appearance of an island whether it is steep-to or likely to be surrounded by outlying dangers. The course we picked was very close indeed to some of the islets, leaving on the starboard hand what looked like a wide strip of deep water, but which, on account of the appearance of the rocks and skerries in the vicinity, I suspected of hiding submerged dangers.

At that early hour it was blowing pretty hard from the north, but it was not rough as the skerries provided protection, so there was little physical danger. It was piercingly cold particularly for Francis, who bore the brunt of this, standing in the bows keeping a look out. We passed some anxious moments while making this approach, but more by luck than skill we succeeded in picking our way between the submerged rocks without mishap. Although the distance was relatively small it seemed a long time before we cleared the dangers and entered the deep water of the sound leading northward to Mariehamn. The engine was then set going full speed, and in a short time we were off the town. We let go anchor fairly near the shore, but found the water so deep that we had to pull it up again and re-anchor even closer in.

It was 5 a.m. when we brought up, and there was not a soul in sight except a paid hand on a steam yacht, who looked extremely miserable. We had a small breakfast of Horlick's malted milk and biscuits, and then turned in until mid-day.

In retrospect it is clear that we ought to have hove-to and waited for full daylight, perhaps having breakfast, as it is always best to approach rocks on a full belly. We could then have used the northern track into Mariehamn (as Mamie and I did seven years later) which is clearly marked by cardinal buoys. It was the lights that were so confusing, as their sectors and characters were not shown. Leading lights are only good for a limited distance as, if overstood, they sometimes end on dangers marked only by unlit buoys. I should add that the Admiralty published a large scale chart of the Åland Isles in 1967 (no doubt based on a Finnish one which we had not with us) showing all 'mod cons', including a radio beacon and light on the islet of Korso well inside the outer dangers of the Kobbaklintarne.

I learnt later that we were not the first to have difficulty in making Mariehamn at night, as a Finnish friend wrote to me afterwards telling of a wreck that occurred in what appears to have been about the same place. He wrote 'Three or four years ago on a pitch-black night just before Christmas a big iron sailing ship, *Virgo* of Mariehamn, tried to make the inlet, running before a following gale. She was on her way home from Australia, and the crew could already see the lights of their homes in the town, when the captain, a few cable lengths from Kobbaklintarne beacon, noticed there was something wrong with the leading lights. He was in the wrong channel!

'The helm was hurriedly put down, but a few seconds later the ship piled up on an ice-clad rock, and was soon broken up by the sea. I remember seeing the wreck there about two years ago.' All hands were apparently lost.

Mariehamn, the capital of the Åland Islands, is situated on a peninsula with deep channels and anchorages on both sides. The small town had a population of about 1,600. It was famous as the home port of the last fleet of big sailing ships. Several of these beautiful barques were lying near us, or farther down the channel; freights were bad and many of them lay at moorings waiting for better times. We noticed the *Olive Bank*, the *Oaklands*, and others equally well known.

We only had time for a brief visit ashore to get a further supply of fuel as we were pressed for time. It was Sunday, August 30th, when we had arrived in the fiord and which left us only one and a half days to get to Åbo on September 1st, to allow time for cleaning up *Sjöfröken*, packing our things and catching the 2.30 p.m. train for Helsingfors, where the *Ilmatar* would take us back to England.

We weighed anchor at 3.30 p.m. and, after following somewhat complicated but well-marked winding channels and crossing the Lumpar Fiord (which resembles an inland lake about 6 miles square and can be surprisingly rough), we entered the exceptionally narrow channel of Bomarsund where, after a brief encounter with a rock, we brought up for the night. This sound is one of the best known in Finnish waters, and along the western shore stand ruined fortifications, resulting from the attack and forces landed by the combined British and French fleets during the Crimean War in 1854. Navigation by these big ships, mostly under sail, through the intricate

16. Ruins of Bomarsund fortress in the Åland Islands, destroyed in 1854 by a combined Anglo-French operation.

narrow channels into Lumpar Fiord, must have been a great achievement. We were told that some of the soundings on the very chart which we used, had been made by the British fleet and it had not been necessary to correct them since. The shores of Bomarsund are composed of the usual smooth granite, and backed by trees; the only signs of habitation were the pilot's house and a few timber cottages of the fishermen, perched upon the steep ascent from the shore to the trees, nor were there any boats or ships lying in the anchorage. The ruins, of which there are several, add a touch of forlornness to the scene, which on a fine still evening is very beautiful.

Next day we weighed anchor at eight o'clock; it was a lovely sunny morning, but we had to use the engine occasionally in order to press on for Åbo, pursuing a winding course for the most part between barren skerries. Fortunately the wind shifted in our favour and by lunch time it was blowing hard enabling us to pack the engine away. Even so, darkness fell before we reached Åbo, and a pitch-black night it was too, although we had no difficulty in following the lights which had clear red, white and green sectors.

At 10 p.m. *Sjöfröken* picked up her mooring at Åbo, after covering eighty miles in fourteen hours. Our holiday was over and what a happy one it had been.

*   *   *

Our next, and last, cruise in the Baltic was started on May 27th, 1938, which was early in the season, when all the buoys were newly painted after the long frozen winter. We were so far north that it was only dark for about three hours from midnight to 3 a.m., and even then there was enough light for navigation. I had chartered on nominal terms, granted to me as an author, the first of four new ten-ton yachts built by the Åbo Batvarf for Oy Cruising in Finland Ab at Helsingfors. Her name was *Mary Anne* and her dimensions were 39ft 7ins LOA, 25ft 6ins LWL, 8ft 7ins beam and 5ft 4ins draught. She was not fitted with an engine nor did she have, or need, a capstan for her 60lb anchor. Sloop rigged with a sail area of only 470 sq ft (compared with the 770 sq ft in *Sjöfröken*'s yawl rig) she was very fast but as easy to handle as a dinghy by the two of us, besides being a good sea boat.

From the Nylandska Yacht Club at Helsingfors, Mamie and I sailed west along the Finnish coast to Utö; from there we sailed some 18 miles through barren skerries north-west to Karlby (Kökar), which Sir Henrik Ramsay, then Commodore of the Nylandska YC, had recommended as right off the beaten track, even of Finnish yachtsmen. And so it proved to be, as on arrival we were completely puzzled by the number of islets between which the anchorage lay. Providentially a fisherman in a motor boat suddenly emerged and kindly turned back to pilot us in. He took us up between two islets so close together that I feared he had made a mistake, but it was not long before a little fiord opened up with a village at its end off which lay a schooner. We anchored near her on mud bottom. Kökar was an out-of-the-world little community living in a village with a church and one small shop; it was set among miles of barren rocks and skerries.

After spending a sunny Sunday we sailed to Degerby and renewed acquaintance with Mariehamn, which is easy to approach from the south-east and seemed much more prosperous than in 1931. After provisioning there, we continued a circumnaviga-

17. Start of the cruise. *Mary Anne* at moorings off the Nylandska Yacht Club at Helsingfors (Helsinki).

tion of the island of Åland where, on its north side, we were in the Gulf of Bothnia which stretched away to the north-east almost to the Arctic Circle. The most interesting part of the circumnavigation lay on the north side, where there are no harbours and a rugged coastline of reddish rock indented by small fiords. From the sea it looks uninhabited, except for a pilot house on an islet, but the track was marked on the chart and we had a splendid sail. The sun was shining and the air was full of the bracing vigour of the north. We were both on deck marking off the headlands and islands as we passed them, and with a fresh fair wind *Mary Anne* averaged 7 knots under mainsail and boomed-out genoa. Once we sighted a patch of black, looking like black seaweed floating on the sea, and coming nearer we saw this was made up by a convoy of fifty or sixty ducklings, escorted by seven or eight 'Mammas', emigrating from an outlying skerry to an island. In the afternoon we came to the entrance of a picturesque-looking fiord to the SSW of an island named Boksö and decided to bring up there for tea or possibly the night. After sailing about a mile and a half up the fiord we found an enchanting anchorage in four fathoms. After tea we rowed a hundred yards and landed where green grass grew to the water's edge. Then we went for a walk, picking our way uphill between trees and outcrops of reddish coloured rock. When we had climbed to the top of the highest ground the view was magnificent. To the north lay channels between the skerries and beyond them the wide expanse of the Gulf of Bothnia. To the south extended ridges and ridges of trees, like mighty ocean swells of green over-running the whole land, intersected by streaks of blue of fiord and lake.

Back on board an hour later, there was a flat calm and no question of sailing until the following morning, when we completed the circumnavigation of Åland. The

18. Local trading cutter hauled out on the rocks at Kökar. *Mary Anne* has the lovely anchorage to herself.

following two days were spent in sailing eastwards through the Finnish Archipelago as far as Hangö.

The next lap of our cruise in *Mary Anne* was to Baltic Port (Paldiski in Russian) which was inspired by the Arthur Ransome's description of it in his book *Racundra's First Cruise*. The little harbour is situated in Estonia about 20 miles west of Reval. It was a fine sunny morning, but the glass was falling when we took our departure from Hangö at 12.30 for the 45 mile south-easterly crossing of the Gulf of Finland. We made a fast passage in seven hours, with land appearing long before it was due and with the high lighthouse of Paker Ort spot on. Baltic Port proved to be a small rectangular basin with a narrow entrance which we found to be on the south side. I luffed and *Mary Anne* shot up in the calm water of the harbour and came alongside the quay, with all our fenders and even the lifebuoys employed in keeping her paint off the rough timber baulks of which it was constructed. There were only a cutter-rigged trader, a schooner and two small steamers in the harbour.

When the alarm clock went at 7.30 next morning it was blowing a north-westerly gale, a bad direction on this coast. After breakfast we went ashore to have a look at the little town; it did not appear to have changed much since Ransome's time there. The grass still grew in the streets and lilac in the hedges. We took an immediate liking to it; the church was the principal building and from the sea makes a conspicuous landmark. There were a few shops but we soon found our way to the inn where we were

entertained at eleven o'clock with beer and vodka and then stayed for lunch. The inn
was owned by the harbour master, a great local character in Arthur Ransome's book;
he told us a lot about Baltic Port. During the Spanish Civil War in 1936–37, the
warehouses by the harbour became veritable arsenals. Baltic Port had been visited by a
then famous adventurer who, as captain of a British ship, was sailing under the Greek

19. Sunny weather. Mamie gives lunch in the cockpit.

flag; having changed to the Jugoslav flag she was chartered by a French firm to take munitions to Spain. She broke her charter and the ship was intercepted, painted grey on one side and black on the other, and wearing the Greek ensign. The ship was put under arrest and the gallant captain was gaoled. Let out on 1,000 Kroner bail, he returned to Baltic Port. There he had sat at the same table where we were now idly listening. After his breakfast he walked out and, catching a train, broke his bail and was smuggled to Finland. That is why in Baltic Port they looked twice at a ship under charter; we ourselves had only been allowed ashore on condition that we did not catch a train. For some reason I had been taken for a professional, perhaps due to my thick pilot jacket, coupled with a capacity for vodka.

In the afternoon we went for a walk, choosing the sea path, which took us past the ruined fortresses of Peter the Great. These overlooked the sea, and were encircled by the remains of the moat. We picked our way over mounds, across old gun emplace-ments and the dry moat; it was stiff climbing in places but inspiring. At length we came to the ruins of a fortress where we could look down; from across the Baltic the seas came foaming, and below they broke at right angles across the submerged barrier, which was all that was left of the mighty harbour conceived in the mind of Peter the Great. There thousands of convicts had laboured. With their hands lashed to barrows they had toiled at heaving the rocks seaward to make the breakwater. Many slipped and were dragged down by their heavy loads to be drowned; others, worn out by

20. *Mary Anne* at Baltic Port (Paldiski). We must have been one of the last yachts under the British ensign since Arthur Ransome to visit the harbour, now in the USSR.

hardship and poor food, threw themselves into the sea. Thousands died, it is said, so the work was never completed. There was nothing left to show of this ghastly labour, save the seas breaking on the rocks and the buoy to warn mariners of the danger.

In spite of the strong winds the sun came through at intervals and on the grass-covered slopes grew wild flowers, so that each gust of wind was full of scent. Lilac grew there, and clumps of white pinks, and cornflowers, strawberry plants, delphiniums, anemonies, vetch and all kinds of rock plants. We continued our walk to the Paker Ort lighthouse which stands on cliffs and is over 160 feet high; we climbed to the top up a narrow spiral stone staircase leading heavenwards. On return to Baltic Port we had dinner at the inn, where the company consisted of a rough looking peasant and an artist who spoke English. The latter was Russian and had been an artillery officer; in the 1917 Revolution he had fought in Siberia and, driven east, had made his way to Harbin and Japan. Absolutely penniless, he found his way back to Riga, earning a little by selling pictures, working his passage part of the way as a fireman, and walking most of the rest—'but what matter' he said, 'I was young in those days!' It was late when we returned to *Mary Anne*. The night was a wild one with spray breaking over the north of the quay. There was no sign of life except for the night watchman who saluted as we passed him.

It was still blowing hard next morning but by eleven it had moderated and the sun had broken through so, without waiting for left-over swell of the gale to subside, we got under way and made a fast 32 mile passage to Reval. We brought up on a mooring at the Estonian Yacht Club where we were welcomed again and it was a great pleasure to meet the friends we made there in 1931. It was a lovely sight from the dining room to see the yacht club fleet arriving below from a week-end, one by one, momentarily obscuring the windows by their creamy canvas and black sail numbers. This was a scene I shall always remember, but not without sadness for our friends, as the clouds of war were gathering fast in the Gulf of Finland.

21. Our last visit to the Estonian Yacht Club at Reval (Tallinn), now in the USSR.

We cast off from *Mary Anne*'s mooring next morning, and to the Estonian Yacht Club and the Tallinn Yacht Club we dipped our ensign for the last time as we ran past. We had a good passage to Finland, stopping the night on the way in an anchorage under the lee of Högh, an island just south of the Porkkala peninsula. The next day we completed our cruise in fine style running before a fresh to strong SW wind under reefed mainsail and no jib, weaving our way through the outer skerries, covering 25 miles to Helsingfors in three and a half hours. At 5 p.m., with Mamie at the helm, *Mary Anne* rounded head to the wind and came gently to rest at her mooring off the Nylandska Yacht Club.

As it was the mid-summer holiday the club was closed and all the ships in the harbour were dressed with branches of birch. The unusual greenery on the masts and funnels of the work-a-day ships looked very festive, and when we went ashore we found that even the trams had been decorated.

So ended our cruise. It had been a perfect holiday, and I do not recollect ever having better sailing. So often on our earlier cruises we had bad weather and head-winds. On this occasion the wind followed us round and was almost always fair.

CHAPTER FIFTEEN

THE WAR YEARS

I do not mention my diabetes in the ordinary way but it is necessary to do so now as the disability greatly influenced my war years.

It was diagnosed shortly before the outbreak of hostilities by the usual symptoms of an acute thirst which could not be quenched. I forget now, but I think I was treated for some months on a strict diet. I was working long hours and had lost about a stone in weight when my doctor sent me to see the great specialist of the time, Dr R D Lawrence, a family man who suffered the same complaint himself. He said that if I continued the way I was going I was unlikely to live for more than six months. He put me on insulin at once and explained the system of diet, which I faithfully tried to follow until I took up ocean racing after the war when, of necessity, I broke many of the medical rules for short periods with little effect.

A year before the war (at the time of the Munich Crisis) I had applied for membership of the supplementary Royal Naval Volunteer Reserve and had been accepted, so when hostilities broke out I expected to receive a commission and go to the King Alfred naval establishment for training like most of my friends. The disability which had developed in the meantime had ruled me out of active service, but there were other branches of which I might have been eligible. Time passed without hearing anything from the Admiralty, so I remained in accountancy practice with my firm and was also appointed under the Ministry of Food War Emergency plans as County Accountant, Ministry of Food (Meat and Livestock Division), for Hampshire, Isle of Wight and part of Dorset. Although not exactly in my line, it was a responsible appointment, involving complete records and payments for all animals going to the slaughter-houses, and their parts whether sold or condemned; I had also certain executive duties. The Ministry work was at first done at the Portsmouth Office, but in 1940 it was transferred to a large house in Fareham rented for the purpose and to provide room for the increased staff; above us the vital Battle of Britain was being fought out in the air. I would have found the work too much for me alone but my partner, Stanley Saunders, took much of the load off my shoulders. Besides being a better accountant than I was, he had the advantage of a knowledge of the meat trade.

Among voluntary duties I served first in the volunteer Home Guard, later to become well known as Dad's Army and, when the threat of invasion diminished, as an air raid warden at Bursledon during the heavy air raids over Southampton (where our former office was destroyed, fortunately without casualties) and Woolston, the latter being less than three miles from our home. I gave up being a warden when on 27th October, 1942, I was commissioned as an honorary Lieut RNVR (Special Branch) for part-time duties as commanding officer of the Fareham and Gosport Unit of Sea Cadets which brought me nearer to the navy; the elementary training of cadets before their call-up was certainly a useful war job. Meanwhile Mamie had worked in the Red Cross and later drove a YMCA tea van visiting the gun sites in the neighbourhood. After a big air raid on Portsmouth dockyard, the YMCA was requested, at short notice, to send the tea van into the naval dockyard. I accompanied her as I had returned home while the van was still being restocked. We were accommodated for the night in the first-aid post at the dockyard. As anticipated there was a repetition of the big air raid of the previous night. However, where we were it did not seem too bad, although it was very noisy with all the anti-aircraft guns in full operation including those in a nearby destroyer and other warships. Early next morning the dockyard workers arrived and were served with tea, buns and cigarettes; they nearly pushed the van down in their eagerness. And no wonder, for when the time came to drive back to Bursledon we found it difficult to find our way either in Southsea or Portsmouth town, so much of it having been razed to the ground during the night. It had been a very big air raid but centred on the town instead of the naval docks where we were.

The end of the year 1942 was a sad one for us. Mamie lost her widowed mother, who died at her home in the Isle of Man in December, and within six months my grandmother and guardian, who had been living in a flat in Ryde, were taken ill and died. I owed most of the good things in my life to these two wonderful Victorians. In retrospect I feel that I took far too much for granted and gave far too little in return.

I think it must have been in 1943 that Winston Churchill made a broadcast calling on everybody to get closer to the war. I responded immediately by applying to the Admiralty, where I was given an interview and selected to fill an urgent vacancy in the book-writing department of HMS *Excellent* to edit gunnery books, for which I had the qualifications of practical experience of writing books, a degree in engineering and quite good first year diplomas from the school of practical engineering. I had already obtained the consent of the area accountant of the Ministry of Food to the appointment of my partner, Stanley Saunders, to take my place as County Accountant, but the department of the Ministry of Labour in London, which dealt with professional appointments, put in an objection and intimated that if I persisted I would be called up.

Nevertheless, I did persist and hence was called up, but I failed the medical and was placed on 26th February, 1943 in Medical Grade IV, the lowest category. I at once offered my services again to the Admiralty, but as I was now officially Grade IV, they could no longer give me a commission and instead offered me the same post as a civilian experimental gunnery officer. I accepted and in due course presented myself at Bordean, near Petersfield, a large country house, standing in delightful surroundings, where the gunnery book-writing was centred. The commanding officer was Commander Gilbert, a descendant of the Gilbert of Walter Raleigh's time, and the books were written by technical experts, as those concerned with gunnery control were very advanced. However, I was put on the comparatively simple ironmongery side, in editing, preparing and seeing through the press manuals on the guns themselves, among them the last edition of the 15-inch gun manual. The establishment was quite a large one, what with authors, editors, technical artists occupying a large drawing office (most gunnery books included detailed drawings) and of course the Wrens, the distaff side of the navy. The work was interesting but there were some serious practical difficulties about diet, and within a year the insulin injections had to be quadrupled and my doctor insisted upon my resignation.

After leaving Bordean we let our house at Bursledon and moved to London in January 1944 where our daughter Arnaud was completing a course in secretarial work at St James' and later joined the ATS, the women's branch of the army. I had the use of a room in the office of a fellow chartered accountant in the City for professional work and was also able to keep in touch with Robert Ross & Co Ltd, whose distributors, Rolls House Publishing Co Ltd, had an office off Chancery Lane. My Company published a few books during the war, mostly shilling paper-backs, but also a volume on careers, for which the Ministry of Information gave a large order as men and women in the forces were already thinking about peace-time job possibilities. I also continued part-time voluntary work at the headquarters of the Sea Cadet Corps in Cockspur Street. We lived in a flat near Earl's Court, but this was put out of action one night by incendiary bombs in a heavy air raid, so we moved to the lodge of the Waldronhurst Hotel at Croydon and I went up and down to London by train. Then came the flying bombs. Mamie was on very active service as she was serving whole-time in Civil Defence, driving an ambulance and doing first-aid. The 'doodle-bugs' caused casualties and much damage in the Croydon area, particularly the more advanced V2 type which gave no warning. It was while we were at the Waldronhurst Hotel that I wrote *Sailing Days* in the evenings.

CHAPTER SIXTEEN

AFLOAT AGAIN

I was lucky in 1945 for, when I returned from other duties, the naval authorities had given me a permit to sail in order to prepare a badly wanted new edition of my book *Creeks and Harbours of the Solent*. The previous year I had bought a Tumlare yacht called *Zara*; she lay at Haines' yacht yard at Itchenor in Chichester Harbour and was a sister ship of *Zest*, which had been lent to me shortly before the war. As there may be few Tumlaren afloat today, I will give some particulars of the class. Designed by Knud Reimers of Stockholm, they were 27ft 2ins in overall length, 21ft 8ins LWL, 6ft 5ins beam, 4ft 2ins draught. The sail area was 215 sq ft set in a high aspect ratio rig which gave them a wonderful windward performance, but the hulls were a little too fine aft and could be pooped in exceptionally bad weather. The cabin was small but just tolerable for up to three crew.

It was on VE Day that I travelled cross country from Bursledon to Itchenor by bus and taxi. The day was fine and from Itchenor Hard it was a cheering sight to look over the creek with the blue wavelets glinting in the sun where *Zara* lay, her freshly enamelled red topsides and new varnish making a sight to gladden any eye. There was still a lot of work to do before she was ready for sea but I made sail the following day rather late on the tide. The wind was light and it was night before *Zara* crept into a snug berth in Wootton Creek. This VE night made a wonderful sight, in fact an historic one, viewed from the deck of my new boat. I could see across the Solent to Portsmouth where fireworks and rockets were illuminating the sky, and a distant sound of music carried over the sea. In the nearer distance the warships, including HMS *Warspite*, were making patterns with their searchlights and shooting flares into the sky. Ashore there were bonfires and sounds of celebrations. I stayed for awhile fascinated by the scene. Then, as the hour was getting late, I went below and turned in glad, after the six war years, to be sleeping once more in the cosy cabin of a little ship.

I started the revision of my book *Creeks and Harbours of the Solent* as soon as possible when I got back to Bursledon; Eric Hiscock occasionally came sailing with me in *Zara* when I was engaged in checking over the harbours. I had known him for many years and he was my proposer for membership of the Royal Cruising Club. I should add here that, during the war, when I was provisionally accepted for Bordean, it chanced that Eric, much to his regret, had been discharged from the RN Patrol

Service owing to bad eyesight; he had been serving as a chief petty officer engineer in an armed yacht on anti-submarine patrol. After that he and Susan were working on a farm, so I wrote inviting him to take over editing *The Yachtsman* for the duration, which he generously agreed to do. In this I was lucky as both Eric and Susan are perfectionists in whatever they do.

When Eric sailed with me in *Zara*, he was interested in the boat's performance, but did not pretend to like extreme light displacement semi-racing boats for cruising purposes. As soon as possible, he fitted out his well-known gaff cutter *Wanderer II* and seven years later started on his great circumnavigation of the world in *Wanderer III*. However, I will not write more about *Zara* other than to say that later in the year I had a good single-handed cruise in her to the West Country, but got dangerously pooped in West Bay on the return passage when running for Portland Bill. I managed to get the water out of her and beat 20 miles to Teignmouth when I brought up at the Morgan Giles yacht yard. Mr Morgan Giles (father of Admiral Morgan Giles MP, who used to crew with him in the 14ft International dinghies) gave me a warm welcome after an admonishment for the folly of being at sea in such weather in so unsuitable a boat. However, *Zara* was too small for my wife to enjoy sailing except for short cruises, and our son Ross, when he joined me next year, had outgrown her so he had to crawl about on hands and knees. The time had come for a larger vessel.

In 1946 I heard by chance of a 7-tonner which was being laid down at the Dorset Yacht Company Ltd at Hamworthy, Poole. When I visited the yard I found that the design was by Fred Parker who had been awarded second prize in a *Yachtsman* designing competition for a fast 23ft waterline cruiser. The other dimensions were 34ft LOA, beam 8ft 1in, and draught 5ft 2ins. I was very much taken by the design as, considering her size, the accommodation was remarkably good for family or other cruising as well as racing. The price quoted was moderate and delivery was promised in June, so I signed a contract on the spot and, when she was completed, we named her *Mary Aidan*. She proved a first-rate boat for Solent racing in the Q class and competed in the first 'Round the Island Race' after the war. Her performance was equally satisfactory when cruising.

In a cruise to the West Country with my daughter Arnaud and a friend, we were caught out in a gale on the return passage from Brixham bound for Alderney. The weather deteriorated rapidly in the late evening on arrival off the Casquets and, being then totally unfamiliar with rocks and tide races NW of Alderney, I gave up the attempt to make harbour and kept well out to sea before running off to the eastward. The night which followed was pitch black with heavy rain squalls and a very rough sea in the strong tidal streams. As the wind increased to Force 8 we followed the gamut of gale tactics: close-reefing, running under staysail alone, running under bare pole at 5 knots, running trailing a steadying warp astern belayed in a loop from port and starboard cleats on the counter, and finally lying a-hull. Altogether it was an unpleasant experience but it provided a good test of *Mary Aidan*'s ability as a seaboat and also of my crew, as morale was high the whole time and neither was seasick. A chapter on the gale is given in my book *Heavy Weather Sailing* as a number of useful lessons were learnt from it.

Mary Aidan had one disadvantage as she measured only 23ft on the waterline, whereas 25ft LWL was the minimum to comply with the rules for racing under the Royal Ocean Racing Club; this was later reduced to 24ft.

In pre-war years I had always taken an armchair interest in ocean racing; it seemed to me one of the most genuine forms of sport, especially the 605-mile Fastnet Race, the Grand National of ocean racing. Racing such as this in any weather appeared to be the ultimate in sailing, providing a test of boats, crews, navigation and racing skill.

Although I was very pleased with *Mary Aidan*, the possibility of taking up ocean racing was never far from my mind. It so happened that a virtually new boat, complying with the RORC minimum waterline length, had just been completed by A H Moody & Sons Ltd, and she came on the market when her owner decided that he (or his wife) wanted something larger for cruising with his family. I decided to buy her and this proved to be a major decision of my sailing life, as it enabled me to combine the two, and sometimes conflicting, worlds of cruising and offshore racing and get the best out of both. I then rather sadly parted with *Mary Aidan*, selling her within a month without financial loss as she was just the kind of boat that many people wanted.

The name of the new boat was *Cohoe* – the Indian name for a species of small fast Canadian salmon. She was an enlarged version of a Tumlare, designed by Knud

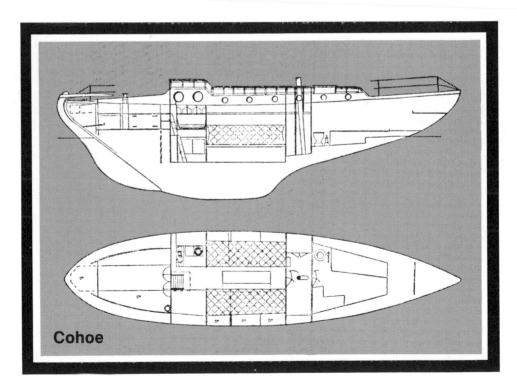

8. *Cohoe*.

LOA	32ft 2ins	Beam	7ft 4ins
LWL	25ft 4ins	Draught	5ft 2ins
Tons TM	7	Tons disp	3.5

Reimers, with a 30 sq metre sail plan instead of the 20 sq metre of *Zest* and *Zara*. The shape of the hull was very similar, with moderate overhang forward, wine-glass sections and a Scandinavian stern with outhung rudder. But the stern was much fuller than in the smaller design, giving greater buoyancy aft, and she was thus less liable to be pooped. An innovation was her equipment with stanchions and lifelines round her deck, and I bought a wireless for receiving weather reports.

Her designed dimensions were 32ft 2ins length overall, 25ft 4ins length waterline, 7ft 4ins beam and 5ft 2ins draught. She worked out at 7 tons Thames measurement, but she was only 3½ tons displacement, and in reality a considerably smaller boat than *Mary Aidan*.

I stress the word 'designed' displacement, because modifications had been made which added considerably to her actual displacement. The height of the topsides had been increased and a long coach-roof and a doghouse had been added; this greatly improved the accommodation below but at the expense of stability. There was a full-length cabin with a berth on each side, and aft under the doghouse there was a galley with a primus stove to port and a quarter berth with chart table over it to starboard. Forward of the saloon was a compartment with cupboards and storage space separated by doors from the forecastle, in which there was a pipe cot, sail and anchor stowage and a Baby Blake WC. Although *Cohoe* was narrow (Humphrey Barton described her accommodation as 'like living in a tunnel'), the arrangements below were comfortable, and there was fair headroom with over 6ft under the doghouse and 5ft at the forward end of the saloon.

The cockpit was a comfortable size and self-emptying, and situated below it was an 8 h.p. Stuart Turner engine. To compensate for this extra weight aft, a quarter of a ton of lead had been added to the forward end of the keel. Many of our friends, especially cruising men of the older school, were critical of *Cohoe*, saying that a yacht of such light displacement was unfit to go outside the Solent. I once even overheard her described contemptuously as a 'toy yacht'.

CHAPTER SEVENTEEN

CHANNEL ISLANDS

Although I bought *Cohoe* in the summer of 1946, it was not until autumn that Mamie and I were able to get away on a maiden voyage in the boat.

We only sailed as far as the Beaulieu River on the first day, where we brought up in the sheltered reach off Ginn's farm as there was a bad weather forecast. It was about the time for Equinoctial gales and next day came the cyclonic storm with winds said to attain 50 to 80 knots in some parts, and at Beaulieu it was certainly at least a severe gale. In course of this our dinghy disappeared but, when the wind abated, Eric Hiscock, whose *Wanderer II* was lying farther down the river, managed to row over and help us. Together we motored in *Cohoe* and searched everywhere for the missing boat but without success. It was not until we had returned from our cruise nearly a month later that we received a report that the boat had been cast up on the shore near Newtown, Isle of Wight, quite undamaged and with her oars still in place.

Next morning we returned to the Hamble River where Cosby Smallpeice, who owned *Josephine* a sister ship, very generously lent us his own dinghy so that we could continue our cruise. This was painted a bright turquoise blue and fitted exactly on our deck. Little did I anticipate the troubles which would arise from the colour of that paint; of this, more anon. The weather continued bad over the week-end and it was not until Monday, September 24th, that we received a good forecast from the local meteorological station. What a rush it was for us both to get away after this unexpected change of plan, and to get provisions and make the other last minute preparations so familiar to all cruising men before making a passage.

I pause here to explain that for us the cruise which lay ahead was quite a new adventure. The boat was brand new and her performance untried for the kind of sailing which lay ahead. Experienced as we were from cruising in the tideless Baltic, in the North Sea and on the South Coast of England, we were bound for the Channel Isles and the Gulf of St Malo, a rock-strewn coast where the tidal streams are all-important, both for navigation and the state of the sea in relation to the force and direction of the wind. An added factor to the game was that the Germans had destroyed many of the French lighthouses during the war and how far they had been restored was not then known.

It was 2230 (henceforth I shall use 24 hour time when at sea) on Monday September

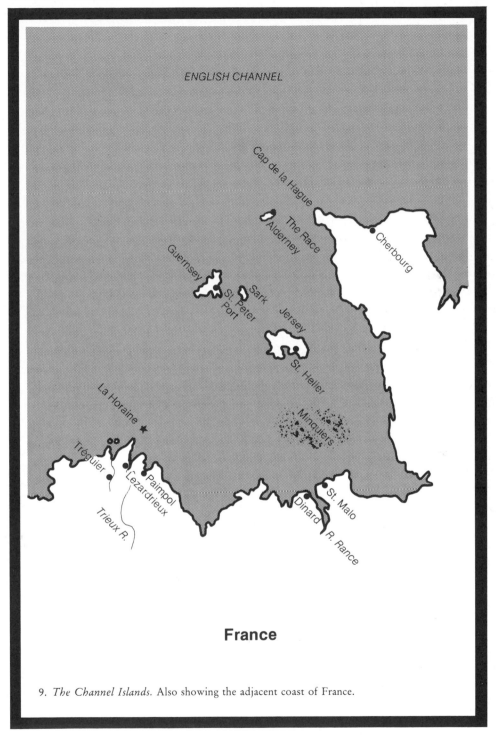

9. *The Channel Islands.* Also showing the adjacent coast of France.

24th, when we slipped the mooring we had temporarily picked up near the entrance of the Hamble River, and *Cohoe* began her voyage bound for Alderney.

It was a fine night when I took the first watch, so that Mamie could go below and get some rest before her turn in the early morning. There was a wholesail breeze and it was pleasant sailing down the Solent. With the help of a strong fair tide progress was good and at 0130 next morning we had passed the Needles, and I had streamed the patent log off the Bridge buoy and taken our departure for Alderney. Half an hour later Mamie came on watch for a two hour spell, and soon after 0600 the tide turned foul and the sun rose as a fiery orb in the soft grey sky to the eastward.

Watch arrangements were much the same as in our Baltic cruises and as before largely a matter of give and take; often there were long periods when we were both on deck.

The sea was fairly smooth and the weather hazy, and at noon we sighted land ahead in the distance. This is always an exciting moment even for the most prosaic of navigators, and we had a drink to celebrate. After our landfall the wind fell softer and the coast gradually became clearer; we made out a line of cliffs terminating in a headland to the west, off which there was a lighthouse. It was Cap de la Hague and our landfall was correct, for the tide was due to change again and sweep the sloop to the westward towards Alderney, which obstinately remained hidden; and it was some time before we sighted it. We then tacked as I was a bit tide-shy and wanted to keep away, as the westerly running stream takes a turn hereabouts to sweep into the Race of Alderney. It was when crossing this rather uncanny eight-mile strip of water that a squall blew up. I had already lowered the genoa and also taken a bearing of Alderney Lighthouse, so I was prepared. Fortunately so, for the rain completely blotted out everything. For a time it was distinctly anxious work as the boat sailed on through the deluge towards Alderney, to which I was a stranger. However, all went well and, in due course, we sighted the long breakwater of Braye Harbour and, giving this a good offing to avoid the submerged extension, *Cohoe* stood into the harbour where the Harbour Master hailed us as we entered and directed us to a berth alongside a small MFV, where we moored at 1600. *Cohoe* was the only yacht there, sharing the whole harbour with the MFV and three French fishing boats.

We stayed two nights at Alderney, spending the day in walks up the steep road from the harbour, past the bombed houses and inns, to the little town of St Anne's. There we did some provisioning and for the first time since the war started seven years earlier I was able to walk into a shop and buy as many packets of cigarettes as I wanted. In the afternoon we found an obliging taxi (I think there were only two) in which we were driven round the Island to see the sights. It was a worthwhile trip for the views from the old forts and headlands are magnificent, especially looking from Fort Homeaux towards the French coast, seeing Alderney race writhing in the channel between, and the patches of white-crested overfalls. Then we were taken past Longy Bay and back to Braye and thence to the west coast.

Alderney was only just beginning to recover from the German occupation. Their fortifications remained and in some parts the land mines had not been cleared and there were still notices written in German to be seen. There were two big cemeteries, one for Germans and the other for Russian prisoners who had either been shot shortly before liberation or come to an untimely end in some other manner. What was surprising to find in so small a place was the number of buildings which had been damaged, many apparently wantonly; the owners were back repairing such as could be restored, and as one walked in the streets one could always hear the tap, tap of the hammers of busy people preparing for better times.

On the day of our arrival at Alderney, a large MFV had come into harbour from Guernsey, and we were moved to lie alongside her. As a result, I made the acquaintance of her mate who had been a Guernsey pilot and was very interested in *Cohoe*.

'The sea gets up quickly without warning,' he said. 'If there is a weather-going tide, a steep breaking sea follows almost immediately the wind freshens. If caught out in a gale there is rarely room to heave-to as rocks are never far to leeward. The tides vary, splitting round the islands on every-varying courses at each hour, and there are severe overfalls in many parts.'

Clearly he did not regard *Cohoe* as ideal for this sort of sailing, but I think he under-estimated her abilities, as was done by many people unfamiliar with small, light displacement yachts. He then fetched his large-scale charts from the MFV, to show us how to take the short cut through the Swinge without getting into the tide race. His directions were so complete that I got confused with the names of some of the rocks and leading marks, but nevertheless I got the hang of the pilotage and was duly grateful.

Next morning we cast off at 1100. The barometer was 1017, the wind light and variable SW by W to WSW. *Cohoe* ran gently out of the harbour and was soon in the Swinge. High water Dover was 1242 on that day, but for nearly four hours before this there was a westerly eddy. We could only fetch part of the way to the Corbet Rock, which is the principal consideration in the Swinge, as it reduces the navigable channel to a width of only three quarters of a mile. After passing this we had to make several tacks. The first of these took the boat across the turbulent part known to locals as 'The Overfalls' (where the stream attains 8 knots at springs) to Burhou, the low green jagged-edged island around which the tidal streams pour. But our acquaintance, the pilot, knew his stuff. At that state of the tide there were tide rips, but nothing alarming and certainly no race. We were delighted to have had such easy conditions for our first passage.

Once clear of Les Étacs, the craggy group of islets and rocks off the south-west of Alderney and the dangerous isolated rock of Pierre au Vraic, we were in open water, but the wind was light and progress slow. In the afternoon the high island of Sark was the first landfall, followed by Herm and Jethou, and the islet of Grand Amfroque, which stands out boldly and looks larger than it really is. Guernsey itself, the largest and nearest, remained coyly hidden in the haze, only the reflection of the sun on some glasshouses giving any hint of its whereabouts until we were within a few miles of it. We carried the fair tide through the Little Russel, passing the sandy and rocky coast of heather-covered Herm which looked a picture on this sunny but rather hazy day, and arrived off St Peter Port at about 1800. On arrival we were hailed and, having given particulars of the yacht, were directed up the harbour to anchor about a cable off the inner basin.

Before we had been ten minutes at anchor we made the acquaintance of two

Guernsey sailing men, P K and A J Barber who knew the local waters and channels intimately; not only on the surface but below, for it was A J B's hobby to go down in a diving helmet to inspect the rocks and shoals and marine life. The following morning we were hailed by P K who motored us to his home where we enjoyed the luxury of hot baths. We then went shopping. Food was rationed but there was an abundance of everything else. At 1500 A J B arrived to take us for an afternoon introduction to the islets off Herm, mostly under engine, there being little wind. He steered *Cohoe* across the Little Russel to a position south of the Bréhon Tower. Then the fun began. Pushing the tiller into the reluctant hands of Mamie, A J B conned the ship towards Herm; she had to steer perhaps within 30ft of a rock, and as the boat approached we suddenly entered a tidal eddy running precisely contrary to the main stream we had left. Just like that – at one moment in a northerly stream and at the next a southerly one, with a clearly defined line separating the two. A J B was not even keeping to the recognised pass marked on the chart, but made deviations or short cuts of his own which brought *Cohoe* close to sinister looking rocks. Some of these rocks he described as a 'Boue', which means a flat rock – unless it is a term of abuse, for the French dictionary gives the meaning as 'dirt, mire, mud or filth.' A J B kept warning us of this or that boue, and we became quite boue-minded.

With a strong fair tide and the aid of the engine we rapidly passed through the Passe Percée between Herm and the small island of Jethou on its south-west. Having cleared this we were piloted northward on the east side of Herm, passing a lovely sandy shore, paved with millions of shells, many varieties of which are not to be found elsewhere in British waters. A J B then piloted us to the islets and rocks lying to the north-east of Herm, which are known locally as 'The Humps' and are familiar to Guernseymen. It seemed to me as a stranger to be a perilous passage, but finally we were steered into a tiny cove between the islets of Godin, Canuette, Galeu and Pierre de la Moue. There was barely room for *Cohoe* to swing at her anchor but the depth was 6ft at MLWS, on sandy bottom. We had tea, after which we landed on the rocks before weighing anchor, and *Cohoe* made the return passage to St Peter Port the same way as she had come, except we went to the southward of Jethou instead of using the Passe Percée. So ended a delightful day. I was wonderfully lucky in meeting A J B and having him to introduce me to cruising in the strong tidal streams of the Channel Isles. In the following year he came again and piloted us round the tricky waters of Sark.

Next day, Saturday, we bade farewell to our friends and weighed anchor at 1515, with a fair tide for St Helier, Jersey. The wind was light easterly and the sea smooth, but the visibility was poor at times. It was about 1800 that we first sighted Jersey and not long afterwards we identified La Corbière lighthouse, which we rounded at a distance of about a mile at 1900. The wind had been steadily freshening as we tacked along the south side of Jersey and, by the time we had passed Noirmont Point, it was quite dark so we proceeded under engine. The approach and entrance to St Helier proved quite easy at night as there were good leading lights. At the harbour entrance we reported and were directed to No 4 steamer berth, but shortly afterwards we had to move further up where *Cohoe* would have to dry out at midnight. A friendly onlooker made fast our warps and, after coiling down, I went to join my wife below for a late dinner.

We were not left long in peace before being hailed by somebody on the quay. I could see the white top of a peaked cap and recognised the Assistant Harbour Master to whom we had already given full particulars.

'It's a funny thing,' he remarked, 'but a yacht of your description has been reported as anchoring in Portelet Bay and people were seen landing in a dinghy about 5 o'clock.'

'We have not landed anywhere,' I replied, 'and what is more we had not even sighted Jersey at 5 o'clock.' I asked where Portelet Bay was, and gathered it was on the west side of Noirmont Point. I thought the incident was closed, but half an hour later he was back again.

'I suppose your dinghy is not green, by any chance,' he asked? He could not see anything but the white bottom turned up on the cabin top.

'Well,' I replied 'as a matter of fact it is blue, but a greenish kind of blue.'

He then told me that the dinghy seen to land in Portelet Bay was green. He explained that it was against the Jersey laws for any boat, even from Guernsey, to land anywhere before clearing at St Helier. He went on to say that what worried him was that the yacht had been reported as coming from the *south*, the direction of France, adding that there were people trying to get from one country to another, there was smuggling, and also the possibility of escaped prisoners stealing a vessel. I do not think that Mamie or I looked like escaped prisoners, but I suppose all such things were possible in the unsettled time so soon after the war. He also added that they had to keep a sharp look-out for Colorado beetles in the case of boats coming from the Continent, which we were evidently suspected of.

'Please attend at the Harbour Master's office at 11 o'clock tomorrow morning and bring any evidence with you,' were the official's final words as he left.

We duly kept the appointment, where we were confronted by the Harbour Master, a Custom's officer and an Immigration officer. The Harbour Master was courteous, but explained that he had to enquire into the matter as three pilots had given a written report that 'a yacht answering to the description of the *Cohoe* had anchored in Portelet Bay this p.m. (5 p.m.) and a person or persons had gone ashore in a green coloured pram dinghy'. A memorandum attached to the report read that the three pilots had since inspected *Cohoe* moored at half-tide steps in St Helier harbour and maintained that she was 'the yacht which anchored in Portelet and crew went ashore'.

The Harbour Master put through telephone calls at Mamie's request. The first was to La Corbière lighthouse on Jersey. The answer came that visibility was bad and no yacht answering the description had been seen. The next was to the Harbour Master at St Peter Port. He was not available, and the watchmen could only state that *Cohoe* had been at St Peter Port in the morning but he was not sure of the time of her departure. This answer should at least have disposed of any idea that *Cohoe* had come from France on some possibly nefarious assignment. If she had been at St Peter Port in the morning, as the watchman said, how could we have possibly sailed from there on a foul tide, say to St Malo, the nearest French port and thence to arrive back in Portelet Bay by 5 p.m., a distance of about 100 miles. The next telephone call by the Harbour Master was to one of our friends we were with before leaving St Peter Port, but we were unlucky again as he was not available, so all our alibis had failed, although he telephoned to the Harbour Master in the evening confirming we had not left before about 3 p.m.

At the conclusion of the 11 o'clock meeting with the officials on Sunday, the Harbour Master decided that a report from me should be attached to the papers and a further meeting would be held at 10.30 next morning, at which one of the pilots would be present. In the meantime *Cohoe* must not leave the harbour. He promised to arrange a deep water berth for us so that we could get some sleep without the trouble of drying out again.

It was not until next morning that the great mystery was solved. It appeared that a local yachtsman had acquired a new boat which he kept in St Aubin's Bay, and presumably had not yet been seen by the pilots. Being a nice Saturday afternoon he had sailed round a couple of miles to Portelet Bay and this accounted for the mysterious lady and gentleman who had landed from a green dinghy. As a result of this information Monday's 10.30 meeting was cancelled, so I did not have the opportunity to ask why the pilots thought the mysterious boat had come from the south. They must have had some reason, as pilots are usually most friendly and helpful to yachtsmen.

The Assistant Harbour Master called on us to apologise for the trouble we had been put to, and to talk over the unreliability of circumstantial evidence.

'To think,' he concluded, 'that people have been hanged before now on circumstantial evidence!'

CHAPTER EIGHTEEN

LA FRANCE APRÈS LA GUERRE

It is a strange coincidence in my life that I, a failure at school in the French language and with terrible pronunciation, should eventually spend at least a part of almost every summer cruising on the French coast for over twenty years, writing or revising my pilot books covering almost every harbour or anchorage on the coast from Barfleur to La Rochelle in the Bay of Biscay. Happily for me, Mamie on the contrary speaks the language well; for three years from the age of nine she had been at a school in Ascot with a French headmistress, where it was compulsory to speak French most of the time. Thus pronunication came naturally to her from childhood.

After this digression I return to St Helier. True to his promise the Harbour Master had given us a berth alongside a Southern Railway steamer, but there was a tremendous lot to be done for, having arrived late on Saturday, we had not been able to provision over the week-end before sailing to France. We divided the labour, Mamie taking over the shopping and thus leaving me to get water and fuel and to see to clearance. There was no difficulty about the latter as the Immigration official arrived on time and quickly stamped our passports and wished us bon voyage. Mamie was less fortunate as she discovered she had lost the coupon book and without this she could not get any bread. However, two seamen on the steamer were very obliging, one filling up the tank with fresh water and the other getting us a loaf of bread.

By 1430 we had finished lunch and set sail for Dinard, a distance of about 45 miles allowing for rounding to the westward of the Minquiers, the group of rocks and islets which lie about mid-way on the passage. It was a peculiar day, quite sunny with rather poor visibility and occasional rain storms; the wind was a moderate southerly. We had made the detour round the Minkies, as they are called, and tacked at about 1930 to bear away to the south-east. The neap tide was fair but not so strong as I had expected, bearing in mind the tremendous range of tide. At 2045 I obtained a fix and shortly afterwards we came on the line of the leading lights, which we found had been re-established. An hour later we could just make out the outline of Ile de Cézembre, which stands on the east side of the entrance of the river Rance, but I cannot recall that we saw the red group flashing light on the dangerous Le Grand Jardin group of rocks SW of the island. Mamie was very tired, so as the night was fine I altered course out of the fairway and let go anchor. It was then that Mamie inquired whether we were in the Swept Channel?

I routed out the Admiralty Notices to Mariners which I had obtained at the Custom House before leaving Guernsey, and saw instantly that we had anchored in the mined area. However, I thought it best to stay where we were, so we spent the night sleeping soundly among the mines, as we thought, although we learnt later that all in the vicinity had been cleared.

The next day was the first of October. We were really getting into autumn. At 0930 we got under way and as the wind was light and we were late on the tide we started under engine. Care is needed by strangers when negotiating the channel between Les Courtis rocks and Le Jardin group of rocks to the SW of Ile de Cézembre but, with the aid of a large-scale chart, we were soon through it and sailed up the well marked channel to Dinard. After temporarily picking up a vedette's heavy mooring, a lady sailing a half-decked boat passed close. I hailed her politely in my best French; she replied in English advising us to move and anchor off the Yacht Club de Dinard where, being neaps, there would be enough depth of water for *Cohoe*. The lady was the charming Madame Vergère, a great hostess of British yachtsmen at the time. She introduced us to Comte de Gasquet James, then Rear-Commodore of the Club, and to a number of the members, among them to Mademoiselle D'A who had been an active member of the Resistance during the war and owned a dog affectionately known as 'Smelly Nellie'. The honorary treasurer was a great help. He took me in search of the Douane, whom we ran to earth at a café where he was having a glass of wine, it being mid-day. However, despite being off duty he conducted us to his office and quickly settled the formalities. The dues amounted to Frs 4·20 (the equivalent of tuppence) for which I received a certificate and had the passport stamped. When Mamie and I went ashore again in the afternoon she was delighted with Dinard and we ultimately remained there for three days in lovely weather, spending much of our time at the club, looking around the town and shops, and in the evenings going to restaurants. This was the first holiday for Mamie since before the war and I had promised it would not be too strenuous.

Nevertheless, time passed quickly. Mamie visited the Mairie, where she obtained French coupons printed in gay colours for rationed foods and wine. I took the battery to a garage to be recharged, although our consumption of electricity was small as it was only used for the navigation lights and temporarily when we went on board at night until the oil lamps were lit. I also put *Cohoe* alongside a stone jetty and at low water scrubbed her bottom which was very foul as she had lain for some weeks in the Hamble River while fitting out.

On Friday October 4th we bade farewell to our friends. The club boatman took a poor view of the weather, so we eventually decided to sail up the River Rance, passing between the Pte de la Vicomte at SE end of the Anse de Dinard and the island of Bizeux; this was, of course, many years before the hydro-electric barrage had been constructed. There were few dangers to navigation and these were well marked so, although we had no large-scale chart, we had little difficulty in sailing up the river. Our first anchorage was near Pte de Jouvante where there was an hotel. The place seemed quite deserted however, except for an owl hooting in the woods and a small dog howling dolorously until far into the night. Next morning we sailed further up the river, and just beyond the Pointe de la Landrais we found a little bay, where a creek ran out between the sands. Near the point was an excellent stone landing slip. As the weather was bad we thought this an opportunity not to be missed and anchored *Cohoe* as close in as we dared in the NW corner of the cove. We rowed off in the dinghy and landed at the slip, hauling the boat up beyond the reach of the tide. On the right of the landing place stood a shrine with a statue of the Virgin, recently erected in thanksgiving for the end of the war. We found a road running up towards the village and an hotel to which we had been recommended, standing on a terrace overlooking the river and the cove where *Cohoe* lay. The tourist season was over and we had the hotel to ourselves, except for Madame and her family, who promised us lunch in a half-an-hour's time and suggested we should take a 'promenade' while waiting. During our walk we noticed little shrines placed on the walls of many of the cottages, rows of beans hung up to dry, heaps of cider apples, and numerous dogs.

Lunch was worth waiting for, as we discovered when we found it ready for us on our return to the hotel. Would we have 'homard'? The answer was 'oui.' The lobster arrived. When I say lobster I mean a whole lobster, and an enormous one at that, hot with masses of delightful sauce. It was such a repast that I stopped eating and much to the surprise of our hostess, took a picture of the meal; it was excellent, other courses being a kind of Welsh rarebit, grapes, cheese and coffee. The bill, including wine, was the equivalent of under £2 for the two of us.

The hotel was a family affair run entirely by Madame, Monsieur and daughters. We learned that in the war it had been requisitioned by the Germans, and the owners had lived in a cottage in the village. During the liberation they found themselves between two fires as the Germans retreated before the advancing American troops. They and their children had found shelter in a trench in the fields for several days at the crisis while the fighting was going on around them. When we were there the hotel had just been re-opened and was sparsely furnished, as the Germans had taken nearly everything. We returned in the evening and my wife had a bath in a very large upstairs room, bare except for a hip bath in the centre. When we came there on the next occasion we found that the hotel had been completely redecorated and refurnished with antiques collected from the district, but I think it has since closed down.

On Sunday, the next day, we weighed anchor and at noon *Cohoe* was off Ile de Cézembre. Once at sea we found the wind to be very light and it took us four hours to cover the ten miles to Cap Fréhel, which is the outstanding headland in these parts. By then we had decided to sail to Lézardrieux on the River Portrieux, a navigable distance of about 40 miles from Fréhel, allowing for a deviation to La Horaine lighthouse which is the outer mark of innumerable rocks to the north-east of the river entrance.

In the late evening we had sighted the Grand Léjon lighthouse which stands on a group of rocks off the Baie de St Brieuc, some 10 miles off the land. When night came no light flashed from its summit, so presumably it had not been restored after the German occupation. I then began to wonder what lights we would find restored in the difficult approaches to Lézardrieux. The next few hours were to be really exciting and well remembered by both Mamie and me.

Soon the light airs were replaced by a freshening wind from the NE and *Cohoe* leapt to life responsively. At 2115 Mamie called me on deck from my charts, to say that we were approaching the dangers SE of the Horaine, the light on which had happily been restored. The wind was now decidedly fresh so we lowered the genoa and set the staysail. The tidal stream was pouring out of the Gulf of St Malo, and with the yacht sailing fast we must have been making 10 to 11 knots over the bottom, which means over a mile in six minutes. Not far to the west of us lay the sinister sounding Plateau de Men-March. Soon we came into a sort of local tide race where *Cohoe* plunged in lively style through the overfalls. Things were moving. Before we had time to realise it we heard the grunt of the whistling buoy off the Men-March shoals, so navigation was spot on, and some fifteen minutes later we were shooting past La Horaine lighthouse through the overfalls north of the plateau it marked.

We sailed west and, with a strong westerly running stream, we quickly came on the leading lights which had been restored, La Croix (the outer one) only recently. Channel markings had been altered to port red, starboard black, exactly opposite to pre-war colours, but of course we could not identify colours at night. We passed between unlit dangers of Plateau des Sirlots to starboard and the Pen-Azen rocks to port. Mamie was steering while I was keeping track below of *Cohoe*'s position on an Admiralty chart spread on a quarter berth under a weak electric light, putting my head on deck from time to time to see that all was well.

22. La Croix structure was under repair, but the light itself had just been restored when we first arrived off Lézardrieux at night just after World War II.

We were running at a high speed over a foul tide in the channel and it did not take long before we could make out the outline of Ile Bréhat to port. Soon the sea, which had been fairly high, died down into a short wind-over-tide popple. The worst was over and ahead lay some fascinating pilotage. Occasionally the form of a beacon tower or islet would loom up in the dark, looking much closer at night than it really was. Before passing de la Croix lighthouse we altered course to starboard to bring the next pair of lights into line. Then ahead appeared an island; in the dark it appeared so close that the yacht must hit it, but as she drew near we could see a gap and *Cohoe* ran happily through, to follow up the inner reach of river with land on both sides. At 2230 we let go the anchor near the Perdrix beacon tower a mile below the village of Lézardrieux, very pleased with the passage.

It is always a happy experience to wake up in new surroundings, which one has entered during the hours of darkness. When we went on deck next morning we found that *Cohoe* was in a narrow river. On each side there were rocky shores, above which rose hills and woods. On the west side was a bay, a little quay, and a lighthouse. A farm stood on the hill and some peasants were working in a field. After breakfast we set sail to run up the river and anchor off Lézardrieux, which turned out to be a village with a small breakwater sheltering a landing which dries out. Perched up high and dry alongside a quay was a little steamer and nearby was a stone jetty. The place seemed to have suffered considerably during the war; there was an immense gap in the break-water, presumably where it had been mined or bombed.

We launched the dinghy and rowed ashore, landing at the slipway, over which there was a curious arch. Walking on, we passed through some kind of shipyard, which we later learnt was the property of the highways department of *Ponts et Chaussées*. The little steamer was used for the supervision of the lights and beacons, and at the quay were numbers of topmarks for buoys and beacons. Strictly speaking nobody was allowed within the gates of the shipyard, but as the breakwater had been blown up there was nowhere else to land and no objection was made to our using the slipway for the dinghy. The foreman was very obliging and showed us the tap where we could get fresh water, very good fresh water, he said. This concession had to be withdrawn in later years.

Continuing up the village road we passed some cottages and inns, a wash-house where several women were busy with the household chores, and opposite two or three sheds where carts disgorged quantities of apples for cider making; cider apples are rotten and not at all like the alluring fruit one sees on cider advertisements. Continuing up a hill we soon found ourselves in the main street of Lézardrieux; it was a typical French village with cobbled streets along which the children run to school, the wooden soles of their sabots clattering on the stones. The women wore black dresses and white bonnets. At one end of the main street, which was almost wide enough to be called a square, was the big church which dominates the scene. The Mairie was on the right-hand side and there were many cafés and small shops.

Finding a shop with the word 'petrole' chalked on a blackboard, I left Mamie there and returned to get an empty petrol tin, not knowing then that *petrole* means paraffin and the French for petrol is *essence*. It was well that I did so, as I found a coastguard in a boat alongside *Cohoe*, and he had come to take particulars of her. I showed him our passport, the ship's papers, and the certificate I had obtained at Dinard. No sooner had the coastguard left than a policeman arrived and I went through the whole process again. In this case there was a spot of trouble. It appeared that the Certificate at Dinard had not completed the formalities. The Gendarme kept on asking for a 'Passeport pour yacht'. My own passport was not enough and he explained that a boat must have a passport also. I rowed him ashore in the pram dinghy (he nearly capsized it when jumping in, but played a noble part in baling it out afterwards) and then he took me to a little shed near the harbour which served as an office. There he filled in the form of 'Passeport pour yacht'. The price for this nautical passport, which was much the same as the modern green card, was equivalent to about one penny so I could not feel badly stung.

In France at that time one needed coupons for nearly everything. The system was introduced during the German occupation, so Frenchmen, rarely slow-witted in avoiding regulations, evaded the enemy-enforced law by the black market. For the majority of articles there were two recognised prices, one with coupons and one without. For such things as clothes or oil for an engine, the surcharge was not severe, but for cigarettes or petrol the black market price was multiplied several times. Hence our earnest desire to obtain coupons through legal channels. We had visitors' tickets for food and obtained most of the provisions we needed at Lézardrieux. We got good meat without difficulty at the butcher's, and at the baker's we bought fine great loaves of bread, and we were glad to be able to present the necessary coupons, for there was a notice on the counter to the effect that there was no 'pain' for the ticketless.

Next day we hired a taxi and motored over to Paimpol in pursuit of petrol coupons. Paimpol proved to be an attractive looking little sea port. It is much larger than Lézardrieux with bigger and better supplied shops, and has a good locked-in basin where a boat can lie at the quay close to the hotels and shops.

We visited the Inscription Maritime, where we were given all the petrol coupons we needed, but the snag was that they could not be used for filling up tins at a garage, and the petrol could only be obtained through the Customs. The nearest place to Lézardrieux where it was available was at Loguivi, a little harbour only accessible near high water and inconveniently placed for us. After getting the coupons we did a little shopping at Paimpol and Mamie secured a Basque beret which delighted her very much. We managed to buy a few cakes which were not easy to get in France, but nowhere could we obtain butter, which we badly needed. As there was no train or bus to Lézardrieux until the evening we walked back; it was quite pleasant along the winding country road, which climbed up and down over the hills. Before one gets to Lézardrieux a big suspension bridge is crossed, giving a fine view of the reaches of the river. It was a sunny day and the newly painted beacons looked bright against the fast running waters of the river. We could see *Cohoe* at anchor about a mile away and very small she looked.

Our stay at Lézardrieux proved to be much longer than we had anticipated when we ran gaily into the river on the Sunday night. By Tuesday the forecast for easterly headwinds was 'fresh to strong', and the following day it was 'strong to gale'. We were weather-bound for the rest of the week and had a lot of trouble with our anchors dragging–excellent as they had proved to be everywhere else.

The worst day of our stay was the Thursday when the wind was gale force, the sky overcast and it was very cold. However, we made an excursion, catching a bus at noon and alighting on the quay at Tréguier. The town is larger and more interesting than either Lézardrieux or Paimpol; we enjoyed visiting the beautiful church which was formerly a cathedral and has a very high spire. After that we attended to the more mundane matters of shopping; we wanted butter for which we had coupons, but we had no better luck than at Lézardrieux or Paimpol.

It was not until Sunday, October 13th, that the wind moderated, although still pretty fresh from E by N. It was a sunny day and we were busily occupied with the usual preparations for getting to sea so it was not until 1500, rather late on the ebb tide, that we weighed anchor and left Lézardrieux bound homeward for Guernsey.

23. After anchoring temporarily near the Perdrix lighthouse, *Cohoe* ran up the Trieux River in the morning and brought up on the east side.

We tacked down the river as we were short of petrol and it took two hours to clear the entrance. At 1700 we were 2 miles NNW of La Horaine lighthouse, the same position as we were when entering the river at night. At spring tides there can be what may be termed local but full-blooded tide races, too small to be shown on the tidal atlas. One of these lies between La Horaine and the Plateau de Barnouic, where the tidal stream is compressed into a 6 mile gap between the two plateaux. Sunday, besides being the 13th day of the month, had one of the highest spring tides in the whole year. I had already taken in two reefs and set the storm jib. Mamie was below off watch. Then we hit the overfalls. The sea was boiling, every wave white-crested and malicious. I nursed *Cohoe* gently through with sheets checked off, holding only enough steerage way to enable me to luff over the worst of the seas. In a very short time she was swept by the tide to the eastward. When the Barnouic lighthouse bore NW, I put the helm down, choosing the right moment between seas, and tacked *Cohoe* back on a northerly course.

By 1930 it was night, and two hours later the light on Roche Douvres plateau lay on the port quarter, bearing SW, some 5 miles distant. The remaining twenty miles were easy, but we did not bring up in St Peter Port until about 0230 in the morning. The following day we sailed for Brixham, where we were delayed by bad weather. A few days later we returned to the Hamble River; it was night before we arrived at Bursledon, where we brought up alongside the barge off Moody's yard, thus concluding *Cohoe*'s maiden voyage.

CHAPTER NINETEEN

FIRST OCEAN RACES

It was not until 1947 that I was able to make a start in ocean racing. *Cohoe* needed little alteration for this; I had the foot of the genoa cut down to avoid penalty under the rules, and replaced the engine by a light two-stroke 6 horsepower motor with a feathering propeller to save weight, much to Mamie's annoyance, as it was nothing like so good for cruising. In a light displacement boat as small as *Cohoe* it is essential to keep the weight down, hence the maximum number of the crew had to be limited to three including myself; the addition of a fourth body, plus oilskins, changes of clothes, water and provisions, would have been too much. Our routine was for each of us to take two hours at the helm, then two hours stand-by below (available instantly at call) and finally two hours off. A boat of *Cohoe*'s size needed only one man on deck to steer and handle her, except when setting or lowering the spinnaker. I usually did the navigation by dead reckoning, except on the Bay of Biscay races when I sometimes had an astro-navigator in the crew. Cooking in the early races (not always five star grade) was divided between us.

Our first ocean race was the 1947 Southsea to Brixham, over a course of 200 miles from Southsea to Le Havre light-vessel and thence to Brixham. There were twenty-eight entries, of which eight were in Class III, including *Cohoe*. My crew were Roger Heron, at that time a partner in Laurent Giles and Partners (all the partners, including Jack Giles, George Gill and Humphrey Barton, were good friends of mine) and the third member was Jim Hackforth Jones, also from Lymington. The race started from Southsea on June 27th at 1845, and the first leg of the course to Le Havre light-vessel was eventless, as there was a light free wind, although it was foggy during the night. After rounding the lightship on Saturday forenoon, the next leg was diagonally across the English Channel for the second time, WNW to Brixham. At first the course provided a close reach, but the barometer was falling and during the evening the wind quickly veered to dead ahead. It freshened steadily and by midnight, when *Cohoe* was in the middle of the Channel, most of the Class III boats must have been well reefed.

At dawn on Sunday morning it was blowing harder still and conditions were dismal. In *Cohoe* the angle of heel was extreme. She was a tender yacht, heeling readily, but once heeled to a certain point the leverage of her keel stiffened her and she went no further. However, it is tiring work when a yacht is sailing on her ear, and on deck

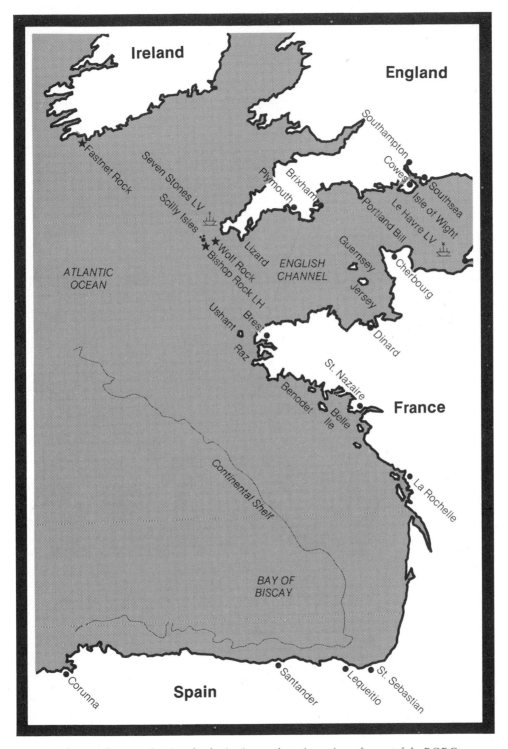

10. *Ireland–Bay of Biscay*. Showing the destinations and turning points of some of the RORC races.

sheets of spray fly aft into the helmsmen's eyes. *Cohoe* lay on the port tack close-reefed and I thought the wind was about Force 6 to 7; a big sea was running as the tide was weather-going. The sun came out when we made landfall, sighting the cliffs of the Isle of Wight to starboard. Several boats were in sight but none was in our Class III. Still on the same tack we lay into Bournemouth Bay and by the time we reached Swanage we were pretty tired of beating against the wind, and the tide was due to turn against us. I realised then that if we were to tack in a strong wind against a foul tide off St Alban's Head we should make little progress so we decided to anchor in Swanage Bay.

There we had the luxury of changing into dry clothes and eating a hot meal. We pumped the bilges fully dry, and kept the primus going, which helped to dry out the cabin, for everything below was wet. We mended a torn sail and carried out a number of small repairs. Then we turned in for a couple of hours rest before getting under way again to catch the early inshore stream at St Alban's Head. We felt a little ashamed of ourselves at sheltering but our self-indulgence was rewarded, as when we were tacking up to St Alban's we sighted again a large Class II yacht which had stood out to sea, where she not only failed to make progress but had been set back by the tide for two or three miles.

By then the wind had moderated and the rest of the race provided a third night at sea, but plain sailing. We were tired and despondent by the time we arrived at Brixham and could see a forest of masts rising above the long breakwater, suggesting that all our competitors were ahead of us. We anchored off the yacht club and Roger Heron rowed off in the dinghy to learn the worst. When he returned he was smiling.

'*Cohoe*'s won', he announced excitedly. 'No other Class III boat finished. We've also beaten all Class II on corrected time.'

24. Entrance to La Rochelle; the historic tour de la Chaine on left and Tour St Nicolas on right.

Thus ended our first ocean race. Sixteen entries had retired. Some had given up because owners or crews had to be back on Monday morning, and others because they had been damaged in the strong winds, among them the 44 ton yawl *Eostra* which had been dismasted. Miles Wyatt's *Bloodhound* was winner in Class I, and Ian Carr's *Phemie* won Class II.

The last event of the season was the Plymouth–La Rochelle Race, which was an exciting prospect, taking us to the Bay of Biscay for the first time.

The first leg of the course was 115 miles from Plymouth to Ushant, which is the most westerly island in France and the most formidable, with its rock formation jutting out into fierce tidal streams.

After rounding Ushant the course crossed the Iroise leading to the entrance of Brest. These are historic waters which, over the years, I came to know intimately. It was here that Admiral Sir Edward Hawkes, with a fleet based on Brixham in Torbay, maintained the blockage of Brest, summer and winter alike, from 1755, often working in gales off a lee shore in unwieldy ships incapable of going to windward under short canvas.

The Iroise is bounded on its south side by the Chaussée de Sein (known as The Saints), a reef of rocks extending some fifteen miles seaward from the Pointe du Raz, off which there is the Ar Men buoy which is a mark on the course which must be left to port. It is here that the Bay of Biscay is entered and the weather usually becomes warmer. From the Ar Men buoy to the Pertius d'Antioche, which is the entrance channel between the Ile de Ré and Ile d'Oléron leading to the finish line, was a SE leg of 180 miles. Intermediate landmarks we expected to pass given a free wind were the Pointe de Penmarch, the big island of Belle Ile, and the Ile d'Yeu. The total length of the race was 355 miles.

On this first La Rochelle race I had with me my son Ross and a navigator, Lieut H A Barbary, who had served in MTB's during the war. Navigation was by dead reckoning, although some years later we had the aid of RDF, and a good series of radio beacons was established on the French coast of the Bay of Biscay. The race started at Plymouth at 1715 on August 16th and the weather was mostly light and without incident, except for a violent and spectacular storm of thunder and lightning in which all the yachts were involved, about 20 to 30 miles or more south of Belle Ile. There had been a dreadful sunrise described as 'a dipsomaniac's dream of hell – red, green, purple, yellow and black.' *Cohoe* did not heave-to but we were worried as we had never before seen or heard anything like it; it proved to be a line squall which only lasted for an hour and a quarter.

Our principal Class III competitor was *Freckles*, a bermudan ketch owned by Dr J H Sewart, a cruising man from Barry accustomed to the rough seas of the Bristol Channel; his excellent crew included his family, all of whom became great friends of ours. *Freckles* was not so close-winded as *Cohoe* but unbeatable when she could set a mizzen staysail. We fought it out over the whole 355 miles, often being in sight of each other, once being in a near collision during a squall at night. *Cohoe* won the race on corrected time, and with it the Class III Points Championship. We were surprised and elated by this success in our first year of ocean racing.

Michael Mason's lovely yawl *Latifa* won Class I, and in Class II A W Goudriaan's *Olivier van Noort* was first with John Illingworth's *Myth of Malham* a close second.

After crossing the finish line we motored into La Rochelle in the evening, passing between the ancient Tour de la Chaine and Tour St Nicholas at the entrance and through the lock gates into the inner basin in the centre of the town. Thus ended the first La Rochelle race after the war, and the French club Société des Régates

25. Ocean racers in La Rochelle yacht basin were few in number in 1948.

Rochelaises gave us all a tremendous welcome and generous prizes, coupled with bottles of brandy. There was a big reception at the town hall and a notable banquet.

I like La Rochelle, which is a large and interesting town. With the yachts lying in the basin in its centre (as they used to) we got to know all our competitors, meeting them also in the restaurants of which there are many. I also made lasting French friends there. When the celebrations were over the crew's leave usually expired and they had to return to their jobs. On this occasion I think Ross and I sailed *Cohoe* home to Bursledon, but often Mamie, with or without Arnaud, joined at La Rochelle to cruise home. It was during cruises such as these that I gathered information for my books *North Biscay Pilot* and *North Brittany Pilot*. I was one of the few sailing men lucky enough to be able to combine ocean racing with an equal amount of cruising, thus getting the best out of two worlds.

*   *   *

In the last year before the war the winner of the Class III Points Championship was *Mindy*, and her highly experienced owners, T B (Buster) Brown and T Lloyd, had no intention of letting the newcomer *Cohoe* win twice running. After winning the North Sea Race, *Mindy* came south in 1948 to regain the Championship which she succeeded in doing. No matter, as we had two notable races in heavy weather and finished the season second to her on points.

The first race that year was the Dinard Race. The course is a very interesting one, starting from Cowes and taking the fleet past the Casquets to Les Hanois lighthouse on the SW corner of Guernsey, and thence into the Gulf of St Malo, skirting the Minquiers group of rocks, and so to the finish at the fairway buoy off the entrance to the River Rance and Dinard. Although shorter than other RORC races, the course can be a tricky one, as I had already discovered when Mamie and I cruised these waters earlier.

For this race I had as crew my son Ross, then a Cambridge undergraduate, where he rowed No 5 in the first May Boat which was head of the river. He also won the Fairbairn Junior Sculls in 1949, putting up the then record time for the course and was awarded Leander colours. The other member of the crew was Gerald Harding, who had been severely scalded when cooking on *Cohoe* during the rough Channel Race of the previous year. He became a 'regular' aboard *Cohoe*, and a much valued one owing to his determination and cheerfulness under all conditions of weather.

The race started during the morning of Friday July 16th in light airs and easy conditions, which held while the fleet was crossing the Channel close-hauled during the afternoon and night. Landfalls were made at various points on the Cherbourg peninsula, depending on the windward ability of the individual boats. Here the wind freshened and there was a forecast of strong winds backing to the SW, accompanied by heavy rain and moderate to poor visibility.

At the Casquets the following morning, Saturday, we had to reef the mainsail and set a staysail in place of the genoa. The sea was beginning to build up, as it always does very quickly in those waters. Conditions were soon gloomy in the extreme. There was dense rain which cut down visibility, and when we were beating off the Guernsey coast it was barely possible to sight land on the inshore tack before entering the danger area of the outlying submerged rocks.

It was not until late in the evening that *Cohoe* fetched Les Hanois lighthouse off the SW of Guernsey and it took a long time to work round the point against a foul tide.

At about 2200 the wind strengthened rapidly. The official forecast was one of strong winds which I logged as Force 7. Three reefs were taken in the mainsail and the storm jib was set. The rain was fierce, the night was black and the visibility was so poor that no lights could be seen. There was then a weather-going tide and a wild sea, so I decided to heave-to for three hours between Les Hanois and the dangerous Roches Douvres, before entering narrow waters in the vicinity of the Minquiers plateau of rocks.

With the storm jib backed, *Cohoe* lay quietly rising and falling in the seas. All the tumult was over, the slamming, the noise, the spray and the motion. I took the quarter berth, as I always do on these occasions, for a skipper has to be handy to go on deck, and in the quarter berth he can hear what is going on, put his head out from time to time and be ready for instant action if occasion demands it. But in rough conditions it is an uncomfortable position, as so much water descends upon the occupant.

It was ironical to be wasting a fair tide and to be waiting for a foul one, but in Channel Island waters with a weather-going tide, there is an exceptionally steep breaking sea. Then it can be like sailing in overfalls.

About three hours later (between 0100 and 0200 on Sunday) the tide turned and became lee-going, so the apparent wind and seas moderated as a result. The seas were higher, but they broke less and the visciousness was taken out of them. The visibility must have still been poor, as no lights were in sight. We let draw and sailed on, still seeing nothing, though we must have passed very close to the Roches Douvres without spotting the light. We gave a wide berth to the Minquiers, setting a course between this plateau of rocks and the French mainland to the west. When dawn turned into day the weather gradually improved and the sun came out, but we sighted no land until we came off Cap Fréhel and altered course for the remaining few miles to Dinard. We had sailed 50 miles and rounded the Minquiers blindfold, in what was recorded at Guernsey met office as thick fog.

Oddly enough the end of the race followed the precedent of the Brixham Race. After crossing the finish line we sailed up the river, feeling tired and depressed. Then as we approached Dinard Roads we saw yachts at anchor. As we passed the nearest we hailed her, inquiring what other Class III boats were in. The answer came clearly: 'None'. *Cohoe* had won boat for boat without calling on the handicap allowance due to her small size and despite her loss of time when hove-to. The only other boat in her class to complete the course was *Alethea III*, a 9-ton cruising yacht owned by Vernon Sainsbury, who later became Commodore of the RORC. The winners in Class I and Class II were Mike Mason's *Latifa* and *Golden Dragon* owned by H S Rouse, one of the most popular and warm-hearted of ocean racing skippers. Only thirteen of forty-two starters in the three classes had completed the course. Many of those who retired suffered damage to sails (often still of pre-war vintage), parting of stays and other breakages. *Seafalke* had a man swept out of the cockpit, but recovered him and went on to win second place in Class II. *Seahorse* was reported to have had two men over the side, but also got them back aboard safely. It may be noted that when men go overboard they nearly always retain a hand for themselves and a hold on something, be it a shroud, a lifeline or a rope.

*   *   *

The next heavy weather race in 1948 was the Brixham–Santander event, which proved to be one of the toughest in my life.

The start was from the Brixham Yacht Club's line at 1530 on Friday August 6th, and there were thirty-one entries. As usual *Cohoe*'s crew consisted of three all told: Geoff Budden (who sadly died some years after the race, while still a comparatively young man) came as astro-navigator, my son Ross as mate and cook, while I was skipper and dead reckoning navigator. We followed our customary system of two-hourly watches; one man steering for two hours, then going below for two hours as stand-by, followed by two hours off watch. In practice our duties overlapped and there was precious little uninterrupted sleep for any of us in this race.

The yacht was not in good racing trim, for in the Dinard Race she had bent the fitting at the foot of the forestays, and the bolt through the mast at the head of the stays had cut its way like a blunt knife downwards through the wood, so that the forestays were slack. In the intervals between the races there had been no time to have the mast out for complete repairs but, thanks to Moody's yard, temporary repairs had been made, together with a new mast band since most of the cleats had been broken or torn off.

The weather forecast was unfavourable as a depression was coming in from the west and there was a southerly gale in the Bay of Biscay. For the first twenty-four hours the racing fleet beat to windward off the English coast. The night was thundery and squally causing a number of retirements. The following afternoon (Saturday) *Cohoe* and Class III were out in the English Channel standing on the port tack for a position west of Ushant. The barometer had fallen 7 millibars and the wind was backing and freshening. At 1730 we lowered the mainsail, lashed it down, and set the storm trysail and storm jib. At this time, the wind was no more than Force 6 and shortening of sail had been precautionary in anticipation of events to come.

It is of interest here to look at the barograph readings of the Class II winner, *Golden Dragon*. It will be seen that the slope of the fall steepens rapidly, dropping 22 millibars in three hours (a slope of 10 millibars in three hours is usually associated with a Force 8 gale), but the depression would not have reached the Class III boats until an hour or more later.

In *Cohoe* it was shortly before 1800 that the wind increased to well above Force 6 and this, coupled with the falling glass, the driving rain and the menacing conditions, decided me on reefing the trysail. At this time Geoff was at the helm and Ross was below off watch. I was stand-by and I pulled down the forward earing and made fast. Then in order to take the strain off the leach pendant I checked off the main sheet. Next I returned to the cabin top to swig in on the aft reefing tackle.

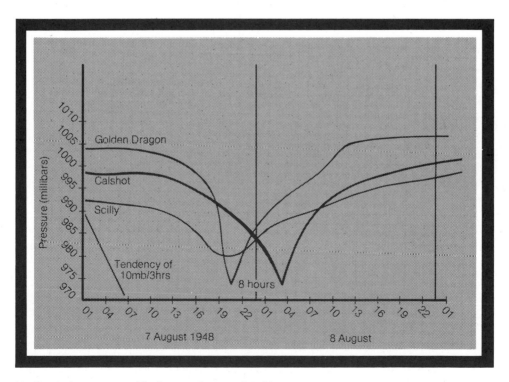

11. *Santander race storm.* The barograph trace of *Golden Dragon*.

The next moment I found myself overboard. Fortunately as I fell I held on to the reefing tackle. I suddenly realised that Geoff was overboard too, for I saw him floating aft, but hanging on to something. Meanwhile the yacht was well balanced between her storm jib and the trysail which had been checked right off. She was sailing herself on a 5-knot reach to the west.

At that instant, it being the six o'clock change of watch, Ross had put his head on deck. His appearance was providential, for he was in time to haul aboard Geoff— whose position was precarious, as he had fallen in head foremost with his head towed under water by the speed of the boat. In some miraculous way he retained his grip on a lifeline which had gone over the side with the stanchions so both were trailing in the water.

My circumstances were less pressing. I had managed to get a foot aboard and wedged it into some wire rope, presumably the runner. But, suspended between the reefing tackle at the outer end of the boom, which was squared off, and my foot at the other, my body was in the water and I was unable to extricate myself—so I was glad of a hand to get back on deck again.

It had been a narrow shave, for both Geoff and I were wearing heavy oilskins without life jackets, and had we lost our hold there would have been but a slim chance of survival, as with the trysail half-reefed it is doubtful whether Ross could have manoeuvred the yacht in such a sea to find and pick up survivors single-handed. It was something little short of a miracle that there was no casualty. What had happened was that an extra large wave catapulted both of us against the lifelines simultaneously. These collapsed under the impact of our combined weight as the eye securing them aft was torn from the deck, and one stanchion was rooted out, taking with it part of the toerail.

All in all the damage was light. Geoff had lost his glasses and for some while he feared he had broken a bone in his hand. I had some nasty looking scratches on my skin and ankle which bled a bit. Ross probably came off worst, as it must have been a shock to come on deck and find he was alone with not a single man left on board.

Once back on board I finished the reefing of the trysail, apart from tying in the reef points which were not urgent, and then went below to join Geoff changing into dry things, and to bandage my foot, leaving Ross at the helm for it was now his watch. It is easy enough to talk of dry clothes, but after one has been racing for twenty-four hours to windward there is often precious little left that is dry. Geoff had run out of clothes, but fortunately I had a reserve kitbag forward and Ross had a few spare dry garments.

Meanwhile the barometer was starting on its spectacular plunge and the wind increasing all the time. I decided to prepare for the worst and went back to join Ross on deck. We lowered both the reefed trysail and storm jib, then secured them. Next we experimented with a small sea anchor, which had a steadying effect when streamed on a long nylon rope from the stern. However, I do not think the sea anchor lasted long as during the worst of the storm the boat lay a-hull under bare pole, beam to the seas, and when the gale was over we found that the anchor had disappeared and only the nylon rope remained.

When Geoff had been recovered on board he expected to be stand-by for two hours, and so he had taken the quarter berth to be within call from the cockpit. Quarter berths are the wettest in the ship so Ross and I, on completion of our work on deck, were lucky to have the cabin berths, one on each side of the saloon; the canvas leeboards were lashed up, so we could not be thrown out. Our principal discomfort was damp. Geoff had got wet again in the quarter berth when the companion door was opened as I attended to the lights on deck; Ross and I got soaked when taking the sails off her, and no more dry clothes were available. The cabin was wet too, not from leaks but from water carried below by our clothes when Geoff and I had changed after being thrown overboard and from general condensation. Our cumbersome clothes added to the discomfort, especially the oilskins which we had to wear in case we should suddenly be needed on deck.

The glass was still falling fast. At midnight the greatest fury of the storm fell on us. The wind and rain flattened the sea. The yacht heeled as though under full sail. On the deck above our heads blasts of rain hammered fiercely. Then the wind shifted. How heavy the sea was I do not know, for waves cannot be seen at night except for the flashing white phosphorescent tops. It was certainly violent and large. One exceptional wave woke us up later as it threw the boat almost on her beam ends. Some said afterwards that the seas ran 'mountains high'. As for the wind, it was the highest I had known up to then. In all this *Cohoe* behaved very well. She was lifted bodily great heights in the air and then down she would go. Down and down so that one tensed oneself for a crash; yet at the bottom of the trough she never slammed, but gently came to rest before rising once more to the next crest.

So passed the night and by dawn on Sunday the wind had moderated, but in *Cohoe*'s cabin conditions did not seem much quieter. The sea after a gale is often more truculent than during it. A boat is no longer steadied by the wind on her mast and the motion is worse in consequence. At 7 o'clock in the morning I got up. I felt amazingly well and refreshed, for we had had a good deal of sleep—more than we got at any other time in the race. I decided not to make sail again until we got the 0800 weather report. The glass was rising, but with a jump which might presage more bad weather. At 0800 Ross got the report, though feebly, having to press his ear to the instrument. The forecast was fair, with promise of a veer in the wind. Once the weather report had been received we immediately made sail, and before we had been long under way we sighted a sail. At one moment it would appear high in the sky and at the next it would be lost in a valley. A lumpy swell was still running. *Cohoe* passed close under her stern and we identified her as *Mehalah*, our largest Class III rival, lying hove-to under trysail and storm jib. Unfortunately our arrival on the scene was a sign for feverish sail-making and she was quickly after us.

We found that owing to a crossed screw thread in the wide diameter cap of the water tank, there had been leakage when we had been heeled in the heavy weather and only three gallons of water was left, plus $3\frac{1}{2}$ gallons in a can. To allow adequate reserve for delays in calms or gales, or even dismasting, we rationed water to three half-pint mugs of water a day instead of the usual 4 pints per man. To encourage thrift all tea, hot drinks and orangeade were cut out for the rest of the race.

As the wind became light and did not veer we made a landfall in France 50 miles east of Ushant, which we did not round until Monday afternoon, and it was not until nightfall that we entered the Bay of Biscay, leaving to port the Ar Men buoy. On

Tuesday *Cohoe* struck a glancing blow on a floating log, of which there were many, as a timber ship had lost her deck cargo during the gale. In the early hours of Wednesday, midway across the Bay, we had left the Continental shelf and entered charted depths of some 2,000 fathoms.

As soon as it became light we discovered that the bolts of the track for the weather runner had sheared, to which I made a temporary repair. Later in the day, Geoff managed to get a noon latitude by lashing himself to the mast while he took the sight, but in the afternoon the sky was overcast and we sailed through a series of squalls so further sights were not possible. During the evening it blew a near gale. The wind had veered and freed; under double-reefed mainsail and storm jib we were soon logging 7 knots again. The sea was very rough with steep breaking pyramid-shaped tops. It became necessary to lash the helmsman in the cockpit, and at nightfall I shortened the watches to hourly spells. Early on Thursday morning, at 0130, Ross identified the loom of a lighthouse; it was the double flash of Cabo Major at the entrance to Santander, and soon the blaze of town lights could be seen.

At 0355 we let off white flares as we crossed the finish line. The eventful race was over and, when dawn came, the sun rose over the mountains of Spain, 440 miles and five and a half days from our departure in England.

✳   ✳   ✳

G P Hall's *Eilun* proved to be the all-over and Class I winner, a well-merited victory as she was an old Fife boat adapted for ocean racing and smallest in her class; her owner was one of the most experienced seamen in the race. Dr E Greville's *Erivale* won Class II; during the night following the accident in *Cohoe*, Peter Padwick, one of *Erivale*'s crew, was catapulted over the lifelines but managed to get his arm round a stanchion. The owner grabbed him by his ankle and got him back on board, when he continued winching as though nothing had happened. In Class III *Mindy* was first, *Cohoe* second and *Mehalah* third.

As to the weather, a very vigorous secondary had established itself in the early hours of Saturday morning and crossed the Bay of Biscay and the English Channel approaches. The storm was so severe and caused so many casualties that it was featured as the 3-column leader on the front page of the *Daily Telegraph*. The centre of the low (which had deepened to 976 millibars) passed directly across the competitors midway across the western end of the English Channel.

The reason why the ocean racers came off so lightly was probably because we were all in deep water about half way between England and France, clear of the proximity of land. This is in contrast to the experience of the 1979 Fastnet Race, where little safety was found in such deep water; fifteen lives and five yachts were lost and nearly two-thirds of the starters retired. Ross and I made a thorough research into the storm and the losses it entailed, which added four new appendices to my book *Heavy Weather Sailing*. The well-known meteorologist Alan Watts contributed a weather analysis, including barograph traces showing that the storm of 1979 was not accompanied by the dramatically steep fall of pressure experienced in 1948. The wind in the 1948 Santander Race certainly rose to storm Force 10 (48–55 knots), and was reported to have been logged as Force 11 (56–63 knots) by the Clan Liner MV *Stirlingshire* which passed through the racing fleet when homeward bound from Australia. Alan Watts examined that gale as well, and confirmed Force 11, but added 'even though . . . such wind strength could not have been sustained for long.'

Once ashore we were all entertained magnificently for three days before we set out again on the next race to Belle Ile.

*   *   *

Once the immediate post-race formalities were over, there was always plenty to do ashore: friends were on every hand, sightseeing was enjoyable and hospitality was generous. Whenever he was on board, Alan Mansley was made what I might call our social secretary; the following story shows the kind of initiative that got him this job.

Cohoe II was lying alongside the quay at St Malo after a roughish Dinard race. We had suffered some damage, including a jammed roller reefing gear which was beyond our own repair resources, and we had spent all day vainly scouring the town for engineers who were able and willing to weld and machine it. Next morning Alan put the boom on his shoulder and was a long time ashore; he came back with a wide smile.

It seems he had spotted a Soviet freighter in the inner basin, and he promptly walked up the gangplank. He was met at the top by a formidable Russian woman, who was sufficiently taken aback by the sight of an Englishman with a boom at the slope to take him to her Captain. The Russians did a perfect repair by mid-afternoon, and refused all offers of payment or, indeed, hospitality from the crazy capitalists.

CHAPTER TWENTY

PUBLISHING

I adopted publishing as my full time occupation only after the conclusion of World War II, when I engaged in two different forms of the profession or trade. One was periodical publishing of *The Yachtsman*, where the revenue was principally derived from advertisements, and the other was book publishing, where the income came from sales to the book trade.

The Yachtsman continued to be published by the Yachtsman Publishing Co Ltd, of which I was the principal shareholder. The publication continued as a quarterly in pocket size and was distributed in London by the Rolls House Publishing Co Ltd, which owned an architectural magazine and was the distributor of a number of other periodicals. The very able director responsible for sales was Mr Rutherford and the financial director was a chartered accountant named Mr Scott, who became a valued friend when I was in London. Both gave me considerable help and advice gleaned from their long experience of the publishing world.

Eric Hiscock continued as associate editor until the summer of 1946, when he took over my rights in the pre-war *Yachtsman's Annual* which he ran for two years under the title of *The Yachting Year*. However, Eric's *forte* was that of an author of cruising books based on his experience as a long distance voyager with his wife Susan, first in their 23ft gaff cutter *Wanderer II*, followed later by their circumnavigation of the world via the Cape of Good Hope in the 30ft sloop *Wanderer III*, over the years 1952–55 and again in 1959–62, this time via Suez. Eric's achievements, with seven notable books in print at the time of writing, are due to his perfectionism, a characteristic he shares with Susan over anything they undertake; his outstandingly good colour photography affords an example of this.

When I took over editing *The Yachtsman* again, I found it difficult to cover all sides of the sport adequately, within the scope of a pocket sized quarterly, particularly racing. However, I devised a method of tabulating results of the principal events, such as Cowes Week or Clyde Fortnight, giving a black square for a first place, a black triangle for a second and a white triangle for a third. By this means a whole season's results of ocean races could be covered in less then one and a half pages. *The Yachtsman* circulation rose from under 1,000 copies when first acquired before the war to an ABC certified figure of around 10,000 copies quarterly, which was quite good in the forties, a time when yachtsmen were few in number compared with today. The advertising revenue also grew steadily and the magazine began to show an acceptable, if not a princely profit.

Editing a yachting magazine was a congenial occupation, and I met a great number of people, being invited to launches and trials of new yachts of all sizes and types, press lunches and all kinds of social activities, which I shared with the editors of the other yachting periodicals who became good friends of mine.

Coming now to books. When I started publishing after the war it was a difficult occupation for newcomers, such as myself, as we were in open competition with the leading old-established publishers who had big back-lists of successful books and, consequently, much lower overhead expenses at a time when price counted far more than it does today. I am afraid that sooner or later there were many casualties among the new publishers, but my Robert Ross & Co Ltd prospered in a modest way by deliberately keeping small and selective. I had the advantage of a specialised list and being fairly well known in cruising and yacht racing circles, besides already being the author of eight yachting books.

The first yachting book we published was my *Sailing Days*, which was a happy one and a success, partly because it came out at the right time when everybody wanted to forget the war. This was soon followed by Ian Proctor's classics *Racing Dinghy Handling* and *Racing Dinghy Maintenance*. Ian Proctor later became an associate editor of *The Yachtsman* before he started a business of his own building alloy metal masts for dinghies, which before many years grew to cover masts and their fittings for every type of yacht from dinghies to ocean racers.

However, what finally set the company on its feet was Captain John Illingworth's masterly work *Offshore*. The book was planned with him at a party in the Town Hall at La Rochelle at the end of La Rochelle Race, 1947. This must have been a tremendous task at a time when he was Commodore of both the Royal Ocean Racing Club and the Royal Naval Sailing Association besides racing his famous *Myth of Malham*. It was due to his extraordinary energy that he managed to complete the book to schedule, writing it, as he said, 'at all sorts of times, in all sorts of places, in yachts and ships and trains'; it was written and published within two years of its inception, a record for so large a work with nearly a hundred diagrams or plans, some of which had to be traced and reduced for reproduction from blue prints.

Among other early publications were *Cruising Yachts: Design and Performance* by T Harrison Butler, an eye surgeon by profession and the enthusiastic designer of small cruising yachts mostly ranging in size from 5 to 10 tons; no less than 76 of these are listed in Lloyd's Register of Yachts. T Harrison Butler was a pioneer of the controversial metacentroid theory and a big kindly man with many friends in the world of cruising. *Sailing Yacht Design* by Douglas Phillips-Birt became a standard work on the subject which is still in print. Douglas was a qualified naval architect, a whimsical character with a great sense of humour and an authority on yachts and their history. The third of this trio of books was *Practical Yacht Construction* by C J Watts, the chief draughtsman of Camper & Nicholsons, Northam, who had spent his whole life on the design and construction of yachts of all kinds, large and small.

Besides manuals, the company was fortunate in having first refusal of a considerable proportion of narratives of long distance voyages, and was the publisher of all Humphrey Barton's books. Of these the most successful was *Vertue XXXV*, named after the boat in which he made his famous east to west crossing of the Atlantic in 1950. His book was written on his return to England and we published it in time for the pre-Christmas demand. Likewise my own book *North Atlantic* was written and published in the same year; in it I gave a full account of the 'expedition' arranged by the Royal Naval Sailing Association in 1950 for the entry of a team of three small boats in the Bermuda Race, followed by the RORC Transatlantic Race to bring them back to England, the first ever for which such small boats were eligible.

Altogether Humphrey made over twenty Transatlantic passages, mostly alone with his wife after his retirement from Laurent Giles and Partners, all of whom I used to know well, especially Jack Laurent Giles himself, who did the designing for his firm. Humphrey was one of my oldest sailing friends and a close contemporary, being only a year my senior. He was the founder of the Ocean Cruising Club and for many years the affectionately respected Admiral of the Club, of which I was also one of the founder members. He was a great seaman, having been awarded the Cruising Club of America's highest honour, the Blue Water Medal, and his remarkable practical knowledge of yachts and everything that goes into them was unique; in manner he was outspoken, never hesitating to say what he thought.

Some of the other narratives I published were *The Wind Calls the Tune* by Stanley Smith and Charles Violet, describing their eventful second voyage in the *Nova Espero* across the Atlantic; *Alone through the Roaring Forties* by the Argentinian Vito Dumas which covers the adventures in his single-handed circumnavigation of the world; and *The Four Winds of Adventure* by Marcel Bardiaux, which followed later and tells the tough story of the first part of his solitary voyaging across the five oceans.

It is perhaps worth noting that in the era to which I refer there was little sponsorship of long voyages. The owners footed the expenses themselves and sailed independent, often on a shoestring.

Although the title of this chapter is publishing, I think I should comment here on my own pilot books, although the earlier ones were published by other firms.

The first booklet was *Creeks of the Isle of Wight*, which was published in 1928 at the price of two shillings as a reprint of a series of articles in *The Yachtsman*. By modern standards it was an amateurish production as the charts were drawn by me and the photographs not notably good. Nevertheless, published over 50 years ago, it was the pattern for all my pilot books which followed.

The same material contributed a part of *Creeks and Harbours of the Solent* which was a well-produced volume published by Edward Arnold in 1933 and which ran to seven editions in their hands. Next followed *The Shell Pilot to the South Coast Harbours*, which was first published by Faber & Faber just before World War II under the title of *Sailing on the South Coast*. At that time the Shell County Guides were edited by John Betjeman (later Sir John, the Poet Laureate), who commissioned the book and took it under his wing. Judging by his broadcasts, he has changed little from when I knew him, retaining his individualistic and semi-humorous outlook on the world, nor has his voice changed one iota over the past forty years. Sponsored by Shell, the book has always been modestly priced and thanks to this it is by far the 'best seller' among my pilot books, and I gather that it is still one of the most successful of the many Shell Guides.

The first pilot book I published myself was H G (Blondie) Hasler's *Harbours and Anchorages of the North Coast of Brittany* in 1952. I first met Blondie in 1948, when he came to live near us at Bursledon. He is one of the most unassuming men I have met, and never even mentioned his distinguished record as a marine commando in the war, and was putting all his energy into sailing. He had won the Class II RORC Points Championship in his 30-sq metre *Tre-Sang* in 1947 and bought *Petula*, an 18-ton yawl the following year. I had started on the preparation of a book on the coast of Brittany when cruising with Mamie, but I had not got far with it when I was invited to race my boat *Cohoe* the following year in the Bermuda and Transatlantic races. This was a chance of a lifetime, so I asked Blondie whether he would step into the gap and take over authorship of the proposed book, which he generously agreed to do.

The result was a masterly volume incorporating all his ideas on what a good pilot book should be. I co-operated to the full and the charts were overprinted in blue for shallows and red for lights. The book was highly commended by all who used it, but copies sold slowly as only a limited number of yachtsmen cruised as far as Brittany at that time. I think it took ten years to sell a small edition at the modest price of under £3; hence it was unremunerative to author or publisher. Blondie naturally felt unable to prepare a new edition and passed the rights over to me, so I prepared a completely revised edition illustrated by photographs in 1965; this sold better but it was not until 1972, when the third revised edition was published and the title altered to *North Brittany Pilot* that, with the boom in yachting, it began to sell really well.

In the meantime, my book *Channel Harbours and Anchorages* had been published by Edward Arnold in 1956. This book was a success because it covered the middle section of the English Channel on both sides, all within easy reach of the Solent.

The last pilot books I published myself were *Biscay Harbours and Anchorages*, volume I in 1959 covering Brest to Lorient and volume II in 1960 covering Lorient to La Rochelle.

Both these sold slowly because, like Blondie Hasler's, they were pioneering and before their time, in the sense that the number of yachtsmen cruising in the area was then relatively small. A second abbreviated edition combining both volumes was revised by Professor A N Black and published in 1970 under the title *North Biscay Pilot*, of which a second impression with amendments appeared in 1977.

The survey work for pilot books adds greatly to the interest of cruising, for it provides a purpose and the fascination of seeking new harbours and occasionally unorthodox anchorages. I used to sail about 2,000 to 3,000 miles a year and I came to know the French Coast intimately from Barfleur to La Rochelle. The books were rewarding in that they evidently gave pleasure to cruising folk and were frequently referred to as 'bibles' but, if so, I think one of the ten navigational commandments is to regard sailing manuals with reserve because there is always a latent risk of error; moreover, changes occur with ever-increasing frequency.

The desk work in the preparation or major revision of a new edition of a pilot book is exacting, but also rewarding as it is so interesting. Take for example the completely revised and enlarged 1977 edition of *The Shell Pilot to the South Coast Harbours*, covering 57 harbours or anchorages. Alan Irving kept a record of time he spent on drawing the new harbour plans which amounted to over 1,000 hours. My own work on corrections to the text and plans was continuous owing to the constant stream of changes while the revision was in progress. I did not keep any time records, but I suppose I maintained about a sixty-hour week from start to finish, burning much midnight oil in the process. Finally, I submitted a copy of my typescript of each chapter to the relevant harbour masters for approval, and they proved most helpful in their comments and advice.

But here I must tell you of the best harbour master of all from an author's point of view. It was many years ago when Captain Meadows was the harbour master on Newtown River in the Isle of Wight. I heard a rumour that he proposed to alter the position of the leading marks, which consisted of two posts in line. Mamie and I sailed over to see him. Meadows was a big and exceptionally powerful man, who had retired from the Thames river police and then lived all the year round in his yacht of about 7 tons, which he sailed single-handed without benefit of engine.

'I hear you are going to alter the leading marks, Captain Meadows', I said. When he confirmed this, I asked him what changes would be made.

He looked hard at me before replying. 'Well, it's this way. Most strangers coming to this river seem to follow your directions.' He paused for a moment or two before adding 'So I am going to move the marks to where they are in your book!'

Returning now to the business of publishing. In 1952 I came in touch with George G Harrap, one of the leading old-established publishing companies, and reached an arrangement with them for the trade distribution of our books. I was sad to part with Rolls House who had done so much to establish me but, by then, I had published about a hundred works, including a growing list of books on ships and the Bosun series of semi-paper backs, so we needed wider representation in the book trade. The late Walter Harrap was then the very able chairman of the company and gave me much useful financial advice, but it was his nephew Paull Harrap, then sales director, that I knew best. He was a good deal younger than me but had been brought up in the world of publishing. He was a hard worker and, besides being a director, did a considerable amount of public work in the world of publishing. Golf was his outdoor hobby, but he gave enthusiastic support to our yachting books. Harraps gave me every possible facility and I soon got to know all the senior members of the staff. The company had a particularly good team of representatives, among them Charles Seyd, a lieutenant commander in the naval reserve, who had been on active service during the war and was particularly interested in nautical and yachting books; he always called to see me when in the Southampton area.

Harraps advised me to change the name of my company from Robert Ross & Co Ltd to Adlard Coles Ltd, which I did the following year, although with some hesitation.

About the same time I moved my editing and general work to an office I rented in Brunswick Terrace, Southampton, owned by the firm of chartered accountants in which I had formerly been a partner. Patrick Madge, the partner who had replaced me in the firm, became the financial director of my company (and also a shareholder), taking over all accountancy matters, including payment of author's royalties, salaries, printers, engravers, etc. He had the advantage of being a sailing man himself and owner of a 7-ton South Coast One Design; later he was one of the crew of *Cohoe III* when she won her class in the 1957 Fastnet Race. Patrick was a tremendous help to me and, with the financial side delegated to him and the distribution of books delegated to Harraps, the arrangement was admirable, leaving me free to get on with the actual publishing, which was growing rapidly.

In addition to *The Yachtsman* and yachting books, I published books on ships, ranging from half-crown booklets for shiplovers to volumes such as Laurence Dunn's *Ship Recognition: Merchant Ships*, so successful that six editions of it were printed. The editor of our shipping books was Captain Colin Stewart, extra master, whom I first met during World War II when he was a serving officer in the Royal Navy. After being invalided out of the Service he joined Trinity House, serving in the well-known pilot ship *Patricia*. Under his supervision his wife Jean drew the charts for my earlier pilot books, including both volumes of *Biscay Harbours*. Colin is the highest qualified editor I have been privileged to have on the publishing staff. He left later to take an appointment with the Hydraulics Research Station at Wallingford. So, instead of editing books and drawing yacht harbours, he is responsible for large scale models of big ship harbours and yacht marinas from any part of the world, testing them for the ill effects of wave disturbance. He also gave me great help as a consultant on oceanographical matters and wrote the appendix on Wave Theory and Facts which appears in *Heavy Weather Sailing*.

The expansion of the business created demands for additional capital. I did not wish to take in substantial outside capital, as it usually entails loss of control and I wished to remain independent; furthermore, differences of opinion can arise between directors in such a colourful and personal occupation as publishing. I sold *The Yachtsman* and the *Yachtsman's Annual*; the latter to *Yachting World* through the good offices of the then editor, Group Captain F E (Teddy) Haylock. Douglas Phillips-Birt, who used to do the design pages of the annual, then followed me as editor.

I put great energy and enthusiasm into the publishing of authors' books. I had two cardinal principles; one was that authors should be paid their royalties punctually on or before the dates they fall due; the other was the timing of books which must be on schedule and never miss the bus in the absence of exceptionally good reason.

I will refer to later book publishing developments in Chapter 26. In the meantime I can describe the occupation as fascinating, creative and exciting, each new book being a venture and occasionally a speculation.

CHAPTER TWENTY-ONE

THE BERMUDA RACE

It was at the annual dinner of the Royal Ocean Racing Club that Captain John Illingworth, Commodore of the Club and the Royal Naval Sailing Association (RNSA), told me that the 1950 racing programme would include a RORC transatlantic race organised in collaboration with the Royal Bermuda Yacht Club, in which Class III boats (minimum length 24ft on the waterline) would be eligible. It would follow the biennial Bermuda Race of the Cruising Club of America (CCA) and give the British entries a transatlantic race from Bermuda back to England.

The rules of the CCA differed from the RORC, as the minimum length for eligibility was 35ft in overall length, but as a gesture of friendship towards Great Britain a special concession had been made, for the 1950 race only, to the RNSA 24ft waterline class. Two were entering, *Samuel Pepys* as the official entry of the RNSA skippered by Commander (then Lieutenant-Commander) Erroll Bruce, and *Galway Blazer* owned by that distinguished sub-mariner, Commander Bill King, who some twenty years later completed his single-handed circumnavigation of the world. Being a member of the RNSA I wrote to Rod Stephens, Commodore of the CCA, asking whether the concession about overall length could be extended to *Cohoe*. I received a nice reply giving very good reasons why the Committee felt unable to make an additional exception to the length rule. This was disappointing but the general arrangements could stand; instead of racing to Bermuda I could sail over the course independently arriving there in time for the start of the Transatlantic Race, so I carried on with preparations for this.

The principal alterations were: removal of engine and propeller to provide room for an additional water tank and provision storage, and forward the installation of a 26 gallon copper water tank shaped to fit; companionway doors were done away with and replaced by battens fitted in grooves; cockpit self-emptying drains replaced by larger ones; extra pump installed below operable without going on deck; new stanchions and lifelines fitted; sails overhauled, two new jibs provided, and an extra spinnaker boom; wireless sets, tools for every contingency and medical stores had to be bought. Personal requirements were sports and open shirts for semi-tropics, heavy weather clothes for mid and east Atlantic. Miscellaneous items requiring attention were insurance, visits to dentist, passport visa, fingerprints, currency, measurement certificates and paperwork of all kinds.

26. *Samuel Pepys*, in foreground, and *Cohoe* racing in the Solent the year before being shipped to Bermuda.

(*Beken*)

Meanwhile everything in London was being organised by the RNSA and Erroll Bruce with his characteristic energy. The Chairman of Royal Mail Lines had given his blessing to the idea of a British team going to race in American waters, and the small yachts, now numbering three with the addition of Major James Murray's 10 tonner *Mokoia*, were to be shipped as deck cargo in the Company's 5,000 ton motor cargo liner *Araby*; the crew members of the team other than those joining in America would be taken as supernumeries. What a help it all was!

About a fortnight before the boats were due to be shipped I was astonished and delighted to receive an official invitation from the Chairman of the CCA Sailing Committee for *Cohoe* to participate in the Bermuda Race. I read the letter again carefully wondering whether there could be a mistake, but there was no proviso about her length which I had reported to Rod Stephens, so I assumed that a last minute concession must have been granted. I acknowledged the letter, and as there was not much time left I acted immediately. The CCA rules allowed much bigger headsails than the RORC. It was the rush period for sailmakers, but for such an important race Ratsey and Lapthorn made a long footed CCA genoa and the Greenock Sail Company supplied a light nylon spinnaker within a week. The invitation also involved a switch-round in my crewing arrangements.

On Monday evening April 18th I received a real shock, as a letter arrived from the CCA Chairman of the Sailing Committee regretting that *Cohoe* could not be accepted for the Bermuda Race unless she was lengthened to 35 feet. Without going into details there had been a misunderstanding for which I do not think anybody was to blame. But immediate action was called for. *Cohoe* stood under the crane in Moody's yacht yard, awaiting the lorry and trailer to take her to London docks on Wednesday morning.

Withdrawal from the Bermuda Race would now be difficult. It would let down my crew members who had refused vacancies in other Bermuda racers which by now would be filled. Besides this, no man, once he has undertaken a project, likes to accept defeat.

Early next morning I called on that wonderful yard foreman of Moody's, Mr Bunday, and together we visited the moulding loft where a new sister ship had been laid off. The chalk lines on the moulding loft floor indicated that a three foot overhang could be faired in at the bows above the waterline.

'I'll see what I can do,' said Bunday. 'Ring me up at 11 o'clock.'

So it was left and when I picked up the telephone to hear the verdict, the reply was crisp.

'The job has already started', he said. 'Come over to see it.'

When I arrived at Moody's yard I found it to be a hive of activity. The plan provided for an extension of the bows by Birmabright alloy plating for the deck and sides, shaped over a honeycomb of decks and bulkheads and stringers, strengthened by brackets, angle-pieces and vertical frames. The new bow began to take shape in the afternoon, when the electric screwdrivers were whirling and hundreds of screws were biting in. Before it became dark the electricians arrived and floodlights were erected. Nearby, in the big laying-up shed, the Birmabright plating was receiving its final tailoring. The work continued all night. The men felt they had been challenged to do the impossible and the impossible they achieved. The job was finished by 5 a.m. the following morning and at 8.30 a.m. the lorry and trailer arrived punctually to take *Cohoe*, complete with a false nose which would have done credit to a leading plastic surgeon, on the road to London docks.

However, the difficulties were by no means over. An unofficial dock strike had started and no goods were being allowed to enter the Royal Victoria Dock. *Cohoe* was diverted to a warehouse at Clapham, and *Samuel Pepys* and *Mokoia* to one in north London. Eventually Service personnel were called into the docks and the boats were loaded by the *Araby*'s cranes operated by the ship's officers. Altogether the merchant ship's departure had been delayed ten days and it was 10 p.m. on Tuesday, 2nd May, when she cast off and started on her voyage to Bermuda, with the three boats strongly secured abaft the main deck in their cradles to the satisfaction of the Chief Officer, the Captain and finally the Chief Superintendent of the Line.

The passage was a happy one. Captain Bolland was a big, broad-shouldered man standing over six feet in his socks, with a bluff outspoken manner coupled with a great sense of humour. We had the run of the whole ship and came to know all the officer's the bo'sun, the carpenter and many of her crew. There was sun and good weather the whole way. On May 7th the *Araby* was off the Azores, passing between the

27. *Cohoe* lengthened forward to 35ft to qualify for the Bermuda Race. Her normal bows can be clearly seen ending near the foot of the forestay.

(*Bermuda News Bureau*)

mountainous islands of Corvo and Flores, and on the morning of the 15th May she arrived at the HM Dockyard Quay at Ireland Island, Bermuda. The work of unloading commenced immediately, after which the boats were towed alongside the *Araby*'s foredeck and their masts were lifted, dropped into place and stepped; all went as smoothly as though the ship's crew had spent their lives dealing with yachts in a yacht yard. There was not a scratch on any of them.

After that they were towed round to the southern end of the harbour where moorings had been specially laid for them. Jack Keary, a retired group captain, who was to be the mate of *Cohoe* in the races ahead and had shared the passage in the *Araby*, spent most of the morning and afternoon setting up our rigging and in the evening we rowed over to the cruiser HMS *Glasgow*, flagship of the West Indies Squadron. The crews representing the RNSA had been made honorary members of the Wardroom Mess and were to live aboard the cruiser during our stay in Bermuda. Jack and I must have presented a strange spectacle in shirts and shorts liberally covered with grease and soot from the *Araby*'s winch cables as, loaded with our clothes in sailbags, we staggered up the gangway to the spotless quarterdeck. There we were welcomed by Lieut-Commander Basil Smith, branch secretary of the RNSA, who took us below to decarbonise under showers and plenty of hot water. Each crew member had been given the cabin of one of the officers living ashore. The hour for dinner was approaching. When stationed in Bermuda, officers wear Red Sea rig for dinner— consisting of an open-necked shirt, black trousers, a cummerbund and half-wellingtons. In *Cohoe* there was barely room for all the sails, much less cummerbunds. However, we were helped out by the loan of borrowed plumes.

We enjoyed our stay in Bermuda, both in the cruiser and in visits ashore to Hamilton, a pleasant town with very good shops standing so close to the harbour that it seemed almost overshadowed by the big ships alongside the town quay. We were made honorary members of the Royal Bermuda Yacht Club, which is one of the oldest British yacht clubs and has always fostered racing ranging from some of the most remarkable dinghies in the world to ocean racers. We made good friends among members of the Club, including 'Shorty' Trimmingham and his brother de Forest Trimmingham, and Warren Brown who later contributed a chapter and much useful information for *Heavy Weather Sailing*.

Besides enjoying ourselves, Jack and I had a lot of work to do in preparation for the voyage to America. In addition to the usual preliminaries there were stores to see to. Lieut-Commander Stephen Sampson (known as Sammy), mate of *Samuel Pepys*, arranged our victualling, which we were privileged to buy through the NAAFI, and fresh provisions were obtained from *Glasgow* herself. *Cohoe*'s decks were covered with boxes and bags, and I could hardly believe it possible that all could be stowed below, but somehow it was done. On Saturday May 20th we filled our water tanks from the Dockyard MFV, and in the afternoon we sailed over to Hamilton to attend a most enjoyable dinner and evening put on by Royal Bermuda Yacht Club. Formalities of clearance and signing of crews were completed on Monday, and on Tuesday Jack and I were joined by Basil Smith, who had volunteered to sail with us to bring *Cohoe*'s crew up to three and to act as navigator. We then sailed round and tied up alongside the quay at St Georges, which is the oldest town in Bermuda.

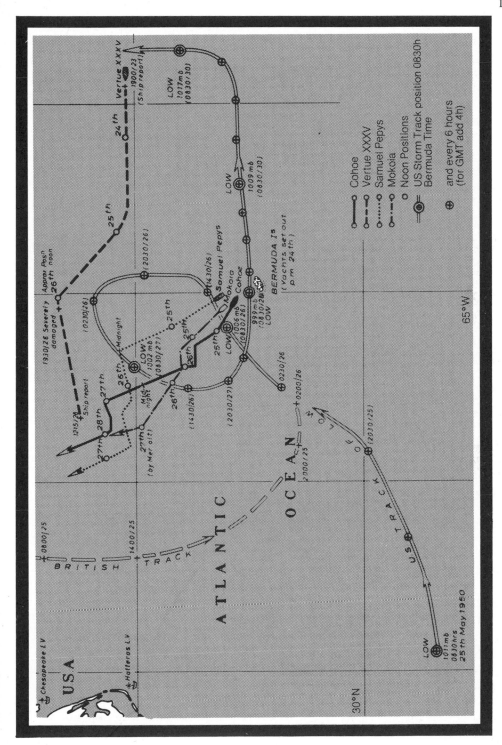

12. *Atlantic storm.* Track of the centre of the low passing just north of Bermuda, with the positions of the British yachts.

It was at 1220 on Wednesday May 24th that the three boats took their departure bound on the 635 mile passage NNW to Newport, Rhode Island. *Samuel Pepys* was fully crewed with Erroll as skipper and Sammy as mate. The bo'sun was Pat Ovens, a Royal Marine commando officer, who was as quick witted as he was strong and wiry. The fourth member was Chief Petty Officer Flux who was the expert in anything to do with yacht construction, besides being an exceptional seaman who had learned his sailing with Uffa Fox and later with John Illingworth. *Mokoia*'s crew consisted only of her owner, Major James Murray, Wing Commander Marwood Elton as mate and navigator, and James's daughter Jean to help.

There was a good weather report and the wind was light until Thursday when it backed east; by 2000 it had attained Force 8 by hand anemometer at deck level, and at least Force 9 on the Beaufort notation which is taken at 33 feet above the surface of the sea. Following my usual practice in gales, all sail was lowered and *Cohoe* lay a-hull all night under bare pole. On deck it was difficult to distinguish between air and water on account of the spindrift and torrential rain. Next morning, Friday May 26th, we were able to get under way again at 0730, running under storm jib. It was a beastly day with a stormy sky, a big and confused sea and pouring rain. The wind remained at gale force except for a three hour respitn,6e when it fell to Force 3 enabling full sail to be carried. Most of the day *Cohoe* was running under storm jib, and at 2140 she entered a confused area with a huge swell from two directions and the seas were heaped in complete confusion.

It was not until over 15 years later that I received from the US Weather Bureau an approximate track of the storm shown to have been an extra-tropical cyclone which made an anticlockwise loop embracing the three yachts. *Samuel Pepys*, some 60 or 70 miles north of *Cohoe* and *Mokoia*, suffered the worst as it appeared that the centre of the low, intensifying as it moved, passed immediately over her on Friday May 26th, when she encountered near hurricane winds and ran off to the west under bare pole streaming warps to keep her stern straight to the enormous seas which she encountered, nor was there any abatement during the whole night; altogether she was in the thick of it for 36 hours.

By strange coincidence a fourth boat was involved to the north in the same storm. She was Humphrey Barton's famous *Vertue XXXV*, forty days out from Falmouth on her east to west Atlantic crossing. On that grim day of May 26th at 1300 Humphrey had logged conditions as being absolutely shocking: 'A wind that had reached a state of senseless fury.' About four and a half hours later on that fateful evening she was struck by an immense sea that threw her on her beam ends, so hard that on the lee side the coaming was split at deck-level for nearly the whole length of the cabin, the doghouse window was smashed and water cascaded into the cabin at every sea. The vessel was saved by a narrow margin through running her off dead before the seas, and by the fine seamanship and tremendous energy of Humphrey in pumping her out and effecting repairs, assisted by his one crew member Kevin O'Riordan.

Returning now to my own narrative. The gale moderated on Saturday May 27th, but it was not until early on Sunday morning that we were able to set the double-reefed mainsail. The wind stayed firmly in the east and the weather-going current of the Gulf Stream caused broken and irregular seas. On Tuesday, with only 100 miles left to

Brenton Cove, the weather played another card against us. It came on to rain followed by dense fog at 1400, the last thing we wanted as we had to cross the shipping routes to New York. At 1800 we heard the sound of diesel engines approaching. Basil was working the foghorn; presently came the swish of a bow wave and suddenly a fishing trawler emerged through the fog 100 yards distant. Forward stood a row of look-outs wearing life jackets who spotted us immediately. The vessel altered course and slowed down close to us. Her name was *Santa Maria* and she hailed from Gloucester, Mass. They told us that our foghorn could not be heard before they sighted us as it was drowned by the noise of the engines.

The trawler gave us our position which confirmed Basil's dead reckoning, so we continued on the course to Block Island. We had to cross the big ship route to New York but it was no more dangerous than remaining where we were because of the trawlers. What a miserable night followed. The fog lay thick in layers, floating above the calm, greasy water. All was silent, no ship was moving. The moisture fell in a steady light drizzle on the sails and ran in streams to the deck; the only light came from the reflection of the navigation lights, red and green, glistening on the bright stanchions, and the gleam of the compass bowl.

On Wednesday morning conditions remained the same, but we had safely crossed the principal steamer route undisturbed, only occasionally hearing the noise of engines in the distance, approaching or retreating. The fog prevailed and *Cohoe* slowly crept forward on her way. At 1230 we heard the sound of engines and presently the hateful swish of a bow wave. Suddenly out of the fog appeared the motor fishing vessel *Alden* moving fast. She was very close before we were seen and her course altered just in time. They slowed up alongside and told us the fog would last another day—they also confirmed our position as 12 miles off Block Island. At 1600 we heard its lighthouse foghorn to port and Basil navigated from buoy to buoy by the sound of whistle or bell. Finally we had a foul tide so it was not until 0300 next morning that we anchored in Brenton Cove and turned in for some sleep.

Shortly after daylight a launch came alongside in charge of the professional skipper of the Ida Lewis Yacht Club, who made us welcome. After breakfast he returned with letters and to tow us to the end of the yacht club pier, where we were met by the Customs and Immigration Officers and representatives of the local newspapers. Formalities were quickly completed and Basil caught a plane back to Bermuda; his help had been a god-send, as also had that of Jack who had cooked regular stews for dinner whether in storm or fog. Erroll Bruce, as captain of the team, came to see that all was well with us. *Samuel Pepys* had arrived two days earlier and *Mokoia* arrived the following day, her crew pretty tired as they were short-handed. None of the three boats had suffered any damage, but the gale had taken the paint off *Cohoe*'s false extended bow. Erroll told us that the British entries had been invited to moor in the US Naval War College harbour, and their crews were offered the hospitality of living ashore in bachelor officer's quarters. At noon a US naval launch came to tow us over and moored *Cohoe* alongside a pontoon next to *Samuel Pepys*. After a shower and a shave and a change into reefer jackets we felt almost civilised again, and in the evening we all went over to dinner at the Naval Club, of which the team had been made honorary members, where we met the British naval officers attached to the base.

The Naval War College was almost a town in itself spread over an island joined to Newport by a bridge. Everything was done for us in the way of minor repairs and hauling up on the slip for rubbing down; we also received much generous personal hospitality. A great deal of work had still to be done on *Cohoe* in preparation for the Bermuda Race, but I managed to take a few days off for a visit to New York. My first call there was on the editors of *Yachting* where I met Herbert Stone, the founder, and all the friendly gang that then ran this great American yachting periodical. With these companions I was taken to the famous New York Yacht Club where rooms had been reserved for the British team. At luncheon I was introduced to Rod Stephens, Commodore of the CCA, and a great international ocean racing man. I also met Sherman Hoyt, one of the most distinguished of American yachtsmen. Humphrey Barton was also there, recuperating from broken ribs incurred when fighting for survival in *Vertue XXXV* in the storm; he was soon to go as sailing master of *Gulvain* in the Bermuda and Transatlantic races.

While in America I took the opportunity of visiting my step-sister Rosemary who lived at Hartford. She was out when I arrived but I was greeted by my charming thirteen year old niece whom I had not seen before. Next day the three of us motored over to Simsbury where my sister and I had lived for a while when we were young children. Simsbury was then an exciting place for a small boy. From the windows of our home I looked out over miles of unspoilt woods and valleys towards distant hills; behind the house lay a track (perhaps first used by indians) running through thick woods. But my best recollections are of water: a big pond in the woods, the home of bull frogs and turtles, and the Farmington River. The latter runs through Simsbury usually as a rather dull stream lying between muddy yellow banks, but I remember it rising on one occasion to a roaring torrent flooding high over the surrounding country and sweeping bridges away like matchwood.

On Sunday I returned to the Training College at Newport; I had to get busy as there was only a week left before the start of the Bermuda Race.

When I was away the American member of *Cohoe*'s crew, Wilson Cross, had arrived. Although young he was already a highly experienced racing man. In my absence Jack and Willie had been working on *Cohoe*. She was now on the slip and had already been rubbed down and received a final coat of anti-fouling. As soon as she was launched *Samuel Pepys* took her place on the slip. There was still much to occupy our time, including varnishing the bright work, repainting the false bow, measurement for rating by the CCA, buying and stowing more provisions. We sailed from the War College harbour on Friday, bidding farewell to our generous hosts, and picked up a mooring off the Ida Lewis Yacht Club. It was there that Tom Tothill, our navigator, joined us; he was an Englishman who was working as a naval architect, tank testing yachts in the Steven's Institute, New Jersey, and had done a great deal of racing and cruising. We were lucky to have him.

The great day for the start of the Bermuda Race arrived on Sunday June 18th. In Ida Lewis Bay it was nice and sunny. One by one the competitors were getting under way and setting sail to reach away to the starting line between Brenton Reef lightship and the US destroyer *Raby*, followed by scores of motor and cruising yachts. The start of the big Class A was due at 1300 and we saw the British entry *Gulvain* (designed the previous year by Jack Laurent Giles) make a good get-away. Next went Class B, and finally the small Class C in which *Samuel Pepys*, *Galway Blazer*, *Mokoia* and *Cohoe* were competing.

The principal navigational feature of the Bermuda Race is the Gulf Stream, which is the great unknown as it varies in direction, strength and in position, as it sometimes meanders off its normal course. As captain of the small boats, Erroll Bruce had arranged that *Cohoe* should take the right wing of the three.

Monday, June 19th. This started with a strong SW wind but by 0830 it had backed to SE and fallen very light, so we came on the other tack. Had we known it, *Samuel Pepys* at noon had covered 132 miles against *Cohoe*'s 128 miles and thus was just over the horizon to the east. The weather was gloomy and rain set in. After a long period of calm, the wind came in fresh from the east and later in the day the yachts entered the Gulf Stream. Here the winds were unsettled, sometimes calm, sometimes fresh and between noon and evening the sea temperature rose from 63°F to 66°F.

Tuesday, June 20th. Conditions remained much the same until 0700: a light air came from the north and the spinnaker was set. Soon afterwards we sighted three sail; it was easy to identify *Galway Blazer* by her ketch rig but the other two were hull down. By 0900 the wind died away and the spinnaker hung lifeless. The sun came out and gave us our first opportunity of drying wet clothes and to get some sleep off watch. Tom got a sun sight and fixed the yacht's position. All day the winds were light and variable; by now we were well in the Gulf Stream, with masses of sargasso weed in the sea and Mother Carey's chickens were busy fluttering close to the water. That night, however, we had no sleep because it was so hot, muggy and damp below.

Samuel Pepys experienced the same conditions. A low pressure trough had intervened in the middle of the racing fleet. The faster leaders of the big Class A carried a fresh breeze the whole way to Bermuda. Many of the medium size Class B experienced only short periods of calm; only the rear guard of smaller lower-rated Class C boats were severely delayed in crossing the belt of calm.

Two awkward incidents had occurred in *Samuel Pepys*. On Monday she had trouble with a leak of cooking gas, so bad that the cylinder had to be lifted out and kept in the cockpit. On Tuesday a leak in the hull which had been giving trouble became so severe that she needed pumping 500 strokes every hour. Loaded with stores as she was, and with every nook and cranny filled with gear and tins, it was difficult to locate the leak, but eventually it was traced to faulty workmanship in her newly fitted cockpit drain. Once found it was quickly put right.

Wednesday, June 21st. The calms were over and replaced on this day by fresh to strong and sometimes squally SW winds. The two-masted rigs, schooners, ketches and yawls were rejoicing in the reaching conditions and Bill King's *Galway Blazer*, the only British ketch, was doing particularly well.

Thursday, June 22nd. During the night the weather remained squally and the sea lumpy, although we must have passed through the southern limit of the Gulf Stream. Here I quote from the entry in *Samuel Pepys*'s log.

'The middle watch started with a blinding flash of lightning, and torrential rain-fall. Wondering at the effect of lightning on a metal mast and wooden hull, we had previously lashed wire earthing pendants to the rigging, and now made haste to throw them into the water. Bailey actually had one in hand when another flash seemed almost to hit us. From the cockpit we could see or hear nothing for many seconds – blinded and deafened. Flux at the tiller shouted, "I can't see the sails, have we been hit?" Then Tony Bailey scrambled back into the cockpit again and we knew that all was well.

The wind increased to 7 in this squall, but the violent rain beat down the waves to flatters, and we were travelling at our fastest, keeping the rail just awash with two rolls and working jib; we covered 27·6 miles in the watch.'

In the morning the wind moderated and in *Cohoe* we got glimpses of the sun through the clouds. Tom obtained a good sight at 1144 and multiple sights at 1653, which was helpful.

Friday, June 22nd. We had little sleep during the night for the exciting part of the race was at hand, with the finish line little over seventy miles away. Bermuda is a difficult landfall from the north-west as the islands are low and the coral reefs extend some 12 miles seaward. From midnight to dawn *Cohoe* sped onwards, clocking seven knots and sometimes more. Dawn, when it came, revealed a grey overcast sky. The visibility was downright bad and offered no prospect of getting sun sights. However, there was a radio beacon at Kindley Field, Bermuda. We had no RDF set, but when in New York I had bought a good wireless with all-band coverage, and in common with other portables it was strongly directional. At 0645, to our delight, we received Kindley Field radio clearly and by revolving the set and watching the compass we were able to get a rough bearing of 168° magnetic.

Soon after dawn a sail had been sighted away on our lee bow and even in the grey light I thought I caught a glimpse of the red in the hull denoting *Samuel Pepys*. Visibility improved and shortly after 0930 St David's Head was sighted. The landfalls of both yachts had been precise. Meanwhile a terrific struggle was ensuing between the two competitors. All handicaps had for the moment been forgotten.

At Kitchen Shoal buoy, with six miles to go to the finish line, little over 100 yards separated the pair, *Samuel Pepys* still clinging to the lead. Passing the buoy the yachts came hard on the wind, close hauled to the finish. Their crews, clad in oilskins, were stretched flat out on the weather decks just like racing in the Solent. Three miles off the finish line *Cohoe* had taken a precarious lead. Wind and sea were increasing and both boats were hard pressed, smashing into head seas, covered with spray as high as their spreaders. *Samuel Pepys* rolled in two turns of her mainsail and set an intermediate jib. *Cohoe* responded by replacing the genoa with a staysail. As we approached the finish line it could be seen that the yachts were practically level. We were timed by the race officers on the lighthouse. It was a photo finish. As we learned afterwards *Samuel Pepys* had won line honours in the private match between the two by 23 seconds. What a race! A difference of twenty-three seconds after sailing 635 miles.

But what counts in ocean races is not of course the actual elapsed time over the course but the corrected time after handicap in accordance with the rating rule; *Samuel Pepys* had thus beaten *Cohoe* well and truly by just over three hours. Under American rules both *Samuel Pepys* and *Cohoe* were too narrow in beam to rate well and *Cohoe* suffered additionally because of her high aspect ratio rig. Two masted rigs rated better and the ketch rigged *Galway Blazer* was fourth in Class C and the only British entry to gain a place. The winners were all yawls, *Argyll* in Class A (in which *Gulvain* was ninth and put up the best time amongst the sloops), *Merry Maiden* in Class B and *Loki* in

Class C, a very beautiful blue yawl designed by Sparkman & Stephens and built the previous year.

Having sailed 1,270 miles we were now back in Bermuda whence we started a month before. What a wonderful time we had been given, and what an exciting race back across the Atlantic still lay ahead of us!

CHAPTER TWENTY-TWO

TRANSATLANTIC RACE

On arrival at Bermuda we were once more given cabins in HMS *Glasgow* until her departure for a cruise on Thursday morning. It was a blazing hot sunny day when she left, with the marine band playing on the quarter deck and her company standing to attention forward; ashore a crowd had assembled to give her and the escorting frigates a good send off. After *Glasgow* had sailed the boats had their headquarters alongside HMS *Challenger*, a survey vessel with a number of scientists aboard.

Among the many tasks to be done before the Transatlantic Race the first in importance was the removal of *Cohoe*'s false nose, for we would now be coming under the RORC rating rules. Chief Petty Officer Flux of *Samuel Pepys* very sportingly volunteered to help. He went over the side in a bo'sun's chair, while Tom and I did what we could from the deck. Soon scores of screws were detached, littering the deck or falling in the sea. Between us we managed to remove the forward end of the Birmabright plates, but the difficulty lay with the aft ones. It was the big three-inch screws which gave the trouble; the timber had swollen and gripped them so firmly that the heads broke.

It was clear that the work could only be completed ashore, and in this the dockyard authorities most generously came to the rescue. Next morning we sailed *Cohoe* round and lay against the quay under the 80-ton crane. Big plaited steel slings lifted her, complete with mast and rigging, high into the air, swung her inland and dropped her gently into her cradle. Two of us set to work immediately, using really good screw-drivers which had been lent to us but, even with the help of two dockyard apprentices who gave their spare time, it took a long time before the last screws were drawn and the false bow lay in pieces at the roadside. Next morning the big crane swung round and, treating *Cohoe* as a toy, lifted her into the sky and gently deposited her back in her native element. Meanwhile arrangements had been made for the big CCA spinnakers and genoas of the British boats to be taken to England in the transport *Beauharnois* by courtesy of her captain. *Cohoe* had thus returned to her original rig and RORC rating for handicap.

Final preparations and provisioning for the Transatlantic Race followed routine, except that far more had to be provided for a voyage that might take several weeks, or much longer in event of disablement. The water tanks held 65 gallons, and new petrol tins and a case of tinned water made up the extra 15 gallons required by the rules to total 80 gallons. All kinds of petty detail had to be listed, even including Beecham (or whatever) pills which cannot be bought in mid-Atlantic. In addition the Rear Commodore of the Royal Bermuda Yacht Club presented each yacht with a large bunch of hard, green Bermuda bananas which would ripen later, and also paw paws, limes, onions and fresh vegetables, so we were not likely to suffer from scurvy!

The race was due to start on Saturday July 1st, but so much remained to be done that (with the permission of the RORC) it had to be postponed to Sunday. In *Samuel Pepys* and *Cohoe* the total complement in each boat numbered four. In *Samuel Pepys* Erroll Bruce was skipper, Sammy Sampson mate, Pat Ovens bo'sun, C P O Flux carpenter and highly experienced seaman. In *Cohoe* Jack Keary was mate, Tom Tothill navigator and I was skipper. Willie Cross remained after the Bermuda Race for the Transatlantic Race but had developed an abscess in his arm and was bitterly disappointed when, on the morning of the start, his doctor had forbidden him to go, for fear of the infection spreading. A replacement had to be found urgently. Ashore at the Club was a young American ex-Marine named John Halstead, who had just graduated and wanted to come in one of the British yachts to England. He frankly admitted to being very seasick but, despite this handicap, he would make a hefty and tough replacement. He was so keen that he already had his passport and papers, but he had to make a pier-head jump to get aboard *Cohoe*, just as *Karin III* arrived to tow her and *Samuel Pepys* to the starting line.

Altogether there were five entries racing together as one class. *Gulvain* was the most notable being a Class I RORC 55ft ocean racer, manned by a crack crew with Humphrey Barton as sailing master; she was unlucky in having no other boats of her class to race against. The other big yacht was Lt Commander G C L Payne's 41ft heavy displacement Scandinavian double-ender *Karin III*. Hers was a sporting entry as she had crossed the Atlantic under her own sail via the trade winds to enter the races; altogether she would have sailed nearly 10,000 miles by the time she returned to her home port of Poole. The remaining three entries were *Mokoia*, *Samuel Pepys* and *Cohoe*, and I shall confine this personal account principally to the last two, as they were about the same size and were racing boat for boat against each other with crews of four including the skippers over nearly 3,000 miles of the broad Atlantic.

Sunday, July 2nd. The race started off St David's Head, Bermuda at 1600, and a large proportion of the nautical population of the island emerged in yachts and boats to give us all a tremendous send-off. In the centre of the arena the five starters ghosted to the line; Class I *Gulvain*, her pretty blue hull surmounted by towering creamy canvas just filling in the light airs, *Karin III* looking very much a ship with her workmanlike gaff mainsail and baggywrinkle on her shrouds, and somewhat astern of here was *Mokoia*, looking very small. Then–gun! *Samuel Pepys* made the best start and a rousing cheer greeted her as she did so.

For the first three days the wind was light and variable, mostly northerly and the weather tropically hot. Below decks the temperature was 95 °F on the cabin thermometer, and on Monday afternoon Erroll Bruce logged that the heat was scarcely tolerable and that *Samuel Pepys* had covered little more than 50 miles in the first 24 hours. The general policy was to follow the great circle route, which is the shortest distance between Bermuda and England, but for the first few days the tactics were to get north of the circle as quickly as possible into the favourable current of the Gulf Stream.

The crewing arrangements in *Cohoe* were unusual as they provided for six-hour watches, the purpose of which was to give the men off watch a chance of more sleep than would be possible in the conventional four-hour spells, much of which would be spent in meals and the tedious task in rough weather of getting out of or into oilskins. There were also occasional two-hour dog watches. Tom Tothill came in my watch and the American John Halstead was with Jack Keary, the mate. The cooking was divided between Jack and me in three-day spells; Tom had the additional work as navigator, and John was the extra hand ready to come from his off-watch spell below if an extra man was needed on deck. As skipper, besides keeping full watches, I had all the usual responsibilities and was available on deck at all times, taking the helm if sails were being shifted.

Tuesday, July 4th. Cohoe was utterly becalmed by midnight, and rolled and rolled in a slight swell with the sails slatting, driving the watch below nearly to distraction. It was not until about noon on Wednesday that a moderate wind came in from the west and the spinnaker was set with an 'anti-snarl' net, always necessary to prevent the spinnaker wrapping itself round the forestay when the boat was rolling. This device with its hanks and sheets easily got tangled up and it nearly drove John demented; he would pick it up and ventilate his feelings by giving it a terrific thrashing on the deck, but the net still retained its twisted smile and had to be taken below to be untangled.

Thursday, July 6th. A nice breeze developed from the west and we were settling down to routine. I wrote up my diary.

'There is nothing but ocean and more ocean, affording a complete mental rest – the absolute reverse of one's ordinary life and work ashore. This afternoon I lay myself down in the sun on the genoa jib lowered on the fore-deck. The yacht is sailing fast and there is a long swell, and the bow is crunching through the waves. One's mind is very clear, relieved of the usual mass of business and personal detail. I remembered many incidents of childhood and early life which I had forgotten, as though the curtain of time had momentarily been raised.'

Saturday, July 8th. Samuel Pepys to the north of *Cohoe* had found better winds. Erroll's entry was:

'The third day of strong following winds, and we almost began to believe we might get this all the way. However, a slight fall of the barometer about noon showed some change must be coming, and dark clouds soon gathered astern. The Gulf Stream set is unusually high after the long period of westerlies. This helps us enormously. Tonight a tot of spirits was issued all round to celebrate Saturday at sea.'

Sunday, July 9th. The competitors completed their first week at sea on this day. It had been a period of calms and light winds succeeded by exhilarating fresh winds and tumbling following blue seas.

The second week opened with what may be called the mid-Atlantic stage of the race when we would soon be off the SE extremity of the Grand Banks, only 100 miles distant.

This is a grim part of the North Atlantic, the region of fog, ice and gales. The boats had come within the limits of drifting ice and would remain in it for about five days.

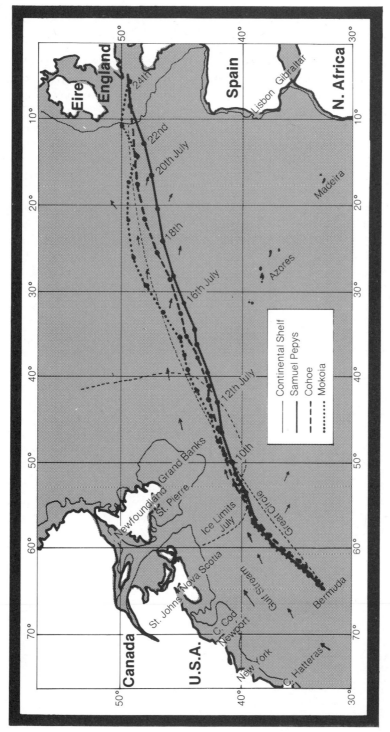

13. *The North Atlantic.* Showing the tracks of the three small British yachts on their race from Bermuda to England, 1950.

The risk of meeting it was not grave, but running fast in rough seas at night it was an added anxiety. Indeed, as late as August that same year the liner *Caronia* reported a berg 300ft high and shipping was diverted to avoid it.

The weather at the time was described by a meteorological expert: 'The Area of High Pressure normally centred over the Azores in July did not move up so far North as usual in 1950. This meant that a series of depressions moved across the Atlantic during July in the approximate latitude of 50° North, giving unsettled weather in latitudes 40° to 50° North. Much rain with fresh or strong winds from a westerly direction therefore predominated. A deep depression moved across in mid-July giving strong gales over a wide area. At 1200 GMT on July 14th this was centred in about 48°N 30°W, and NW winds Force 10 were reported from various weather ships to the westward.'

As well as entering the ice zone we had also come into what may be called the 'Shouting Area'. For the rest of the race the boats were travelling so fast in rough water that their crews could hardly make their voices heard, so loud was the noise of the bow and stern waves, the wind and the sea.

In these conditions the battle between the three small yachts continued far out of sight of each other; *Mokoia* was altering course to the northward and clung to a lead of some thirty miles. *Cohoe* had recovered much of the hundred miles she had lost early in the race and was gaining on *Samuel Pepys*, separated from her by about forty miles of dismal heaving ocean. Sail shifting on the foredeck had become increasingly difficult, for no sense of balance could anticipate or compensate the motion of the Atlantic seas; we never got accustomed to them. Navigation was also very trying as the rolling of the yachts made the use of a sextant difficult, and often the horizon could only be seen on the tops of the waves; all credit to the navigators who managed to get reasonably accurate fixes by miracles of perseverance.

Tuesday, July 11th. On this and the previous day the winds had been variable from northerly directions mostly Force 6, with rough seas, and *Cohoe* had almost overtaken *Samuel Pepys*. Erroll told me that Tuesday was the day when he and his crew approached their nearest to exhaustion. Here is an extract from his diary on the night of July 11th/12th when it blew Force 7 to Force 8.

'During the night the wind backed to west and increased, and after the genoa sheets had twice parted, we lowered mainsail, and set our down-wind rig of two headsails on booms . . . . . . The crew have frequently had impressed on them that once overboard in a rough sea their chances of survival are most remote, in spite of lifebelts, and they must stay inboard at all costs. Some wear a lanyard with a hook, which can be attached to any rigging handy, leaving both hands free to work. However, this is not always possible.

To-day Flux, our most daring and able man on the fore-deck, very nearly went over. After a hard night and with the boat moving violently in a rough sea, he went forward to get in the great spinnaker, now too much for her in half a gale of wind. The sail split and swung in towards him and, thinking that the bo'sun had begun to lower the halliard, he gathered in the sail with both hands. Actually the halliard was still not clear for lowering, and the wind caught the sail to belly out again. Flux was off balance for this and swung out over the sea still clinging on to the sail, and liable to be swept off by the passing waves. The bo'sun (Pat Ovens) was sitting on the fore-deck, back to the spinnaker and legs round the mast. He could not understand my shouts from the cockpit, and thought I was ordering him to get on with the lowering; this would have been fatal to Flux. Just in time *Samuel Pepys* turned so that the mainsail spilt the wind out of the spinnaker and Flux landed with a heavy thump horizontally on the fore-deck.'

Wednesday, July 12th. Fall in barometer and wind backed west. In *Cohoe* we had our worst day of the race. We had a tiring night rolling before a gathering sea; by 0700 the seas seemed so huge and the wind so fresh that we lowered the mainsail and ran under genoa. Sunny and warm but wet sailing and tiring.

By 1500 the motion was so wild that we lowered the genoa and set the storm jib – a pocket handkerchief of only 30 sq ft. Half an hour later we lowered even the storm jib and ran under bare pole. The wind was well under Force 8, but the Atlantic seas were so big that they threw the boat about and punished her severely making steering difficult.

Under bare pole we only made about two knots in the troughs of the waves, but on the crests she ran at four knots and seemed to skid on the breaking crests.

At about 1630 I was called on deck to see the Italian liner *Saturnia*, which was tearing close by on a reciprocal course. She made no sign of seeing us. In fact in those seas our helmsman only saw the liner when she came quite near.

I returned below, leaving Jack and Tom on deck. Then suddenly there was a roar of breaking water. The boat lurched violently, then heeled right over. The cabin went dark, water spurted through the tightly screwed port lights. There was a tremendous noise of rushing water, and a loud report as though the hull was cracked in. *Cohoe* had been knocked down by a big wave and broached to.

She rose again and came to even keel. Jack and Tom were safe and told us what had happened. A large wave (but not much larger than the others) with an immense breaking top had struck the boat on the quarter. This caused her partly to broach to, threw her over on her side and half filled the cockpit.

While staggering under this blow, a second wave, larger than the first came roaring down on her beam. It was this second wave which gave her such a tremendous crack. It completely filled the cockpit, ran as high as Tom's arm where he was clinging to the runner, and threw the boat on her beam ends right down over the cabin top.

The boat recovered and Jack, at the helm straightened her out before the seas. No serious damage was done, and the Whale bilge pump quickly dealt with the onrush of water. It was the heaviest blow that *Cohoe* had ever taken, and no doubt caused by freak seas resulting from the liner's wash crossing the great following waves.

Shortly afterwards it was observed that the *Saturnia* was turning. Well handled, she passed slowly by. She seemed crowded with passengers. We signalled MIK 'Please report me to Lloyds, London' and exhibited a strip of canvas with the name of the yacht *Cohoe* painted on it.

We hoisted our ensign and the liner, acknowledging our signal, made a complete circle around us to satisfy herself that no help was needed. I suppose the sight of a small yacht (3·89 tons registered) under bare pole in bad weather in mid-Atlantic was an unusual spectacle. I for one should have liked to accept help if I had been weak-willed enough to allow it. We had received a severe blow. Everything below was wet. The seas seemed immense. We were all dog tired with the violent motion, the constant sail trimming and lack of sleep; I, myself as skipper had only had a few hours real sleep in the past three days.

So it was with mixed feelings that we watched *Saturnia* stride away over the seas and disappear leaving us once more to *Cohoe*, the Atlantic and the gathering night.

28. *Cohoe* surfing on crests in mid-Atlantic under spinnaker. Wind probably about Force 6 but regular seas; noon to noon run 177 miles.

The sea puzzled me. The wind was strong but I do not think it attained Force 8; yet the sea was big enough to make the boat almost unmanageable. On the crests of the 'big-uns' she would simply be picked up bodily and thrown forward surfing. I took the dog watch during which she nearly broached to three times, and at 2000 I concurred in the mate's suggestion that we should heave-to.

The fact is that the state of the sea does not depend on the force of the wind alone. In retrospect, it is clear that I had made a mistake in running under bare pole, as *Cohoe* would have been partially blanketed in the troughs of the bigger waves which were running as high as her upper spreader. She would have needed at least a storm jib (or better still, proper boomed twin-running sails, which she did not possess) to attain the necessary speed to get a quick response to helm and hold her stern end-on to the approaching crests. If the seas then remained too much for her, the time had come to stream steadying warps astern or adopt other tactics.

Waiting for a 'smooth' I put the helm down and *Cohoe* came gently up into the wind and then fell off, lying a-hull broadside to the seas. As usual she was happy in this position, riding the waves like a duck, although this stratagem may not necessarily suit every type of boat.

I lit the navigation lights and made dinner: three tins of soup and a can of bully beef thrown in. We finished with apricots.

Then we turned in, Jack and John in the cabin bunks, sleeping tolerably, and Tom jammed on the cabin sole where he slept well. I got into the quarter berth so as to be available to get on deck quickly if need arose. It was wet there, and spray periodically came through the hatch, so although resting I slept little. It blew hard in the night, certainly attaining gale force for a while.

It is interesting to compare the experiences of other competitors during the same night. In an article in *Yachting World*, Major James Murray, skipper/owner of *Mokoia* to the north of *Cohoe*, described the seas as being 'as big and impressive as yet seen. Down in the valley of the troughs, we were so sheltered that the sails only filled on the crests.' This opinion I heartily endorse. Meanwhile *Samuel Pepys* who had been some 90 miles to the south-east had, as I anticipated, made the best of fresh and strong winds, running under twin headsails and covering 158 miles, giving her a lead over *Cohoe* of nearly 100 miles.

Far ahead of the smaller boats, *Gulvain* had also run into heavy weather during the night. She gybed all-standing, and when gybing back the topping lift caught round and damaged the lower port spreader. Charles Gardiner, a member of her afterguard, went aloft in a bo'sun's chair and made repairs by means of a light alloy angle bar. Later the upper spreader broke and Bill King went up and repaired it. The rolling of all the boats was bad enough on deck, but aloft in *Gulvain* the motion must have been like being at the end of a pendulum. Great seamanship was required but despite the delay *Gulvain* logged 150 miles in the 24 hours.

Thursday, July 13th. The morning after the gales, I went on deck at 0500. The wind had moderated but the sea was still high, and a wave had flooded the cockpit as recently as half-an-hour ago. The crew were sleeping soundly so I decided to make breakfast and then went on deck to get under way, soon followed by the port watch. We ran

29. Jack Keary steering with John Halstead during the transatlantic race. The seas were irregular.

Cohoe off before the wind and quickly got sail on her, first the jib and an hour later the mainsail and boomed out genoa. Later it developed into a lovely sunny day with a moderate westerly wind and a rising barometer, which gave the rather tired crew a respite and the chance to dry out a lot of wet clothes.

But my mind was far from peaceful. By the evening my conviction that *Cohoe* was far behind became so strong that I determined the spinnaker must be set at all costs, despite the big sea. John Halstead undertook the task. I had observed that he was not sick working on deck in bad weather; he seemed only to be affected when below by the roll and pitch of the boat under light conditions.

At 2000 I gave him a hand and the spinnaker was set, together with the infernal spinnaker net. The big sail was difficult to cope with and, once set, *Cohoe* staggered under the load rolling wildly from side to side. That night the wind rose to Force 6 and we were running faster than at any time I had known. It was soon a black night but above all was the extraordinary noise, like an express train, or the roar of a weir or waterfall. The boat was surfing on the top of the big waves, a great wedge of foaming water shooting out like a fan, and at her stern the wake was boiling almost to the top of the rudder. The speed was anybody's guess, perhaps ten or twelve knots on the crests, but reduced when she fell back in the troughs. Aft in the cockpit the steersman wore a personal lifeline hooked to the stanchions and was changed at intervals of 45 minutes. For the helmsman it was an experience of a lifetime, responsible and tiring. Jack and John did the 2000 to 0200 watch and Tom and I from 0200 to 0800 next morning.

Erroll logged the waves at noon as 'height 18ft, period 9½ seconds, which probably means over 300ft long'. Before midnight two aircraft passed overhead of *Samuel Pepys* and the distant lights of two vessels were sighted. 'All this traffic,' remarked their bo'sun, 'is just like Piccadilly Circus.'

Friday, July 14th. The morning was grey with drizzle. The wind remained strong and at times just as much as the spinnaker would stand. At mid-day the noon-to-noon run was a record of 177 miles, helped by the Gulf Stream. At 1830 in a squall, with Jack at the helm, a very steep sea struck the boat. *Cohoe* lifted bodily out of the water from stem to the mast, while the rest of the hull was immersed and the cockpit filled to the coamings. The boat was surf-riding with an immense bow wave abaft the mast, about 3ft higher than the guard rail. On such occasions steering is not usually difficult as the helm becomes light and the tiller merely vibrates. The spinnaker had to be lowered for repair at 2000. After twenty-four hours in a high wind the guy rope and tack had chafed; these had been replaced but the wire rope halyard where it turned over the sheave had been badly stretched and worn.

Samuel Pepys had shared the experiences of *Cohoe* when surfing. 'This is most exciting to the helmsman,' Erroll wrote, 'as the tiller goes stiff and the bow wave froths up on each side level with the guard rail and water pours over each side deck, as though we were submerging.' Both boats had exceeded their maximum theoretical speeds, *Samuel Pepys* logging 84 miles in 12 hours. In the night the wind veered NW and moderated, enabling *Cohoe* to reach under mainsail and genoa, and the watch below to get some well earned sleep.

Sunday, July 16th. The three small boats had completed their second week of the race and were dispersed over a wide front of 150 miles, *Mokoia* far to the north, *Cohoe* well to the south of her, and *Samuel Pepys* leading on the south-east. The race had developed more than ever into a test of endurance in varying winds and weather.

Monday, July 17th. During the past four days *Cohoe*, by brutal driving, had gained with her heavy nylon spinnaker set by day and by night 17 + 17 + 11 + 26 miles, giving a total of seventy-one recovered of the loss made the previous Wednesday, but here is an extract from Erroll Bruce's diary in *Samuel Pepys*:

'About 0200 the wind suddenly veered after a squall, and the sky cleared to show some brighter stars. Although the barometer was still falling, all my apprehensions of the early night went. There was no sound logic in this, but all seemed well, such is the effect of seeing a star or two. Down came the trysail with a great struggle; set genoa, set reefed mainsail, cram on everything, and she creamed through the breaking seas.

'Calculations at noon showed us to be 997 miles from Plymouth, so now we had entered the last thousand. All along I had planned to take no undue risks, consider wear of rigging and crew carefully until a thousand miles. Then, if all was well, to race as though we were turning round the buoys off Cowes . . . . . So this was the time–barometer very low and dropping slowly, sea rough, wind Force 6. Hoist spinnaker. Perhaps she wouldn't last long, but the needles were sharp and sewing cotton ready.'

Wednesday, July 19th. Tom and I came on watch at 0200. It was a great experience, for the yacht was tearing across the ocean at tremendous speed. The seas seemed pretty enormous, yet *Cohoe* lifted to each breaking wave and steering was light. Shortly after I took the helm at 0330 a solid black cloud was overtaking menacingly and rain formed a kind of mushroom in the sky. Then came fierce squalls with violent rain like a curtain of white over the black sea. It smoothed out the white caps leaving only the long rollers running up astern.

Samuel Pepys had experienced much the same weather and squalls during the night, but about four hours earlier than *Cohoe*. In one of the squalls Erroll reported that the wire strop holding the tack of the big spinnaker to the end of the spinnaker boom parted, and the sail began to thrash in a way that would tear it to shreds in a minute or two. The bo'sun was on watch at the time but the skipper rushed on deck and took the helm. Between the two of them the flogging spinnaker was got down without damage under the lee of the mainsail into the cockpit. Within minutes the broken strop had been replaced by a pair of special shackles.

'Blue spinny ready for hoisting,' yelled the bo'sun.

'Hoist blue spinnaker,' ordered the skipper, and soon it was backing up the mainsail to pull her ahead at seven knots.

When morning came it felt colder; already we had been wearing winter woollies, and everything below including the settees, the blankets and our spare clothes were damp from the salt which impregnated them. There was mildew even in the lockers. On a lighter topic, our beards were growing long, and the unaccustomed feel of them took some getting used to, but none had any inclination to shave. In *Samuel Pepys* it was the bo'sun's (Pat Ovens) black beard that was most impressive, but the mate who was tall and more stringy sported a red growth. On an even lighter topic I must add that in both the boats the bunch of bananas had ripened, but by Tuesday *Samuel Pepys* had eaten all theirs and the mate had substituted vitamin tablets.

Cohoe's noon-to-noon run was 161 miles and *Samuel Pepys* logged precisely the same distance, thus maintaining her lead.

Thursday, July 20th and Friday, July 21st. In these two days *Mokoia* who had been keeping north of Great Circle route came south and crossed *Cohoe*'s track. *Samuel Pepys* remained in the lead. In the noon-to-noon run to Thursday, *Cohoe* gained 21 miles on *Samuel Pepys* only to lose 21 miles on Friday. The crews in both boats were getting impatient with the lighter weather and were hoping for just one more gale.

At 1600 a Royal Air Force Sunderland flying boat circled round *Cohoe* taking photographs. After leaving us she went west for some miles to circle round another object, so we had our first indication of another competitor—probably *Samuel Pepys*. In the evening we crossed the continental shelf. From over 2,000 fathoms we came into only hundreds, according to the chart.

Saturday, July 22nd. In the early hours of the morning came portents of a breakup in the fine weather; the glass had fallen and the wind backed. The hopes in both boats for a moderate gale were soon to be realised and, when it came, the crews responded by driving their boats to the utmost limits.

In the six-hour watch from 0200 to 0800 in the dirty morning with rain and increasing sea, *Cohoe* covered 43 miles at an average speed of 7·2 knots, and in the afternoon *Samuel Pepys* made her record of 7·4 miles in one hour. By 1300 the barometer had touched its lowest and the wind veered west. At 2000 I relieved John who looked as happy as a sandboy at the helm. With night coming on we double-reefed the mainsail. Half an hour later a big sea came up astern and lifted *Cohoe* into a magnificent surf-ride. I thought it time to lower the mainsail and run under the genoa and staysail boomed out. The night was wild, the wind strong. The only relief from darkness came from the orange glow of the compass, the gleam from the navigation light on the stanchions and the phosphorescent flash of the breaking waves. Steering was erratic in the big seas which threw the stern about as she raced on, rolling, pitching and surf-riding through the night. It was the same in *Samuel Pepys*:

'By evening the wind we had hoped for was all we could manage. With full mainsail up she tore along, the water swirling up on both sides of the deck at once, and sometimes slopping into the cockpit. It was all the helmsman could do to keep her under control, so down came the mainsail, and the running rig of twin headsails was set. As this job was finished gale gusts and driving rain came on us, and we were glad to have the sails trimmed in time . . . .'

Sunday, July 23rd. The night had been dark and rainy with the yachts racing all out before a Force 7 wind, gusting higher. At 0300 *Samuel Pepys*, when the wind veered NNW, was down to running under one headsail only. Half an hour later this blew out and her skipper ordered it to be replaced not by a smaller one but by a larger. 'As dawn broke,' wrote Erroll, 'we saw once more how big and frightening the waves looked coming up astern.'

The boats raced on, staggering under their press of canvas. But *Samuel Pepys* was running on a better gybe and, though we didn't know it at the time, was gaining on us. It was not until 0715 that *Cohoe* changed the headsails on the twin forestays and altered course further north for Lizard Head.

Navigation had become the principal interest. During the night a temporary clearance in the sky had enabled Tom to get star sights on Vega and Jupiter and check the position. Erroll in *Samuel Pepys* got a fix from the same stars. In the morning, with temporarily poor visibility we failed to sight the Bishop Rock lighthouse on the Isles of Scilly, the landfall which used to be taken by the liners for their transatlantic records.

With moderating winds *Samuel Pepys* increased sail step by step. Their log read 'Hoisted storm trysail—down trysail, hoist reefed main—hoist small spinnaker—shake out reefs in main—small spinnaker blew out—hoist large spinnaker,' but I do not think I responded so quickly in *Cohoe*.

As the day drew on it became sunny. There was still half a gale of wind and a big breaking sea, but it was a day of sparkle and zest. We passed trawlers, only their masts appearing over the crest of the waves. Big ships were frequently going by. It was strange to see so many, as in the Atlantic only once in a thousand miles had we sighted one. Our landfall was made at the Wolf Lighthouse. Tom as navigator had calculated to leave it six miles to port, and so he did. Before very long the hazy looking headland of the Lizard was sighted rising in the distance, but the wind was falling and it was not until 1932 that we came abeam of it, three hours 47 minutes after *Samuel Pepys* as we learnt later, and by this time we in *Cohoe* were feeling pretty desperate.

The distance from the Lizard to the finish line off Plymouth Breakwater was fifty miles and, with *Samuel Pepys* leading as I felt sure she was, the opposition might well cross the line leaving us becalmed somewhere between the Lizard and Plymouth. Tom and I came on watch at 2000, and would remain so until 0200 on Monday morning. Both of us were getting very tired and we took it in turns to steer in hourly spells, helped by many cigarettes, biscuits and coffee to keep us alert while coaxing the best out of *Cohoe* in the light airs. We were lucky because, as the night lengthened, a light but firm breeze came up from the NW enabling us to reach in smooth water under the spinnaker at five knots.

At 0200 we were relieved by Jack and John, and the Eddystone Lighthouse lay on the starboard bow. Tom and I turned in, and fell asleep instantly. Two hours later Jack called me on deck to take the helm as we were about to enter Plymouth Bay. It was still dark. We altered course; on the quarter the Eddystone Light gave its double flash, and on our starboard bow the Breakwater Light at the finish line winked its rapid single flash. The genoa was hooked on forward, ready for hoisting. A quarter mile from the line down came the spinnaker and up went the genoa.

Now at last the finish line was at hand. There stood the tall lighthouse at the breakwater end and beyond it the breakwater fort. The warning flare was ignited and held high over the side. The magnesium blazed in a brilliant bluish white, lighting the mainsail and letting fall a trail of hot ashes into the sea. The message was answered by a signal lamp in the fort.

These were wildly exciting moments at the climax of the long race. Nearer and nearer came the breakwater.

'Stand by,' I called to Tom as time-keeper.

Now! And the second flare sped its message as *Cohoe* crossed the finish line, twenty-one days nine hours fourteen minutes from the start at Bermuda.

Before we had sailed far a motor launch wearing the white ensign came alongside and took our warps. In it were Commander M H Brown, then the Assistant King's Harbour Master, and the Committee of the Royal Western Yacht Club of England, together with Customs Officers. It was a royal welcome, extended to each yacht at the conclusion of her voyage.

Cohoe was quickly towed to the Millbay dock and came alongside *Samuel Pepys*. Sammy sleepily put his head out of the cabin to greet us.

'Well sailed, Sammy,' I said.

'Well sailed *Cohoe*,' Sammy replied, adding 'Erroll thinks you have won.'

And so it proved to be when the Committee worked out the corrected times under the rating rules:

RESULTS
OF
TRANSATLANTIC RACE 1950

		Elapsed Time	Corrected Time	
Cohoe	Adlard Coles, RNSA	21.09.14	14.07.21	Illingworth Cup
Samuel Pepys	RNSA	21.04.17	14.09.26	2nd Open
Mokoia	Major James Murray R CNQ YC	21.13.20	14.20.54	3rd Open
Gulvain	J H Rawlings Sussex MYC	18.03.02	15.20.55	R Bermuda YC Trophy
Karin III	G C L Payne Poole YC	24.13.40	16.16.36	

Nevertheless, ignoring ratings, *Samuel Pepys* had beaten *Cohoe* boat for boat on elapsed time by five hours (equivalent to about 6 seconds a mile over 3,000 miles), a record for so small a boat. In the next Transatlantic Race, two years later, Erroll Bruce skippered *Samuel Pepys* to victory, but he told me the weather conditions were nothing like so bad as those we had experienced.

The 1950 event was an important pioneering race which had considerable bearing on things to come. Among others it led to the recognition of the ocean-going ability of small sailing boats, and indirectly to the Single-Handed Transatlantic Races in which boats of about half the size of *Cohoe* and *Samuel Pepys* were allowed to compete. It was also a practical test of hulls and gear and risks at sea. As captain of the team, one of Erroll Bruce's cardinal principles was that a man overboard (who had lost hold of the boat) in heavy weather could be a man lost; from this developed the safety harness devised by Peter Hayward and later followed by other makers.

My narrative ends with the crews of the three small competitors reunited in Millbay docks. What good friends we all had made, and what adventures we had shared together. Our wives joined in the celebrations, and then Mamie and I had a quiet cruise in *Cohoe* back to our home port of Bursledon.

CHAPTER TWENTY-THREE

CRUISING IN THE BAY OF BISCAY

My second ocean racer *Cohoe II* was a yawl designed by Charles A Nicholson and very well built by Wilf Souter at Cowes in 1952. She was a roomy boat of nearly double the size of *Cohoe*, displacing some 6·7 tons compared with the designed 3·5 tons of the earlier boat; her dimensions were 34ft 10½ins overall length, 26ft LWL, 8ft 6ins beam, 6ft 2ins draught. The hull design may be likened to a modified metre boat, but beamier with shorter ends. She had the broad shoulders and fine run aft common to the designs of Charles A Nicholson, but slacker sections. She gave us just what we wanted, and all the accommodation and locker space which made cruising a pleasure to Mamie.

So far as ocean racing was concerned, in her first year *Cohoe II* did reasonably well, ending the season with a first in the Bay of Biscay race which finished at Benodet on August 21st. There the crew left except for Ross, and we were joined by our respective wives, Mamie and Elizabeth, for a family cruise.

Incroyable Mais Vrai. Even my French could understand that, as I looked at the notice displayed on a gaily coloured booth at a travelling fair which had arrived at Benodet. *Tout Pour Gagner*, it continued, indicating the array offered as prizes, ranging from Algerian Red Wine to Champagne. *Incroyable mais vrai* developed during our cruise into a catch phrase, applicable to all kinds of strange situations, including a good landfall by the skipper.

There was nothing incredible about this cruise of which I write, except the weather, for day after day it was fine. It was so settled that we were able, without large scale charts, to visit many of the islands and ports of Brittany which we had never seen before, some of which are often unapproachable. We sailed to fourteen different anchorages in fifteen days, with only one whole night at sea.

We had agreed to take things easily, for Mamie had not sailed before in that season. Elizabeth was not entirely new to sailing as Ross had invited her the previous year for the Dinard race, rather rashly I thought. The battery had capsized and the acid mixing with the salt water made chlorine gas just under the berth on which his then fiancée was asleep. Engagements have been broken off on more trivial grounds than that.

Our first few days were spent pottering along the coast from the Odet River to the Morbihan. This is a wonderful cruising ground, offering the choice of so many harbours and anchorages that one can sail just as long as one pleases, with always a port close at hand. There is such variety too; proper harbours as, for example at Belle Ile and Ile de Groix, and the natural anchorages in the rivers Odet, Aven, Belon and Etel. To see something of rural France one merely has to sail up any of the rivers to find a beautiful old town.

30. *Cohoe II* at anchor off the Grand Hotel, Benodet.

We first sailed up the Odet River to Quimper, where the pottery, famous throughout Brittany, is made. Some of it is beautiful, and has character; but the best is expensive, and there is much of the 'arty crafty' kind made for tourists. Concarneau, best known of all the fishing ports, we visited for the first time. The old walled city in the centre of the harbour is worth seeing, for inside this small area is crowded a town of mediæval appearance, with narrow streets and houses jostling close together. Except for the shops selling the inevitable souvenirs, it can have changed little since the Middle Ages—a place of teeming life, people, dogs, cats, rats and smells. I had one grudge against Concarneau, its large number of fishing tackle shops. I don't like fish hooks or bait, or lines, which sooner or later get tangled in the log line. What is more, I am not really fond of fish. So, when starting on a cruise I usually manage to forget the fishing lines, and leave them stored in the attic out of harm's way; but at Concarneau the family bought lines galore.

A fog descended upon us when we sailed next day for the Aven river. The coast we were passing is fringed with rocks and with plenty of outlying reefs. They are well marked by towers and beacons, but these disappeared in the mist; worse still, the wind headed. After a long tack seawards towards the Glénan Islands we were lucky on the next leg exactly to find the Corn Vas buoy, for had we been a cable out in our calculations we should have missed it altogether and would have had to stand out to sea for deep water.

There was a temporary improvement in the visibility; but when we approached the entrance to the Aven river, trailing the now inevitable fishing lines, it was still poor. The bar gave momentary anxiety for, without a large scale chart, we did not know exactly where it was. The approach is not difficult. Keep rather to the west side, passing a little village with a small quay which dries out just beyond the Pointe de Rousbicout at the entrance. We found a port hand red beacon; and, after that, it was easy. The Aven is not so well known as the Odet on account of its bar; but I think it is prettier. In the upper reaches, the channel runs between oyster beds; and, in one part, takes a turn within a stone's throw of the west bank. Farther up there is a junction where two tributaries meet; and the one leading between a boulder strewn shore and low trees to Pont Aven is very narrow. We sailed up this the following morning without difficulty, until we touched in the middle of the channel. As it was the top of the tide we thought the risk of going farther was too great, so we sailed back to the entrance where there is a pretty anchorage.

31. Anchored at Port Tudy in the Ile de Groix.

After a brief visit to Port Melin and Port Tudy at Ile de Groix we sailed to the Etel River. This also has a bar, and the Cruising Association Handbook advises that it should be inspected before entry, because the position of the channel through the sands is constantly changing. It was a brilliant sunny day when we arrived off the entrance; but we were rather early on the tide, there was quite a swell running, and a breaking sea on the bar. A mast stands on the west side of the entrance, which has a revolving arrow to indicate when the approach is safe, and on which side the channel lies. The arrow was vertical indicating there was enough water, but we were not quite clear where the channel lay. There appeared to be a gap in the breakers, but even there the steepness of the swell looked ominous. Luckily a French fishing boat came by, and we got a tow through in about 8ft of water.

We liked Etel. It is a pleasant small French town, situated on the bank of a broad and fast flowing river. When we were there a travelling market had arrived, and stalls and booths stretched for a long way on each side of the main road. The gaily coloured awnings and the bright hues of the clothes and other things displayed made a colourful scene on that pleasant sunny day. These travelling markets seem a feature of Brittany and, as they supply every conceivable kind of thing, they must be quite a headache to the local shops.

We wanted to see Morbihan, so it was to this inland sea that we sailed the next afternoon. The water sparkled, ruffled by a fresh fair wind, which took us rapidly along the coast, past Quiberon and through the Teignouse Passage to the entrance. There are no difficulties in the approach, and the deep water lies close to the Pointe de Port Navalo which stands on the east side of the entrance. The tidal stream is reputed to run at 8 knots; but it was not so hard as this when we entered. Nevertheless it swept the yacht quickly past and up between the low-lying islands to the Ile Aux Moines, where we dropped the hook just before darkness fell.

32. Visitors call on *Cohoe II* anchored in the Morbihan.

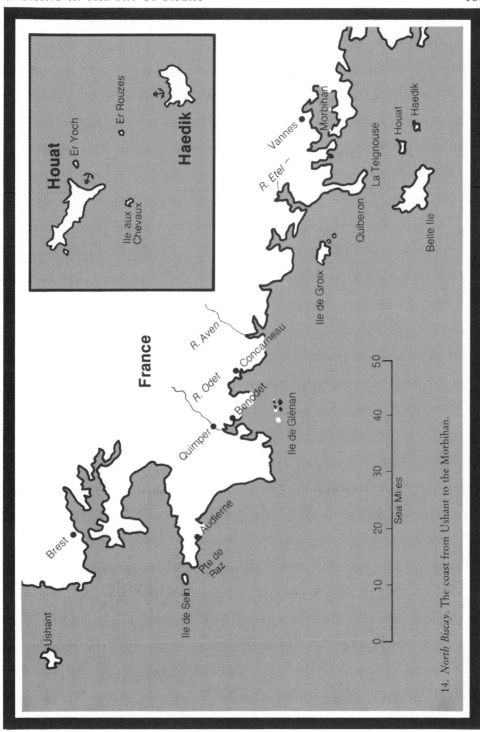

14. *North Biscay.* The coast from Ushant to the Morbihan.

We rowed ashore for dinner at one of the two hotels, where the food was not particularly good, and decidedly expensive. We came to the conclusion that the Ile Aux Moines was rather too much of a holiday resort for our liking. After dinner it was a pitch black night when we walked through the village; and, wherever we went, we ran into piles of empty wine bottles, which no doubt marked the conclusion of a successful season. The fun of the Morbihan really lies in navigating the channels among the islets and the less popular parts. There are miles of channels in which to sail, and there are good anchorages almost anywhere out of the strength of the tides. We went as far up as the last reach just before the canal to Vannes, where we anchored in 6ft of water.

A row in the dinghy took us to the towing path, from which it was only about a mile to the old walled city of Vannes. It is the capital of the Department of Morbihan, and has a beautiful cathedral and many lovely old buildings of historical and architectural interest. We would have liked to have seen more of Vannes, to have spent a few days pottering about in the Morbihan and to have visited the Auray River; but the fine weather gave us a chance of exploring the fascinating looking waters off the Quiberon peninsula.

Quiberon, almost an island itself, juts out into the sea between the mainland and Belle Ile. Extending from its tip there is a continuation of the original formation which manifests itself in a line of rocks, reefs and islets, each bearing a strange-sounding Breton name. Between the rocks there are passages, of which the principal one is La Teignouse, through which we had sailed on our way to the Morbihan. It is well buoyed, and there are good lights at night.

There are many other routes through the rocks, which are used by the fishermen and are marked by beacon towers. Among the islets or rocks there are two larger ones. Houat, which is the nearest, is shaped like the trunk of a body, with two legs forming a 'Y' facing east. Hædik, almost entirely fringed by a rocky bank extending nearly two miles on the south-east side, lies four miles away and is roughly rectangular in shape with an indentation forming a bay on the north side. I am told the names mean duck or duckling, but I believe that the derivation is disputed.

A nice breeze and a fair tide carried us rapidly across the ten miles of sea between Morbihan and Houat. As we approached, the island, some 2½ miles long, looked interesting: it is only about 100ft high, and the coast is rocky with numerous indentations and sandy beaches. The first islet we identified was Er Yoch on the NE side. It is larger than the others and at low water is joined to Houat by a narrow spit of yellow sand. We rounded close to the off-lying rocks, and a most beautiful little bay, named Treac'h er Gouret, opened up. We were delighted to see that we had obviously picked a good spot, for we found that the bay before us was dotted with a fleet of fishing boats at anchor. There were so many that we had to pick our way among them to find a berth with room to swing. We let go the hook in line with a sandy road which was cut through the sand dunes to the shore.

A slight surf was running, so instead of landing on the beach from the dinghy we rowed over to a little harbour which we found on the south side of the bay. It had almost dried out; but there was just enough water for the dinghy at the outer steps. By the harbour there were one or two small stone buildings used for stores, a pile of

33. Tumbledown cottages at Hædik, and the village well.

lobster pots, a few nets drying in the sun, and a small shrine. We followed a sandy road northwards, leading towards the village, and it ran along a narrow strip of sand dunes with the sea on either hand. On the west side there was another bay, a lovely one with clear blue breakers falling on a sandy shore, white in the evening sun.

It was only a short walk to the village, passing a pleasant little hotel-restaurant on the way. In the centre there is the village square and the church, which is the centre of a community of about 350 inhabitants, almost all fishermen. Close by was a war memorial, a well and a general store run by nuns. It all looked very peaceful that evening, with the hens running about among the cottages; but in winter Houat must be a grim place indeed, for it stands in an exposed position, swept by gales. The proper harbour at Houat, which I found on the next visit, lies on the north side and it became one of our regular ports of call.

When we retraced our steps we followed the shore. It was low tide and, by digging with our fingers in the wet sand at the water's edge, we dislodged quantities of small sand eels, a kind of fish which we had not met before. They are lively customers when they are unearthed, or unsanded, but we hoped they would make a good breakfast, as they are said to be excellent eating when fried whole. However, the wives refused to cook them and, even worse, they used them as bait for the fishing lines, on which nothing had so far been caught.

Our anchorage was well sheltered when we entered; but, in the summer weather, there are clockwise winds which the fishermen call 'Vents du Soleil', and during the night a fresh breeze got up from the mainland shore. It was so fresh that the boat pitched violently enough to wake us up, so that we were in rather a bad temper the following morning. But it was another sunny day, and we had a very happy sail over to the neighbouring island of Hædik, the distance is less than four miles, but the intervening water is strewn with rocks and the streams run hard, although not so fast, I fancy, as in the Teignouse Channel. The principal batches of rocks are marked by beacon towers, but there are so many of these that they are a little confusing. We avoided the difficulties by making a detour, and leaving all the beacons to starboard, and approaching from a northerly direction to the Pointe du Vieux Château, the headland at the western end of Hædik, east of which lies the only part of the coast free of dangers.

Although different in shape, Hædik is of the same granite formation as Houat. It is rocky with stretches of sand in the bays. It is even more exposed and, owing to the dangerous reefs of rocks and the poor harbour on the south-west side, communications with the land were irregular. The guide book *Bretagne Sud* sums it up shortly in the words *Elle n'offre aucune ressource pour le séjour.*

We stood in eastward of the Pointe du Vieux Château. Here the shore is rocky; but ahead of us lay a stretch of pure white sand, and on the shore were two beacons marking (according to the chart) the eastern limit of a prohibited anchorage. Immediately beyond this we could see a slip and a lifeboat house, towards which we sailed. The sea was so clear that there was no danger. Rocks below the surface could be seen and, indeed, even the different depths over the sandy bottom were shown by the tints of the green of the sea. We brought up off the slip in a lovely anchorage. The whole place was entirely deserted; not a soul was to be seen on the clear stretches of sand, on which a gentle surf broke with a soft rustle. A short dinghy excursion brought us to the slip. There was no road, and we walked over short dry grass to the top of the island, which is only about seventy feet high. Sea holly and hardy deep-rooted flowers fought for existence in the sandy soil. The village is in the middle of Hædik, only ten minutes' walk from the shore, as the whole island is little over a mile long.

It is very like Houat, but smaller and more compact. There was a beautiful little church, inside which a painted model ship was hung from the roof, a characteristic of many Breton churches; also a school, a well, and a row or two of cottages, some in ruins, for the place seemed poorer than Houat. We met a fisherman who directed us to a débit at a cottage where we sipped aperitifs. There we met a stranger among the pleasant Bretons; an unprepossessing individual who called himself an Egyptian. He was one of the most gesticulating and persistent cadgers I have ever encountered and, full of wine, he even staggered after us when we walked to the old harbour at Port de la Croix. This was on the south-west side and was unapproachable without a large-scale chart, for it was so surrounded by reefs and rocks that even from the shore it was difficult to trace the way in. It consisted merely of a long and a short mole, behind which was a sort of sandy lagoon, which dries 9ft; but the fishing boats lie outside. There were not buildings of any kind near the harbour and, as at Houat, the moles had been breached by gales.

Mamie went out in a boat with two fishermen and bought two enormous live lobsters. We took them back to the inn where they were to be boiled. The price seemed fantastic, but they were carefully weighed on scales and the sum was worked out from newspaper quotations, so I am sure that we were not deliberately stung. Lobsters were far more expensive in France than in England.

We weighed in the afternoon, intending to sail through the Chaussée de l'Ile aux Chevaux. There are many shoals on this course, across which the stream sets with overfalls, though it was nothing like so strong as I had anticipated. After passing between two rocky patches, namely Les Soeurs and Er Rouzes, each marked by a beacon tower, the wind fell light, so we altered course and returned to our anchorage at Houat. It was a peaceful evening, but our wives suggested that the wind might freshen again in the night. After a large lobster dinner and a bottle of wine, Ross and I made light of this and said that if this occurred we would get the boat under sail and quit. Sure enough, the wind freshened in the early hours of the morning and dutifully, but not silently, Ross and I arose and sailed away. It was dawn by the time we were in Teignouse Channel, a grey dawn, heralding another perfect day. We put into Ile de Groix at noon for provisions, and then sailed on our way at a steady 5 to 6 knots in smooth water, silent but for the rustle of the bow wave, and the ripple of water along the planks. We anchored off Benodet at 0100 and spent Sunday ashore seeing the 'Pardon' procession, cashing traveller's cheques, and having baths at the hospitable Grand Hôtel.

Time was getting short, so we got under way again in the evening and did a fast night sail to the anchorage off Audierne, Ross and Elizabeth, who had become a promising helmswoman, doing most of the steering. We set sail again after breakfast; it was another glorious morning but we ought to have started the engine, for the wind was so light that we had lost several hours of fair tide by the time it had freshened and we had made the Raz de Sein.

Being bound for Ushant we took the passage through the Raz between Ile de Sein and Tevennec. It was already apparent that we were likely to be too late on our tide before we approached Ushant, and the Ile de Sein behind its screen of rocks and the beacons looked so enticing that the opportunity of visiting it was not to be missed. On the passage chart the whole island was only about $1\frac{1}{2}$ inches long, and I had to use the magnifying glass to decipher the maze of rocks. However, I saw that on the north side there is a buoy just off one of the channels, the lead-in being noted as 'Third house and beacon in line'.

The tide took us straight to the buoy marking a rock on which the swell occasionally broke, but we could not be sure which beacon was which, nor were we quite certain of the third house. We made a guess by the compass course, and could see an islet which was clearly to be left to starboard and beyond it a larger one named Nerroth to be left to port. We sailed on and once again we were lucky, for a small open fishing boat was making for the entrance at the same time. The skipper slowed his engine when he saw we were strangers, and all we had to do was to follow. It appeared that in addition to the starboard hand rock near the buoy which we could see, there is another submerged one to port. Once past these two, the channel lay just as we surmised. The beacon proved to be what we should call a lighthouse, and the third house is from the left and has a white roof, but the paint was a bit jaded.

Once past the island of Nerroth we entered a delightful anchorage. On the starboard side was the sea wall of the village, a lifeboat slip, and the lighthouse and mole. To port was another mole, and beyond it shoals, islets and rocks marked by beacon towers. The bottom was quite clear, including the crab shells and oddments littering it, and we were pleasantly surprised to hear that there was just enough water to float us at low tide, so that we could remain the night. There were several Audierne fishing vessels at anchor near us, and many more came in towards nightfall. A French boat entered shortly after we arrived. She was from the sailing school at Penfret in the Glénan Isles.

Ross rowed Mamie and me ashore, as we did not want to leave the dinghy un-attended. The waterside population of both the Ile de Sein and Ushant breeds children that start their boating lives at the age of three, and to leave a pram dinghy at their disposal might have been too much of a temptation for their adventurous spirits.

There is something unusual about the Ile de Sein, and its setting contributes towards this, for there are few coasts more dangerous. To the east lies the Raz de Sein, a notoriously rough tidal race, and to the west a long finger extends several miles into the Atlantic, ending with a buoy appropriately known to us as the Ar Men, although the Breton word has a different meaning. The island itself is little more than a sandbank, half a mile wide at its maximum and under two miles in length. What surprised us was the village, which is a small town supporting a large church, houses, schools, res-taurants, small shops and numerous bars, all clustered close together in a small area separated by narrow alleyways. Outside the town every bit of the island appeared to be cultivated in tiny plots, each with a wall of loose stones to protect it from the searching wind. It must be a terrible place in winter, at the mercy of every gale, but on this summer's afternoon it was beautiful, with the sun falling on the harbour walls and on the whitewashed lighthouse and cottages, under a cloudless sky, powdery blue in the summer haze.

On our return to *Cohoe II*, we saw that there was great excitement on board. No wonder, for the first fish had been caught. It was one of those tough little fellows about six inches long, which are all head and bones, though they have pious eyes, always looking upwards. Thank goodness it did not provide an evening meal; but I was sorry to observe that it was kept for bait.

Cohoe II just touched the bottom at low water, and next morning we weighed anchor and sailed outward bound for Ushant. It was a sunny morning but rather hazy. By the time we had cleared the entrance and left the buoy a mile astern we ran into fog. It was a really thick one, so it was impossible to return and the only thing we could do was to continue, with our foghorn emitting its feeble, ineffectual bleat. I hoped it would clear by mid-day, for navigation was decidedly difficult. The wind was light and it headed us, so that we had to make a tack. Dead reckoning is not easy where the tidal streams are fierce and vary in direction at every hour. Ushant, to which we had not sailed before, is a difficult landfall, as the streams run six knots along the northern shores and up to eight knots on the southern, through the Passage de Fromveur.

At noon it was as thick as ever, with visibility varying from 50 yards to a quarter of a mile, and I was on the point of altering course and clearing out to sea, when it began to lift a little; the sky looked lighter and by 1245 the sun came through.

The bay of Lampaul for which we were sailing lies between two headlands which form arms, and from which extend rocky patches for a mile or so. At the extremity of the northern arm is the Roche Nividic lighthouse, and at the southern La Jument. There are rocks off the latter from north-west through north to north-east. After the fog had lifted, the weather remained hazy with a visibility which appeared to be about a mile. I have a great dislike of approaching land in thick weather, whether in fog or rain, and was again strongly tempted to get clear into open water.

However, coerced by our wives who had joined forces in their determination not to spend the night as sea in a fog, we tacked and set a course for La Jument. It was not until about 1430 that anything was sighted. Then Ross spotted a tall pencil of white in the haze. Nothing was in sight to check it by; but the outline agreed with the drawing of La Jument in the *Channel Pilot*, and a DF bearing on Creach lighthouse with the newly acquired Beme Loop radio set confirmed our position, but navigation required great care owing to the poor visibility and the fierce and variable tidal streams. We tacked again and I worked out courses which could clear the rocky shoal half a mile NW of La Jument, and bring us blindfold across the entrance of the Baie de Lampaul to the shoals south of Roche Nividic lighthouse. They proved right, and thus we knew exactly where we were, although Ushant itself did not lift through the haze until we were close to the lighthouse.

By then the wind had freshened and we reached back athwart a sluicing tide which was running north-west. We were doing about six knots in smooth water with the mizzen staysail set, but we could only creep past Roche Nividic against the tide towards Lampaul Bay. We could see tremendous eddies near the lighthouse, and the sea looked as though it were pouring over a sill.

Once within the entrance of the bay, the big Creach lighthouse appeared through the haze high above the land. After that the rest was easy and we moored to a buoy off Lampaul at 1600; and after tea rowed ashore.

Ushant is quite the strangest place to which we have sailed. The entrance to Lampaul is wild in the extreme with fantastic shaped rocks between which the tides pour. Even in the bay itself the low granite cliffs on each side are worn by the sea into clefts, fissures, caves and in one place even into a natural rock bridge. We thought it more impressive than the Ile de Sein, although both are equally unapproachable in bad weather.

To get to the inner harbour we had quite a long row in the dinghy from where we moored. It is very small, but is protected by two moles leaving a narrow entrance, so I suppose in an emergency it might provide shelter, although it dries out. The village of Lampaul stands close by, dominated by the tall spire of the church. The island itself, about ten square miles in area, is large in comparison with the others we visited. Farming, which is carried on almost exclusively by the women, and fishing are the principal occupations of the islanders, and Lampaul is the only village of any size. It is a hilly little place, with rows of stone houses. There are shops of all kinds, and I think it is visited by quite a number of holiday makers, for a steamer service runs twice a week to Brest.

We had dinner ashore as a last celebration for time was short, and then we returned on board at 2300. It was a dark night and Roche Nividic light was not operating; but the fog had lifted. We got under way immediately and made St Peter Port the following evening. Here Ross and Elizabeth caught a steamer for Southampton, and Mamie and I cruised on to Alderney and Cherbourg before rejoining them at our home in Bursledon.

I was very busy when I got back, but a week later I went aboard *Cohoe II* to do some clearing up. There seemed to be a bit of a smell in the cockpit and, in a canvas bucket, I was shocked to find the decaying remains of the little fish caught at Ile de Sein a fortnight before. These fishermen! *Incroyable mais vrai.*

CHAPTER TWENTY-FOUR

OUR IRISH CRUISE

The following year Mamie and I made our first cruise to Ireland, a country whose fascinating coastline differed so much from any to which we had sailed before.

In the intervening winter *Cohoe II*'s rig had been altered. In her first season she had proved rather tender and sometimes evinced a notable rhythmic roll when racing down wind in rough seas. So, with the approval of Charles Nicholson her designer, I had the mast cut at the jumpers thus converting her to masthead rig. This was a great improvement as the smaller sail area was easier to handle by Mamie and me when sailing on our own, and for racing she rated better.

Having won in her class in the 550 miles La Coruña Race, *Cohoe II* had returned from Spain to compete in the 330 miles Cowes to Cork Race. For this event my crew consisted of the stalwart Alan Mansley, Doc Hudson, John Webster and Jim Kentish.

Owing to a SW gale the start had been postponed until Saturday morning, August 8th. On Tuesday when we passed the Eddystone lighthouse off Plymouth a forecast of further gales was given at 1800 and repeated the following morning, by which time *Cohoe II* was down to reefed mainsail, mizzen and storm jib, an efficient gale rig which gave a low sail plan. It was very rough, wet and uncomfortable beating to windward down Channel past the Lizard, and it was not until midnight that we cleared Land's End and altered course for the remaining 150 miles to Ireland. The high winds were over, but the weather still had a card to play, for after 24 hours sailing it changed to dense fog; the following morning John Webster homed on the Daunt light-vessel's radio beacon so exactly that we had to alter course quickly to avoid collision when at length we sighted her. From there to the finish line, which we crossed at 0924, was only a few miles and the visibility improved somewhat. Out of the eleven starters in the race only the Class I *Jocasta* and *Marabu* completed the course, apart from *Cohoe II* which was overall winner on corrected time: it was the first occasion that we had won against Class I in a heavy weather race. Great hospitality was given to us by the Commodore and members of the Royal Munster Yacht Club at Crosshaven over the three days we were there.

In the meantime Mamie had arrived at an hotel at Wexford. She had gone to bed early as she was tired, when a telephone call came through from the Club. She asked the porter to take the message.

He returned, knocking at the door, he called from the other side. 'Your husband's horse has won the race, Ma'am!' With that Mamie jumped into bed, which promptly collapsed and she had to call for the porter to be rescued.

When Mamie arrived at Crosshaven she stayed a day at the hotel there. *Cohoe II* had been in a pickle and was soaking wet as usual at the end of a rough race. The crew spent the last morning before returning to their occupations in England doing a noble clear-up even cleaning the cooking stove with sandpaper, and Jim Kentish had put the engine in order. While this was going on I had been busy rowing the pram dinghy (it was only 6½ft long) bringing off provisions and filling the water tank.

Mamie and I started our Irish cruise on Monday morning, August 15th. Our plan was to work our way west in a leisurely manner as far as Mizen Head and then north-westward to Dingle, where Ross and Elizabeth would join us to sail to the Blasket Islands at the extreme west of Ireland.

It did not take long to get the five miles from Crosshaven to the Daunt light-vessel, where we found a light to moderate SE wind and altered course along a deeply indented coastline for the Old Head of Kinsale. We sailed across a wide bay to the Seven Heads then across another bay to Galley Head. These big headlands with their lighthouses were so conspicuous that navigation was easy, so easy that we rarely looked at the compass and only once streamed the log during the whole of our cruise in Irish waters. Most of the coast is pretty steep-to and well charted on the large scale Admiralty charts.

During the morning sailing conditions were perfect but, after passing Galley Head, we made acquaintance with another characteristic of the Irish coast, with which later we were to become more familiar—mist. First of all it enveloped only the tops of the hills but, before long, a combination of rain, drizzle and mist came down on us. We were then crossing the wide twenty mile stretch across Glandore and Baltimore bays and had passed the Stags, rugged precipitous rocks which from a distance looked like an island. The wind was now fresh and the sea was getting roughish, so it was time to call it a day and seek port in one of the numerous harbours which always seem handy. We altered course for Baltimore passing close to the low green Kedge Island, by which time the Stags had disappeared in the mist and the whole coast was shrouded in grey. However, we had not far to go and soon a beacon on a headland loomed like a white ghost in the fog above us at the entrance of Baltimore, and at 2030 we anchored in the landlocked natural harbour off the village. All was silent. Grey mist over the water, clouds on the hills, and no sign of life ashore. The barometer was falling fast, and after a meal we turned in, glad to have covered sixty miles.

Next day it blew a south-westerly gale, so strong that we were unable to get ashore in the dinghy. All day the wind screamed in the rigging, and forward there was an unceasing patter of spray. Nevertheless, Group Captain Brier's 16-ton steel sloop *Frisk* arrived that day from England with her owner and family, and anchored the other side of the bay under Sherkin Island.

The gale blew itself out during the night so the following morning we landed at the little stone quay, alongside which lay two or three small fishing boats. The village of Baltimore is a pleasant one and, contrary to our expectations, since we had been told that provisioning is sometimes difficult in small Irish ports, we found everything we

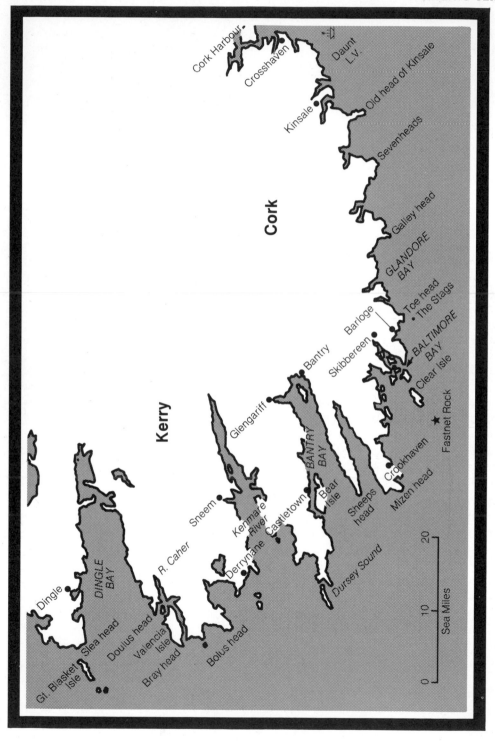

15. *SW Ireland.* Showing some of the ports of call on our 1953 cruise.

wanted. Close at hand was the post office, a grocer who kept a good stock, including home-cured ham, an ironmonger and a farm where we bought milk. There were plenty of pubs where one could buy 'Paddy', the Irish whiskey to which we had been introduced at Crosshaven and liked.

It was a glorious, sunny day and we walked along a narrow road between stone walls to the entrance of the harbour. The hills about us were covered with heather, gorse and flowers, and the water lay below us, with its surface ranging from brilliant blue to dark blue, where it was shaded by the passing clouds. In the distance rose Mount Gabriel and the mountain range.

In the evening we got under way. Without an anchor winch, I have sometimes found chain heavy work in my ocean racers, especially with a strong tide, but one of the advantages of Ireland is that many of the harbours are relatively tideless, so the boat lies head to wind as in the Baltic. It is then just a matter of direct heaving and up comes the anchor, then up headsail and away under genoa and mizzen, leaving the mainsail to be set at one's leisure. Here I must confess that the engine had already packed up. When it was examined by an engineer when we got to Dingle, he reported that the propeller shaft was $\frac{1}{4}$ inch out of adjustment so that the propeller was permanently (and fortunately) feathered, and the water pump was out of action. As he could not repair it the whole cruise and the passage back to England was made virtually under sail. I have no idea how and when the damage had been done; anyway it did not matter (except on one occasion) as the yacht was so handy and it is more fun to sail without an engine.

We wanted to visit Barloge, which we had been told at Crosshaven is a particularly beautiful inlet about five miles east of Baltimore. With a fair tide and a northerly wind we reached rapidly along the coast. Unlike Brittany much of the south-west coast of Ireland is free from offlying dangers. Hence we were able to keep close-in, admiring every detail of the coast and watching the seabirds, until we came to Kedge Island. This lies four cables offshore, and between it and the mainland there are numbers of forbidding looking rocks, but immediately under Spain Point there is a narrow passage used by coasters. As we approached the channel it looked amazingly narrow, with the swell rolling over the rocks in cataracts on either hand, especially on the port side where there are some ledges extending from Spain Point westward parallel with the passage. But for the assurance in the Irish Cruising Club's *Sailing Directions* (our sailing bible in these waters), we should have turned back. To our surprised eyes the width of the channel seemed only about twice the length of *Cohoe* but, like the height of waves, this was probably an optical illusion. At any rate the passage was quite exciting, especially as the wind was blanketed by the cliffs, but the tidal stream quickly whisked us through and *Cohoe* was soon off Barloge.

The entrance lies between Lalawn Point and two rocks off a little island called Bullock Island. The entrance proved by no means easy because the wind was light and, coming off the high ground, it was flukey but, with Mamie at the helm leaving me free to walk the genoa round at each tack, we were soon in the harbour; we then brought up in as lovely an anchorage as it has been our privilege to see.

Although narrow the anchorage is two fathoms deep and has just enough room for a boat to swing, as the shore on each side is fairly steep. To the north the inlet widens into what looks like a lake, before narrowing again into a gorge, which leads to Lough

perfect anchorage, completely sheltered, and next day we enjoyed every minute of our stay. There was a landing place at each end of the harbour, and between the two there was a path over the hill, overlooking the shore, with its miniature headlands, bays and pools, where the sea lies smooth, reflecting every colour of the sky. There was no village and not even a pub, but there was a shop on the road up the mountains, a mile or two away. In my diary I see that I made a plan of the north-western harbour entrance, which shows two white leading marks at 024°.

Our objective was now Dingle; we made it in two hops, the first to Port Magee, in weather which in the afternoon was so thick that we had to use the compass, and the second through Valencia Sound and with a spanking leading wind across Dingle Bay.

Dingle harbour is different from the other ports we visited. A narrow entrance leads into a large almost landlocked bay. The anchorage is far from the town, as near the harbour the charted depths are only about ¾ fathom. However, at neap tides a keelboat of 6ft draught can anchor close in, especially as the bottom is soft mud, or alternatively she can dry out alongside the quay. Here we took the opportunity to get an engineer to examine the engine installations at low water. As already established he found the propeller shaft ¼ inch loose, the feathering not working and the water pump out of action. He said he could not get at the engine for RSM so that was that!

We liked Dingle. There are many shops, most supplying a varied assortment of provisions, oilskins, boots, a bit of stationery, a few toys, nick-nacks, and almost always beer and spirits. It is the market town for the Dingle Peninsula, and every morning donkey carts and pigs arrive from the surrounding district. Mamie had friends there and the community seemed a cheerful one and extremely helpful. Unfortunately, the generosity extended to a present of roots of flowers. Not clean bulbs, but the sort of knobbly things one sometimes sees in florist shops, with plenty of soil clinging to them.

'Won't it be nice to be reminded of Ireland when these flowers grow up in the garden?' said Mamie.

'But what about the Irish bog they will make in *Cohoe*'s stern locker!' I argued feebly. However, there was one good thing about it. Our friend and I took it in turns to carry the heavy carton of roots down to the quay. We got so tired that we went to rest in a pub. There the proprietor introduced us to Maurice O'Sullivan's book *Twenty Years A-Growing*. 'Take it with you,' he said, in his Irish way. 'Just post it back when you have finished with it.'

So when Ross and Elizabeth joined us, the first place we visited was Great Blasket Island, lying at the extremity of the Dingle Peninsula and then the most westerly partially inhabited island in Europe. Though a fine day and only a moderate wind, the Atlantic swell found its way into Blasket Sound and, when we anchored, *Cohoe* pitched and rolled. There were breakers along the rocky shore and big combers breaking on the yellow strand under the lee of Great Blasket. Landing seemed impossible until we saw a curragh disappear between two rocks. Mamie and I followed in the 6½ft pram dinghy (the sea was smooth but for the swell and in the tide rips) and found a tiny boat harbour, formed by a wall joining two rocks, where we landed without much difficulty on the slip. Beside the rough path were two or three upturned curraghs, looking like lean black beetles. The inhabitants had left the island the previous year, except for three and for a few who return for the summer months. Above the Lilliputian harbour there were tumble-down cottages, with here and there one in good repair. We passed them and sheep, hens, a donkey and a few goats as we set out for a walk. Our efforts were well repaid for we had magnificent views over the Sound towards Slea Head and the mainland. Every islet and rock was fringed with foam from unceasing swell, and there was a most spectacular rainbow, where a squall was blowing across.

35. Mamie and Ross navigating in *Cohoe II*. There are innumerable safe anchorages on the south coast of Ireland.

Next day we sailed to the Outer Blaskets, Inish-Vickillane and Inishabro, but the flukey wind off the high islands coupled with the swell defeated any landing. I could have written a book about all we saw and enjoyed in our Irish cruise.

From Dingle we sailed back to Valencia Harbour and anchored temporarily under the lee of Church Island, a little rocky islet with the remains of a beehive monastery at the summit. By then it was blowing a near gale so we ran up the unbuoyed River Caher and anchored. Despite the weather, or perhaps because of it, the scene was beautiful. On the north side was a miniature bay joined by a rivulet. Above this were low walls composed of loose stones and boulders edging fields which made a patchwork, some emerald green and others dotted with golden stooks of cut corn. Occasional white-painted farmhouses diversified the countryside.

We wanted to see the ruins of Ballycarberry Castle standing alone and aloof on its hill, so we rowed ashore landing beside the rivulet alongside which there was a narrow lane. The hedges were ablaze with flowers, clusters of orange montbretia, fuchsia, wild roses and honeysuckle. Presently we found a friendly farmer who accompanied us part of the way.

What a walk it was; it took us across small fields and over stone walls and sometimes across boggy, peat land. We were deep in nature's own country of meadow and marsh, brambles and rabbits, land birds and sea birds. Finally, after passing another farm and another field the massive castle lay before us, part intact and part ruined, deeply impressive on that dark evening with the mountains behind it. The farmer had told us that it dates back to the sixteenth century and that some say its magazine was blown up to prevent it being of service to Cromwell.

It was getting late when we retraced out steps and arrived back at the river. There was now a weather-going ebb tide and all across were white-capped waves, so that we had quite exciting passages in the pram dinghy two at a time.

Next we revisited Derrynane, on the way circumnavigating the Skelligs, precipitous islands stranger than any in a fairy story. At Sneem in the Kenmare River another gale found us in the sheltered harbour. This is a really lovely anchorage. It is far from shops and supplies, but a resident on the east side of the harbour visited us and generously gave up a morning to our needs, motoring Ross and Elizabeth on a shopping expedition to Sneem, and giving us lunch and the use of his bathroom. The next night was spent in a tiny anchorage at Garinish Bay behind two islets just north-east of Dursey Sound. There a fisherman gave us an enormous cooked lobster, not for half a crown, but for nothing. He broke its claws, saying that a big one can exert a pressure of 300-lbs and can break the neck off a whiskey bottle.

'Not a full bottle?' asked Elizabeth.

'Oh, no!' he replied. 'Paddy is too valuable to let a lobster play around with.'

Time was getting short. We started early next day and beat through Dursey Sound and then sailed on to Crookhaven, whence we took our departure from Ireland and made a fast passage to Helford. Ross and Elizabeth left when we arrived at Brixham and, after waiting a day during another gale, Mamie and I sailed to Swanage in $9\frac{1}{2}$ hours, at an average speed of $7\frac{1}{2}$ knots, and back to our home port of Bursledon the following afternoon, Sunday, September 12th.

CHAPTER TWENTY-FIVE

FASTNET AND OTHER RACES

In 1956 I sold *Cohoe II* and placed an order for a faster all-round boat, which we named *Cohoe III*. She was extremely well built at Poole by Newman & Sons Ltd and, like her predecessor, designed by Charles A Nicholson. Her dimensions were 32ft 6ins overall, 26ft LWL, 9ft 1in beam and 6ft draught. Like *Cohoe II*, she was an example of cod's head and mackerel tail hull, with a fine run aft below water. Although over two feet shorter overall than *Cohoe II*, she was much larger, as she ended in a wide transom stern which in some respects is akin to having a larger yacht and chopping the counter off. She displaced about 8 tons and was sloop rigged with a sail area of 533 sq ft as designed but, when I later converted her to masthead rig set to a tubular stainless steel bowsprit, this was increased to 615 sq ft. The features of the new boat were her stiffness and sail-carrying ability in hard weather, and her roominess and strength. Everything about her construction, whether hull, mast or rigging, was above average strength and both her coachroof and stem were stiffened with steel; all this involved some sacrifice of speed in light and moderate winds.

However, what counted most in the sort of severe weather which suited *Cohoe III*, and later *Cohoe IV*, was the crew, so here I would like to refer briefly to Ross who was mate in the Fastnet Races and contributed so much to our successes.

After the 1948 Santander Race he continued sailing in *Cohoe* until 1950 when I was away on the Transatlantic Race. In 1951 he became a mate in Geoff Pattinson's Class I ocean racer *Jocasta*, which won her class in the Fastnet Race and the Points Championship for that year.

Ross took his qualifications of Bachelor of Medicine and of Surgery in 1952, and next year entered the Royal Navy for his national service as a Surgeon Lieutenant; he served at first in HMS *Osprey* and later in HMS *Tyne*, the command ship at Port Said. His most interesting appointment from the sailing point of view was to the Royal Yacht *Britannia* in December, 1958, when he followed Alastair Easton as sailing master of *Bluebottle*, Prince Philip's Dragon class yacht.

It so happened that the following year *Cohoe III* put up the best corrected time in the Morgan Cup Race and won the Queenborough Cup. This race is organised jointly by the Royal Ocean Racing Club and the Royal Thames Yacht Club, where I was invited to the Annual Dinner and prize giving. On this occasion I was given the honour of sitting immediately on the left of Earl Mountbatten, the Commodore (who was so tragically assassinated in 1979). Lord Louis told me that Ross's papers had come before him personally as First Sea Lord, as it was the first time in the history of the Royal Navy that an executive appointment had been made to a medical officer. Ross raced *Bluebottle* for two years and skippered her when she was sent to Canada when HM The Queen opened the St Laurence Seaway; it was a wonderful experience for him. He continued Dragon racing for some years afterwards except when ocean racing in *Cohoe III* and *IV*.

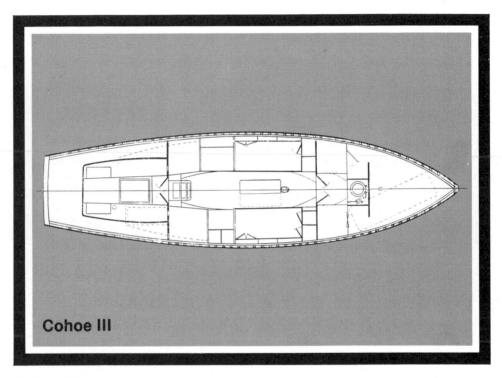

Cohoe III

16. *Cohoe III.*
    LOA   32ft 6ins   Beam   9ft 1in
    LWL   26ft   Draught   6ft
    Tons disp   8

After being promoted to Surgeon Commander in 1966, with a part-time appointment at Southampton University doing research on deafness and balance disorder, he retired in 1970 to take a full-time appointment at the University. Later in 1978 he became the deputy director of the Medical Research Council's newly formed Institute of Hearing Research at Nottingham University. Initially he remained with his own research team and academic colleagues at Southampton, where he became an honorary professor, but in 1980 pressure of work necessitated a move to Nottingham, and for the first time in his life living more than a mile or two from the sea.

Returning to my narrative, the first Fastnet Race *Cohoe III* entered was in 1957 and was said to be one of the roughest in Fastnet history. I had a very strong crew: Ross, Alan Mansley, our met expert, Patrick Madge and Peter Nicholson, the son of the designer and a brilliant helmsman, later the chairman of Camper & Nicholsons.

Forty-one entries crossed the Royal Yacht Squadron's starting line at Cowes on Saturday morning, August 10th in really dirty weather. It was described as a south-westerly gale. Force 8 was reported at the Scillies and Force 6 and 7 at two neighbouring inland weather stations. *Cohoe III* started under staysail and had a few turns rolled in her mainsail. She was carrying relatively more sail than others and the conditions suited her, for she quickly took the lead in her class; by the time she had reached the Needles she had overhauled many of the Class II and Class I yachts which had started earlier.

36. Mamie launching *Cohoe III*. Author left and Charles A Nicholson the designer right.

By the late evening *Cohoe III* in a mass of spray had beaten across Bournemouth Bay, past St Alban's Head, which was shrouded in driving rain, and had arrived off Portland, where she just missed her tide, with *Myth of Malham* and another yacht within sight ahead. It was spring tides and, with 4 knots against us, our speed over the bottom slowed down, and before long night fell upon us. On deck all was dark except the friendly orange glow of the compass and the reflections of the navigation lights. The cold regular four white flashes of Portland Bill lay on our starboard bow. The watch on deck were secured by safety harness, and they needed it, for every sea broke aboard forward, and in the gusts the boat lay far over.

Down below the aft end of the cabin was like a half-tide rock. As each sea struck the cabin top forward, it came streaming aft, flooding through the aft hatch and the companionway doors one of which had broken. Both quarter berths were swamped and the chart table unusable, so I had to spread the sodden chart on the table at the forward end of the saloon.

Navigation was a whole-time job as we were skirting Portland Race, with the spare man on deck taking hand bearings on Portland Lighthouse. It was also physically difficult, as I was thrown about so much. Progress was desperately slow, as it always is when rounding a headland against a foul tide, but hour by hour the bearing changed and I was able to plot each position a little west of the last one. Regularly the boat needed pumping. Masses of water found its way into the bilges. We had two pumps, but the one in use was situated in the cabin with a long hose which was led into the cockpit, so that the water returned to the sea via the self-emptying drains. I took it in turns with the spare man to pump. Only one remained on deck at a time except when taking bearings, for it is a mistake to expose two to the flying spray and the cold of the night for longer than necessary. The watches were four-hourly, but the spells at the helm off Portland were fifteen minutes only.

Beating to windward in a gale the helmsman should luff to the crests and bear away sharply at the top, so that the boat falls into the troughs on the other side at an angle to the seas and regains speed until she luffs again to the next crest. The boat should be kept weaving in the seas. Off Portland *Cohoe III* very occasionally fell off irregular wave formations and came down on her stem with a most dreadful shock. This was not a matter of ordinary, regular pounding as is found in many yachts, but it was the effect of nearly 8 tons weight of boat throwing herself at 6 knots over the crest of a big sea and falling on her stem on water that sounded as hard as a roadway. In the saloon one wondered how timber construction could stand such treatment, and after each impact I would lift the saloon floorboards to check whether there was an inrush of water resulting from damage forward, but my anxiety was uncalled for. Peter remarked that he thought for this sort of work an ocean racer should be double-diagonal planked.

As we soldiered on against both wind and tide progress seemed desperately slow, but inch by inch we edged through off the tail of the race and by the midnight change of watch we had broken through and lay about 2 miles to the SW of Portland Bill.

Shortly after midnight, when the new watch had taken over, I was called on deck, as the helmsman thought we were carrying too much sail. When I took the tiller I found that he was right. The wind had freshened to Force 8 (34–40 knots) gusting higher in the squalls, and though the yacht was sailing grandly she was hard pressed and there was a risk of things carrying away.

It was time to shorten sail. Patrick and Peter rolled the mainsail down, bringing the peak to the upper spreaders, the staysail was lowered and the storm jib set. All this was done as smartly as if in daylight in the Solent. But alas we were now over-reefed, and I had forgotten that the storm jib, an old-fashioned one which was roped all round and never hitherto used, was cut too full to be of service as a racing sail. *Cohoe III* sagged badly to leeward and there are unlighted buoys to the west of Portland Bill. Under reduced sail we could no longer clear them and it was improbable that they would be spotted in the dark in time to avoid collision. We were forced to come on to starboard tack, bringing the weakening foul tide on our beam and thus losing much of the distance that had been so hard earned.

I have clear impressions in my memory of that outward tack. The moon appeared between the clouds racing overhead and at times the boat and sea were bathed in light. The waves were high, but under reduced sail the boat was an easy match for them. A yacht passed close ahead of us, running east under bare poles, her port light shining brightly. (It must have been *Inschallah* who had her deck-house stove in by a sea and, after making distress signals, was escorted by a lifeboat to Weymouth.)

We tacked 5 miles out and I then handed over and turned in. Both quarter berths were flooded out, so I took the root berth in the fo'c'sle, which is supposed to be untenable in a gale. At each plunge of the boat I felt I was left in the air, and put my hand up to prevent being struck by the deck above. Sleep was out of the question, though I managed to get a modest degree of rest.

The wind moderated in the early hours of the following morning (Sunday 11th), falling to Force 7 and, after the change of watch, the staysail was reset and some of the turns in the mainsail were let out. It remained rough going in driving rain over forlorn grey seas the whole way across Lyme Bay, but we made better progress with more sail. To cut a long story short, the over-reefing west of Portland Bill lost us a lot of time, for the delay caused us to miss our tide for Start Point. I put into Dartmouth for shelter during the foul tide.

This enabled us to carry out a number of small but useful repairs. Some of the screws in the mast track were beginning to work loose and it was essential to tighten them up, repairs were made to a broken cabin door and I nailed canvas across the aft end of the coachroof and hatch to keep some of the water out of the quarter berths and chart table. It also gave us the opportunity to get a hot meal on a level table, and with the aid of two primuses to dry the cabin and our masses of wet clothes.

Once in shelter there is sometimes a reluctance to put to sea again, but on this occasion there was no delay, thanks partly to Alan, who kept us up to the mark. We left early on the tide and got past Start Point close to the rocks in the early slack. The wind had moderated and next morning (Monday 12th) we sighted *Elseli IV*, the Swedish entry which rated at the top of our class. The race was on again and over the remaining 500 miles of the course was bitterly contested, the two boats rarely being out of sight of each other.

West of the Lizard the wind went light and *Elseli IV*, with her big masthead rig, gained on us steadily tack by tack. She had left us far astern by the time we had rounded Land's End.

Luckily for *Cohoe III*, the wind freshened again, and we found ourselves hard on the wind for much of the 180-mile stretch across St George's Channel. The wind was about Force 6 to Force 7 (some say Force 8), so it was a tough passage pressed under staysail and whole mainsail. Both boats arrived off the Irish coast on Wednesday morning, 14th, almost at the same time. Meanwhile the wind had veered to the north-west and headed us, so that our landfall was some 20 miles east of the Fastnet Rock, whereas the leading yachts should have been able to fetch it on one tack.

We scored a few miles off *Elseli IV* by standing in to the Irish coast and tacking inside the Stag Rocks, thus getting an earlier fair tide and smoother water under the lee of the land. Off Baltimore we all looked longingly towards the soft contours of Ireland lying so alluringly close on the starboard hand, but there was little time for such idle thoughts, for *Elseli IV* was not far astern, and by the time we had rounded the Fastnet Rock at 1340 she was snapping at *Cohoe III*'s heels.

The run of 150 miles from the Fastnet Rock to the Bishop Rock SW of the Scilly Isles provided closely contested racing between the two of us. *Elseli IV* had lost her spinnaker boom, but running under mainsail and boomed-out genoa she gained on us and steered a straighter course. *Cohoe III* carried all sail with her biggest spinnaker bellying out against the light blue sky and the dark blue white-crested seas. At 1610 we gybed and, with an increasing wind, she became almost unmanageable at times in the big quartering seas, forcing her to tack downwind too much. But for two hours she logged over 8 knots, far in excess of the maximum theoretical speed of a short-ended boat of only 26ft waterline. For a while *Elseli IV* must have done better, for her log showed a steady 8 or 9 knots, and when surfing the needle was up to 11 knots. Gustav Plym describes the surfing in his book *Yacht and Sea* as 'really fantastic and something that none of us had ever experienced before in such a relatively large boat . . . it was fascinating and, to tell the truth – slightly terrifying'.

At nightfall *Cohoe III* lowered her spinnaker and set her genoa. It was blowing hard and the seas were building up. The night was rough and at 0515 next morning all hands were called to gybe on to an easterly course for the Bishop Rock. This was a tricky job in the seas which Gustav Plym described as 'high breaking mountains of water', because of the weight of the wind in the full mainsail and the risk of breaking something or broaching as the boom went over, but the crew managed it smartly, and we sped on over the sea.

When dawn came there was no sight of *Elseli IV* as we raced eastward. The wind had if anything increased, for it was blowing a good Force 7, possibly Force 8, and was reported as being Force 9; *Cohoe III*'s speed had risen again to over 8 knots. This was fortunate, because the two adversaries met again just west of the Bishop. *Elseli IV* had lost time when two slides of her mainsail broke, and she reduced sail to avoid being pooped, but she had steered direct as compared with *Cohoe III*'s involuntary tacking downwind. There was a tumultuous sea in the overfalls west of the Bishop, for here there was the full fetch of the Atlantic into a weather-going tide. *Elseli IV* was being driven through it all out. She made a spectacular sight and at times was almost lost to sight in the troughs of the waves. Gustav Plym, her owner, told me afterwards that she broached-to twice, but neither boat suffered any harm.

The seas were lower south of the Scillies and the wind gradually moderated throughout the day on the 80-mile run to Plymouth, though a gale warning was repeated at noon. Off Land's End the wind had softened sufficiently to enable *Cohoe III* to reset her spinnaker. *Elseli IV* could not respond owing to the loss of her spinnaker boom, and thus *Cohoe III* crossed the line with a lead of half an hour to win Class III by four hours on corrected time; we were sixth overall in the three classes.

It had been a great battle between the British and the Swedish entries, which proved to be the only two small-class boats left in the race. *Elseli IV*'s owner (Gustav Plym) was elected 'Yachtsman of the Year' in Sweden and I received a similar honour in Great Britain.*

Dick Nye in the Class I American yawl *Carina* won the Fastnet Cup as well as five other trophies. Hers was a well merited victory as she had received considerable structural damage forward early in the race, having fallen on a wave when emerging from the Needles Channel into the English Channel, where the tearing ebb tide met the full force of the gale. John Illingworth's *Myth of Malham* won Class II.

Besides *Carina* many other boats had suffered major damage. Our rival *Elseli IV* broke three frames off Portland, *Maze* was dismasted, Chris Ratsey's *Evenlode* damaged her rudder, and five winches on Sir Max Aitken's *Drumbeat* broke under the strain. A serious accident occurred in *Galloper* when a member of the crew coming on deck from below was catapulted overboard by a sea; his rescue was an outstanding feat of seamanship in the wild seas running at the time. Of the forty-one starters in all classes, only twelve completed the course.

*   *   *

In the Fastnet Races of 1959 and 1961 *Cohoe III* won a fourth place in each; the latter event was interesting as a small but vigorous secondary depression moved quickly from the Bay of Biscay across to the Isles of Scilly, intensifying as it went. Many boats, including my own, were caught out between the Wolf Rock and the Scillies.

The wind rose very suddenly and, after blowing out our spinnaker at 1935, we ran under a new Terylene storm jib (which had replaced that stupid bag of a sail used in 1957) without any loss of speed. Everything was blotted out by rain. The gap between the Longships and the Seven Stones light-vessel is 12 miles wide and we tore on in the gathering gloom seeing nothing at all, though we must have passed near the Seven Stones before we emerged into the open sea of St George's Channel.

The barometer touched its lowest at midnight followed by a veer to NNW later. It was intensely black, the rain absolutely torrential and the visibility nil. There was one brilliant flash of lightning, but it lit nothing but the rain-swept smoking seas. When daylight came the wind moderated and the rest of the race was uneventful. The gale caused the RORC Committee some anxiety as so many of the yachts were caught in narrow waters with a risk of getting on a lee shore. However, there were few mishaps as the majority of the racing fleet had found temporary shelter or retired. Sustained winds of Force 9, and possibly storm Force 10 at times, were experienced for about three hours, with violent squalls and gusts (over 60 knots was recorded at the Lizard). Altogether 33 boats out of 95 starters retired before lighter weather followed for the rest of the race.

*   *   *

All previous records in numbers were eclipsed in the Fastnet Race of 1963, when the entries numbered 132 of which 48 were in Class III which alone equalled the total in all

---

* After receiving this award, I used to be invited to the annual lunches given by Sir Max Aitken for leading journalists and previous Yachtsmen of the Year, to consider and vote on the forthcoming award. Max, himself a very experienced ocean racing man, was always a splendid host, and I much looked forward to these happy occasions where I met so many friends and interesting people.

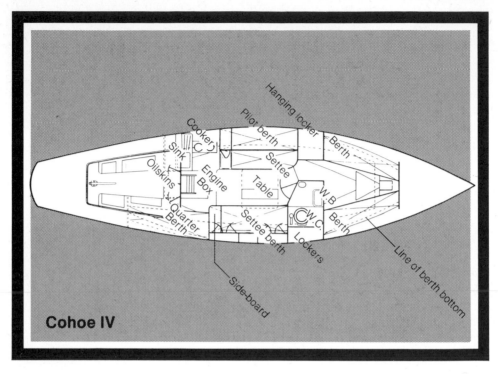

17. *Cohoe IV.*

LOA	36ft 3ins	Beam	9ft 6ins
LWL	26ft	Draught	5ft 11ins
Tons TM	11	Tons disp	7·5

classes in 1957. It was the year when the Admiral's Cup was recovered from America, against hot international competition.

I was racing a new Class III yacht *Cohoe IV*, one of the successful class of fibreglass Nicholson 36-footers. Her dimensions were 36ft 3ins LOA, 26ft LWL, 9ft 6ins beam, 5ft 11ins draught and 7·52 tons displacement. With longer ends she had a more easily driven hull and, when heeled, she had a longer immersed waterline giving her a higher theoretical maximum speed. Her measured sail area was 543 sq ft, compared with *Cohoe III*'s sail area (as increased) of 615 sq ft, and her RORC rating was over a foot lower. The new boat had a nice sheer and was handsome; she looked just right, and with higher freeboard and beam she was much roomier than the older boat. Nevertheless, she faced hot competition as many new and well designed yachts had been added to Class III, and to win the Fastnet Challenge Cup she would have to beat on corrected time all the international competitors entered for the Admiral's Cup.

At 1400 on Saturday August 10th there was half a gale of wind from the south-west for the start; this was quite enough with from forty to fifty entries in each class milling around the line, battling to get into the narrow fair eddy inshore off Cowes Green. It was not surprising that in the mêlée there were two collisions, one of which was serious. The wind and sailing conditions were similar to the early part of the Fastnet Race of 1957, but with rather less wind.

Cohoe IV started under small genoa and two rolls in her mainsail, and in the rough and tumble of breaking weather-going seas in the West Solent, and off Anvil Point and St Alban's Head, she worked out a lead in the same way as *Cohoe III* had done in 1957. In fact, she proved herself to be rather better, as off Portland Bill she was lying sixth in the whole fleet on elapsed time, boat for boat without handicap.

However, *Cohoe IV* probably saved at least an hour by taking the inside passage in the gap between Portland Bill and the Race. When bound westward in moderate weather this affords a short cut, with a fair tide between one hour before and two hours after high water Dover. What was not then so generally known is that this passage can also be used (with care and under suitable conditions) against a foul tide. Besides Ross (who knew Portland and the Inner Channel well by day), I had a strong crew in Alan Mansley, Dr Rex Binning, David Colquhoun and Keith Hunt, an Irishman with a great sense of humour, so no one was perturbed at the idea of the short cut at night through the unlit channel at the wrong state of the tide. At the time this tactic was a pioneering one, but since then it is often adopted in Fastnet racing.

When *Cohoe IV* approached Portland breakwater at 2236 we were lucky, as the wind moderated to about Force 5, permitting the mainsail to be unreefed and the big genoa to be set in smooth water under the lee of the peninsula. The lights on the breakwater were close when we tacked, and behind them lay the bright lights of Castletown with the high dark land mass of Portland itself fading into the sky to the southward. Four of us were on deck: the watch of two with Ross forward acting as local pilot and handling the genoa sheets round the mast when tacking, while I was at the helm and responsible aft.

At first progress was slow, as we had a weak tide against us, but off Grove Point we came into the fair eddy and passed through modest overfalls. The interesting part lay between Grove Point and the Bill, as we tacked between Portland and the Race. Except for occasional breakers it was not rough inshore, because the overfalls in the Race of Portland formed a kind of breakwater. On the offshore tacks the brilliant group flash of Portland lighthouse gave us something on which to take bearings. The inshore tacks were more difficult. The closer we could get to the cliffs the better, but here Portland light was obscured and it was difficult to judge distance at night. We used the echo-sounder constantly. Soon we had over a knot of fair eddy, but the farther south we got the nearer to the land we had to keep. On the inshore tacks Ross threw the beam of our powerful electric signal lamp on the cliffs.

Progress as we approached the Bill was increasingly fast and each tack had to be shorter, for the Race lay close to the south. At the Bill we came close in to the rocks. I have never viewed the lighthouse at night from so near at hand. It was a lovely sight, with big windows, the upper one with a white light and the lower with a red. In the background were car lights and lights in a big building. To seaward all was dark and black as pitch.

It was only a glimpse, because we tacked close to the lighthouse just before midnight and only made a short board before coming round again. Here lies the crisis of the inside passage against the flood stream. At that state of the tide the whole weight of the

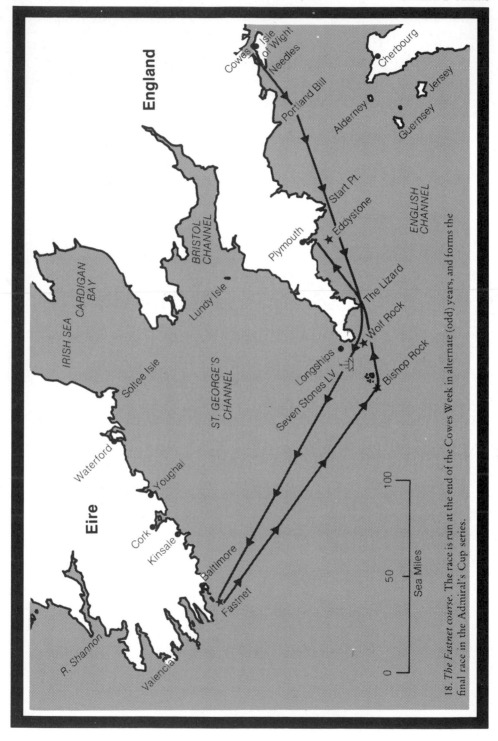

18. *The Fastnet course.* The race is run at the end of the Cowes Week in alternate (odd) years, and forms the final race in the Admiral's Cup series.

easterly-going stream is diverted off the west side of Portland and accelerates south-wards, pouring past the Bill at 5 knots or more headlong into Portland Race, less than half a mile to the south-east.

37. *Cohoe IV*, class III winner Fastnet Race 1963 and 2nd overall.   (*Beken*)

Throwing *Cohoe IV* on the the port tack, we stood as close to the end of the Bill as we dared in the darkness; but very quickly the boat was seized by the southerly set of the stream. We responded by checking off the sheets and reaching at maximum speed, but even with the strong free wind off the Bill and lee-bowing the tide we were set almost a cable south towards the Race, before we gradually broke through into the weaker stream.

The elapsed times taken at Portland were:

1. *Bolero* (Class I) 7·05; 2. *Capricia* (Class I) 7·30; 3. *Dyna* (Class I) 8·45; 4. *Outlaw* (Class I) 9·35; 5. *Stormvogel* (Class I) 9·40; 6. *Cohoe IV* (Class III) 9·50.

Portland Bill marked the end of the short spell of heavy weather, and over the rest of the course there were only moderate winds and almost a calm off the Irish coast and near the Fastnet Rock. *Cohoe IV* won Class III with the French *Pen-ar-Bed* second, just saving her time by two minutes on *Belmore II* placed third. We failed by only six minutes to win the Challenge Cup for the first place overall in all classes, including the competitors in the Admiral's Cup, being beaten by the Class II *Clarion of Wight*, then owned by Derek Boyer and Dennis Miller. This was the closest we ever came to winning the Fastnet outright, but I lost no sleep over it, as we were lucky to do as well as we did; I consoled myself by remembering that we had created something of a record in being placed four times running, with two firsts in our Class. The winner of Class I that year was the American yawl *Figaro* owned by Bill Snaith, but the Admiral's Cup was regained by Great Britain.

In the Class III Points Championship for the year, *Cohoe IV* just won by the narrow margin of 31 points, with 7033 against her very sporting French rival *Pen-ar-Bed* who had 7002 points.

✳   ✳   ✳

The last race of the season was to La Rochelle, where the crew returned to England and Mamie joined me to cruise back to Bursledon visiting French harbours and anchorages for checking my pilot books. On return I sold *Cohoe IV* as I could not afford two yachts on my hands for long. Mamie preferred *Cohoe III* as she was smaller, and I continued to get satisfactory racing results from the older boat.

In 1965 the principal events were the first of the new series of the historic International One-Ton Cup races, which consisted of two 30-miles 'round the buoys' races and a long distance one; these were to be held at Le Havre July 22–28th. The British entries were sponsored by the RORC and, after tough selection trials, the three boats chosen to represent Great Britain were *Golden Samphire* (J A Sampson), *Ilex II* (Royal Engineer YC) and *Cohoe III* with Ross as mate, Alan Mansley, Keith Hunt and David Colquhoun. To be eligible all competitors had to rate at not more than the maximum RORC rating of 22ft; subject to this the events provided the innovation of level racing without handicap. There were fourteen entries representing eight countries. Competition was strong as two Sparkman & Stephens designed yachts were entered, the redoubtable *Hestia* for Holland and the new *Diana III* for Denmark and several boats were specially designed and built for the races.

The principal point-winning event was the long distance race of 240 miles over a triangular course in winds of varying strength. Fortunately for us there was a good

Force 7 during the first night, providing a tough beat to windward to the CH 10 buoy, the westerly mark off Cherbourg in which *Cohoe III* recovered nearly all the time she lost in the light winds in the earlier part of the race. However, the Danish entry *Diana III* won, beating *Cohoe III* by twenty minutes, with *Ilex II* fourth. I am afraid that this was the only race in which any of us was placed.

However, the racing was a most enjoyable experience in which a wide interest was taken. It had been a privilege to participate in the pioneer races on level rating, which were to become one of the great annual events in the international yachting calendar. In 1974, nearly ten years later, the International One-Ton Cup came to Great Britain, being won by *Gumboots*, owned by Jeremy and Jonathan Rogers and Derek Pitt-Pitts.

* * *

I qualified for the old age pension in 1966 (although I did not take it until I reached 70) and I had much more time for sailing than when I was younger. I had *Cohoe III*'s sail plan increased to move her up from Class III to Class II, and that year we had the best possible conditions in the Cowes Dinard Race. There was a fresh or strong head wind for the first 100 miles to the south-west of Guernsey, where we picked up the early inshore eddy as close as I dared to the unnumerable drying rocks north and north-west of Les Hanois lighthouse, which is the most westerly mark before altering course to the south for the Dinard finishing line. The race proved to be one of the best *Cohoe III* ever sailed, as she was the first in her class and second overall, being beaten only by G P Pattinson's Class I *Fanfare* by 35 minutes. Geoff had been a racing friend dating back to the Santander race of 1948.

However, it was in the 500 miles race to Spain, the Yarmouth to Lequeitio event, that any boat of mine was nearly dismasted since 1923. The crew in this race consisted of John Patterson (who often came on long races across the Bay of Biscay), Keith Hunt and David Colquhoun (both of whom had raced in the One-Ton events) and Derek Ide; the latter two, besides being first-rate racing men, were experts in carpentry and metalwork.

After a bad start *Cohoe III* made some 40 miles to Portland Bill in fast time, hard on the wind all the way. This attained Force 6 to Force 7 for two hours (by Brookes and Gatehouse anemometer), but never Force 8 as some yachts reported; later the wind fell to Force 5 and the masthead genoa was reset. Coming in on Portland Bill nothing could be seen in the thick rain and fog until, on account of bad visibility (as I learnt later), at 2040 the light was exhibited early. It stood high up when sighted, not much more than a quarter of a mile distant. We tacked immediately and went through the Race, which was rough although nearly slack at the time. Some two hours later, with *Cohoe* under full sail with a wind of only about Force 4 to 5, the speed on the Harrier speedometer suddenly fell to only 4 knots. On investigation forward by electric torch it was found that the stainless steel bowsprit, to which the forestay was set, had crumpled because a weld had broken. The bowsprit was made of triple part, 1½in diameter tubular stainless steel and was supposed to be unbreakable, although by then it was possibly suffering from fatigue. It was a miracle that the mast had not gone over the side.

All hands were called and *Cohoe III* was run off to take the weight off the mast.

David and Derek carried out the repairs while Keith and John stood by the halyards and helped with the electric torches. First the fore halyard was shackled to the old stemhead fitting (which luckily had not been removed when the bowsprit was added) and set up hard by winch to provide a temporary forestay. Next the turnbuckle was taken off the broken bowsprit and unshackled from the forestay, which was then set up to the stemhead by means of a Terylene lanyard with many turns. The fore halyard was then released and the staysail set.

The repairs took David and Derek an hour, which was quick when everything had to be thought out on a pitch black night running east contrary to our course in what was still quite a roughish sea. We steered under short canvas for Brixham to get more permanent repairs, but when daylight came we found the temporary repairs so good that it seemed safe to carry on with the race rather than to give up, which was then contrary to RORC tradition. The loss of time owing to the accident was about six hours before reaching Ushant and, ill-balanced with a shortened fore-triangle, much speed was lost over the rest of the course except for a period when we were able to set a spinnaker in the Bay of Biscay. As a result we were placed poorly in the race and in the following one to La Trinité, but we enjoyed the visit to the unsophisticated little harbour and town of Lequeitio. Over the season *Cohoe III* was first in the Dinard and Channel Races, and third in the Morgan Cup; she thus managed to be placed third in the Class II Points Championship. During the winter the steel bowsprit was replaced by a new one of different shape.

My last year of ocean racing was in 1967, which was a Fastnet year; yachting was booming and there were so many entries that Class II was divided in the results into (a) and (b) divisions. *Cohoe III* was sixth in Class II(b) both in the Fastnet Race and the Points Championship for the year, which was satisfactory in a class and division which included boats such as Dick Carter's *Rabbit II*.

In the following year I sold *Cohoe III* at rather a low price, perhaps because potential buyers may have imagined she had been strained by hard driving, which was far from being the case. Eventually she was resold to a young couple who sailed her to South America and back. She was in poor condition on return to England from her voyages, but in 1979 found a ready buyer who I am told is putting everything in order. *Cohoe III* was superbly built and I hope many happy cruising years lie ahead for her.

CHAPTER TWENTY-SIX

MORE PUBLISHING

By 1961 our publishing list both of yachting and books on ships was well established. The most notable book we published that year was *Passenger Liners* by Laurence Dunn, an authority on the subject, whose earlier book *Ship Recognition: Merchant Ships* had been such a success. His work on liners made a 466 large page book with nearly 400 plates printed on heavy art paper; it was a magnificent volume and backed by extensive advertising was an outstanding success.

However, the heaviest demand on my time came from a 264 page annual named *Merchant Ships—World Built*. It consisted of twenty sections; an alphabetical register of new vessels of 1,000 tons gross and upwards delivered each year, a list of ship owners of the world giving new vessels completed for them, and seventeen sections covering each country showing the output of each shipyard, together with some 200 photographs or plans and descriptions of the principal new ships. The first edition of this annual appeared in 1954, covering ships completed in 1953, and had acquired a distinguished list of subscribers and advertisers throughout the world, other than in countries behind the Iron Curtain.

The snag about an annual on new ships was that it had to be published as early as possible (mid-May) in the year following that in which the new ships were completed. This left only four months for my final editing (including writing introductions for each section), mock-up of pages and dealing with the advertising side followed by the production, printing and binding. I had the help of four good secretaries in the rush period and the work on the annual was always interesting. Nevertheless it was all high pressure stuff coming on top of my principal occupation of publishing yachting and nautical books and writing my own ones. Besides these occupations I was chairman of a small public company, Southern Counties Hotels (Southampton) Ltd until my former accountancy partner, Stanley Saunders, took over; I continued as a non-executive director until 1979.

In 1961 I continued working long hours when ashore, some eighty-five a week, which was fair enough seeing that I was away sailing so much in the summer months, but in that year something occurred which considerably altered my future publishing life. A distant acquaintance of mine who ran a one-man business was incapacitated in a road accident and his concern had to be sold up. When I heard of this I began for the first time to think about what would happen to Adlard Coles Ltd, if I were involved in a similar accident or became incapacitated by illness as I had no successor. The more I thought about the matter the clearer it became that the time had come to capitalise and sell the business while I was alive and kicking, and capable of transferring the goodwill to the purchasers.

My first action was to see Walter Harrap, then the chairman and managing director of George Harrap & Co Ltd our distributors, who had first refusal of the business in the event of a sale, but we failed to come to agreement on terms. I met a few other leading publishers, all of whom were interested in the idea of a take-over, but the obvious choice was Rupert Hart-Davis Ltd, publishers of the legendary Mariner's Library. I knew and occasionally lunched with one of the directors and through him satisfactory arrangements were concluded in 1962, when Adlard Coles Ltd became a subsidiary of Rupert Hart-Davis Ltd. It was in the nature of a merger of interests in common as I continued as a director with part-time advisory duties. Rupert Hart-Davis, an outstanding personality, was later knighted for services to literature. He had wide experience of pre-war publishing and, when he started his own company after hostilities were over, it became one of the most notable among the 'new' publishers. Among others, Walter Harrap heartily approved of the link up.

When I joined Rupert Hart-Davis Ltd the company had the financial backing of one of the leading American educational publishers, but they suddenly decided to dispose of their British interests and in December 1963 the company was acquired by Granada Publishing and this, of course, included Adlard Coles Ltd being the subsidiary company. I remained chairman of Adlard Coles Ltd and Richard Creagh-Osborne (whose name needs no introduction from me) was editor and also a director. Richard and I were soon invited to lunch by Mr Sidney L Bernstein the chairman of Granada, at their offices at Golden Square, London, where we met him and other directors for the first time. I found him to be a big man of considerable unostentatious charm, with wide interests, including authors among whom he had many friends. As the chairman of one of the most efficient television enterprises in the world he was rather taken aback to hear that I did not own a television set so, perhaps to improve my education in this respect, a week or two later Richard and I were invited to Manchester to see the centre of Granada television activities. A private Dove aircraft was sent to pick us up at Southampton Airport and bring us back. We had an extremely interesting day and were impressed by all we saw.

An unfortunate incident occurred later when full page advertisements appeared in the yachting press starting and ending with my personal name. I considered the wording was couched in flamboyant terms and, as I was chairman of the company bearing my name, readers might naturally assume that it had been inserted with my approval. I put in a complaint to Sidney Bernstein and showed him a photostat copy of the advertisements. He said at once he would not like it himself and immediately ruled that my personal name as an individual must not be used for publicity of the limited company; this was duly minuted and settled the point amicably for good.

In 1967 I signed an author's agreement with the company in respect of the book I was writing entitled *Heavy Weather Sailing* which proved the most successful I have ever written and in its way was a best seller. Since then over 100,000 copies have been printed in the English language alone and translations have been arranged into eight other languages.

Nevertheless, I found various difficulties in working in such a large group and eventually I retired by mutual agreement and left Adlard Coles Ltd on 30th September, 1967. I had been quite open with the directors of Granada informing them that I intended to start a new publishing company. Sidney Bernstein, now Lord Bernstein LLD, was one of the most remarkable personalities I have had the privilege to meet. I had a great respect for him and oddly enough I think he had a measure of respect for me on account of my independence in proposing to start up a new publishing venture a year after the normal 65 year age of retirement; my relations with him and the company which bears my name have remained friendly to this day.

I had not proposed to create another one-man business for, if I did so, I would fall back into the same trap as caused me to sell Adlard Coles Ltd, namely the risk of illness or premature demise. The intention was to form a publishing business in partnership with Commander Erroll Bruce, my erstwhile rival in the Bermuda and Transatlantic races. When he retired from the Royal Navy in 1961 he had taken an appointment as editor of the *Motor Boating and Yachting* which he ran successfully, introducing many new features, and had only retired in order to join our publishing venture. In the capacity of an editor he met innumerable sailing people, and was himself the author of three yachting books, of which the most successful was his work on *Deep Sea Sailing*. Besides this he was very energetic and did much honorary work as a member of the Council of the RYA and other committees; in short he had exceptionally high qualifications for starting to publish yachting books. Erroll and his wife Daphne lived at Lymington, the very pleasant harbour town in the West Solent which was ideal for our publishing as it is a considerable centre of yachting and racing activity, and within easy reach of London by road or rail.

Mamie and I were still living on the Hamble River at Bursledon, so we had to find a new home quickly in Lymington. We were lucky in this as, after a short search with the help of a good local estate agent, Mamie found a small house in Woodside only five minutes by car from the centre of the town, yet situated in unspoilt countryside only a short walk to the old salterns and sea wall facing the Solent, and within hearing distance of the Needles foghorn which I knew so well when returning from sailing foreign in foggy weather.

The new business was set up as a partnership which we registered under the Business Names Act as the Nautical Publishing Company. In the meantime I had visited Harraps, who had been book distributors for Adlard Coles Ltd until my company was sold. My particular friend Paull Harrap, who had been sales director was now managing director, and he and the board agreed to take over the book distribution for the new firm on the same terms as before. Our office to start with was at Erroll and Daphne Bruce's large house in Captain's Row. We now had a name, an address, a secretary, distributors; the only thing we lacked was books to be distributed. Erroll had started on the *Who's Who in Yachting*, but this was a tremendous task as it was to make a volume with some 4,000 entries which could not be published until the following year; it was a mine of information to which I still often refer, particularly so while writing the present book.

However, Douglas Phillips-Birt, one of my first authors and a friend of long standing, came to the rescue. For sixteen years he had contributed a monthly column to the *Yachting Monthly* under the pseudonym of 'Argus', in which he wrote on this and that according to his fancy at the time of writing. Douglas was exceptionally well read and a notably good author, his work being spiced with a great sense of humour. From his Argus material, gathered over the years, he made a selection of the best into two books *Reflections on Yachts* and *Reflections in the Sea* which we published in 1968 as our first two books. It is sad to have to add that Douglas, who had done so much to help, died about eight years later while still only in his middle fifties.

Mamie and also Charles Seyd, the South of England representative of Harrap's, had more than once suggested that we ought to try to get the rights in a book by Alec Rose, who was engaged in making his famous single-handed voyage round the world, but I had taken no action because I felt sure that he would have placed the rights with a publisher before he sailed from England. However, life is a strange thing in its ups and downs and unforeseen turns.

I was seeing quite a lot of Douglas Phillips-Birt while looking after the production of his new books. He lived in Southsea which was Alec Rose's home port, so I asked him whether he had heard of any arrangements about publication of a book on his return. By pure chance I struck lucky, for Douglas replied that he was a member of the Committee who were representing Alec Rose's interests while he was away and that, as yet, no arrangements had been made about a book. With Erroll Bruce's vigorous agreement I acted quickly and Douglas introduced me to Alec Rose's wife Dorothy and to the Committee, which included Sir David Mackworth an ocean racing friend of mine who also knew Harraps who would be doing our distribution. Alec Rose had arrived at Melbourne and a cable was sent to intercept him there and, with his approval, terms for the publication of his book were settled with the Committee. It was thus that we were incredibly lucky to have the privilege of publishing such an important book so early in the history of the new firm.

Alec Rose completed his voyage successfully on 4th July, 1968 and received a tremendous welcome. After being knighted by the Queen he was given many big receptions, so it was some while before he was able to visit Lymington and stay with Mamie and me to write his book. He was a charming visitor but very tired when he arrived after receiving so many honours at the end of his strenuous year of single-handed sailing round the world. We tried to feed him up, and happily we had fine sunny weather so that he could write quietly at a table on the lawn of the garden with only the call of the birds to disturb him. During his voyage he had kept a good log in pencil but this had to be turned into a book, aided by some chapters I had arranged to be written in advance to broaden the subject. He became something of a captive as we were working all out, it being vital that his book should be published well in time for Christmas. It was my job to help him and as fast as the pages were written Erroll Bruce had them typed for revision and final correction. Erroll took over the illustrations and organised the whole of the publicity. All went well and Alec's *My Lively Lady* was launched at a very big party which we gave for him at Covent Garden. It was all very exciting and Alec's book became third best seller of the year, after quick reprints due to the splendid co-operation of the printers.

The Nautical Publishing Company made remarkable progress, and by the end of the first three years the list had grown to over forty books, including fourteen publications in preparation. Among these were included new editions of two of my pilot books, *Creeks and Harbours of the Solent* and *Channel Harbours and Anchorages*, the rights of which had generously been returned to me by my former publishers, Edward Arnold & Co Ltd.

I retired finally from publishing towards the end of 1970 when Sir Peter Johnson took my place, buying my share in the firm which was then incorporated into a limited company with pleasant offices in Station Street, Lymington. The management formed a strong team with Erroll Bruce as chairman, Richard Creagh-Osborne and Peter Johnson, the leading expert in ocean racing rules. I remained with the company as consultant and was invited to be Honorary President, which I accepted with great pleasure.

It is with very great sadness that I have to record that Richard Creagh-Osborne died in 1980 at the age of 52. A former Olympic helmsman in the Finn Class, and champion in many other classes, he was an expert on the racing rules and all sailing subjects. He was a most gifted author and publisher, besides which he had many other literary and artistic interests; his wide experience provided the basis for his brilliantly successful book *This is Sailing*.

As a personality Richard was an enthusiast endowed with a tremendous sense of humour and proportion; busy as he was he always found time for other people. He did not know how to be unfair.

CHAPTER TWENTY-SEVEN

LIFE AT LYMINGTON

When I came home from the Boat Show in January 1969, Mamie said that the expression on my face was like that of the cat that had swallowed the canary. She then asked me what I had been up to, suspecting rightly that I had ordered a new boat.

Cohoe V, as I named her, was a 31ft 'half tonner' designed by Sparkman & Stephens, and one of the standard fibreglass class built by South Hants Marine. She was pretty to the eye, delightful to sail and had remarkable accommodation for her size. David Colquhoun bought a third share in her as we intended to put her through selection trials (which David won later) to be one of the entries representing Great Britain in the International Half-Ton Races to be held in Sweden at Sandhamn. I was very keen on this plan as, in addition to the highly competitive level rating races, I would have so much enjoyed the outward passage renewing my acquaintance with the North Sea, passing close off the Frisian Islands and then to the Baltic of which I had such happy memories.

Unfortunately, I developed a severe virus pneumonia in April which (coupled with another disability) knocked me out of racing for the season and put paid to our ambitious plans. So, instead of *Cohoe V* sailing to Sweden, a season of Junior Offshore racing was substituted. David with Derek Ide as mate proceeded to win almost every race they entered, together with the JOG Points Championship. At the end of the season I hurriedly withdrew my name as joint winner, for I had contributed little other than goodwill. When racing was over I had recovered in health sufficiently to enjoy a cruise with David and Derek checking over Brittany harbours for my pilot book.

Although I had failed to get to Sweden by sea, I got there the same year in a different way – by air. It happened this way. Norstedt & Söner had just published the Swedish edition of my book *Heavy Weather Sailing*, which had been translated by Gustav Plym, our rival in the 1957 Fastnet Race. To mark the occasion they had arranged with the principal Scandinavian yacht clubs for me to make a ten day tour at the publishers' expense giving lectures on heavy weather sailing. Mamie had also been invited but, sadly, could not accept as she was down with shingles and unwell at the time. Everything was planned in the utmost detail and I was sent a schedule of times of departure and arrival at each airport, together with the air tickets and the names of the hotels where I was to stay as guest of the yacht clubs.

I took off from Heathrow on October 7th for Helsinki where I arrived in the afternoon in high spirits as I like the city, and was the guest of the Nyländska Yacht Club from where in 1938 Mamie and I had made our last happy cruise in Finland. Next I was flown over the pine forests and lakes to Åbo (Turku). This was the home port of *Sjöfröken*; her owner Dr Mustelin, had died but his nephew asked me to his home and did everything to make my visit pleasant. The next destination was Stockholm where I spent a pleasant week-end until Mr Nils Dahlberg, a director of my Swedish publishers, arrived back from the Frankfurt book show on Monday. Despite being very busy on his return he took me to the Norstedt offices and for a run in his car to see Stockholm, with its gardens, lakes and glimpses of the sea; a lovely drive on a sunny morning.

My talk to the Royal Swedish Yacht Club was given the following day to a large gathering of yachtsmen, followed by a club dinner where I was introduced to many people, including Knud Reimers, the designer of my first *Cohoe*, one of the happiest and most successful boats I have owned.

Next I flew to Oslo and gave a talk to the Norwegian Ocean Racing and Cruising Club, where the Crown Prince presided in a charming and informal way. Oslo was the farthest north of my Scandinavian tour and from there I flew south to Gothenburg where an ocean racing friend, advocate Stig Konigsen, welcomed me to the Gothenburg Royal Sailing and Swedish Cruising Club.

My final talk was to be given to the Royal Danish Yacht Club. I was due to arrive by air at 1340, but the Commodore telephoned to tell me that there was fog over Copenhagen, so I had to make the journey by train from Gothenburg to Hålsingborg, then across the Sound by ferry and finally by train to Copenhagen. Owing to the fog I was late on arrival; the secretary of the club had almost given me up, but hurriedly drove me in his car to the Strandhotel Bellevue, situated on the north side of Copenhagen. I arrived somewhat dishevelled after the long day's travelling and much embarrassed at keeping the members waiting. However, after my talk to the members, there followed a most enjoyable evening as a guest of the Commodore, Mr Erik Dugdale and his wife. I met many friends at the dinner, including Hans Steffensen who had crewed in the first *Cohoe* and Hans Albrecht the winner of the One-Ton Cup for Denmark in *Diana III* when we were racing at Le Havre in 1965. I have a particular affection for Copenhagen because of happy memories of it when cruising in *Annette* and with Mamie in *Racundra*. I was sorry to leave the following afternoon when I was driven to the airport, and I arrived back in Lymington by 2100 after an eventful ten days marked by a warm welcome and personal hospitality wherever I went.

I found Mamie better and all well at home on my return from Copenhagen; the only problem was that of a boat. I had sold *Cohoe III* in part payment for *Cohoe V*, but clearly my racing days were over and, owing to her narrow keel, she was not suitable for drying out alongside quays when doing survey work on the French coast. David Colquhoun likewise did not wish to retain his share in her, so after keeping her in the Berthon Marina at Lymington we sold her to a racing owner in Bridlington who achieved considerable racing success with her. I was thus boatless for the first time in the past 50 years. Worse still, I had no time to look after a boat, even if I had one, as the shore work on pilot books is considerable and I had three such to revise.

However, I was soon to have a stroke of the extraordinary good fortune that I have so often experienced.

When Mamie and I first came to Lymington we were invited to stay with our old friends Major Bill Martineau (a former commodore of the Royal Lymington Yacht Club) and his wife Joan. When Bill Martineau had the misfortune to lose his eyesight (a disability which he bore with amazing courage) he had given his yacht *Sequel* to his nephew Dr Charles Sergel. As it chanced, Charles had followed me some ten years later to Clare College, Cambridge, where he became a distinguished rowing blue and later president of the CUBC. He had only recently taken up sailing, and invited me to sail with him as pilot to introduce him to the French coast or anywhere I needed to go revising my various pilot books. It was a wonderful arrangement at any rate for me!

Sequel was a roomy, comfortable 11-ton centreboard sloop, 34ft overall and 9ft beam, designed by Maurice Griffiths. She had a small easily handled sail area (Bill had intended to sail her often single-handed) and for cruising she had the great advantage of having only 4ft draught with the centreboard up, and was equipped with legs to take the bottom in shallow harbours. Another feature was her exceptionally good ground tackle, including fairly heavy anchors and chain, together with a heavy Worth traveller which, suspended from the chain when at anchor, immensely strengthened the holding power and prevented snubbing. The auxiliary engine was a 2-cylinder air-cooled Enfield diesel, of which we made considerable use, as a record number of harbours and anchorages had to be visited; it was also useful in the cold early morning hours or in bad weather as it warmed the bridge deck and hence one's bottom if sitting on it. In short, *Sequel* was an ideal boat for what was proposed. She was based on a mooring at Keyhaven, except during winter when she was laid up at Elkin's shipyard, Christchurch.

Charles himself, a tall athletic looking man, with greying hair and by nature extremely kind, made friends wherever we went. He soon found that sailing for a purpose such as checking harbours and anchorages, particularly out of the way ones, gave an added incentive to cruising and he enthusiastically threw his whole energy into it.

Our first cruise together started on Thursday August 13th, 1970, and *Sequel*'s crew consisted of Charles, his wife Betty and myself. The first port of call was Omonville, west of Cherbourg, followed by a week-end at Sark where we anchored under the lee of the island in La Grève de la Ville, as close to the shore as we dared. During the night it blew a gale which strengthened early on Sunday to a good Force 9, and the wind came down from the high land in violent gusts striking *Sequel* so that she heeled as though under sail.

We were glad of our good ground tackle, lying between the big bower with heavy chain supplemented by the Worth traveller, and a sizeable kedge anchor. The weather improved on Monday when we sailed to Jersey, picking up a good mooring in St Catherine Bay on the north-east side. The harbour is a pleasant one although there are few facilities and fierce tidal streams in the offing. It is open to easterly winds and sure enough, next morning, we received a forecast of a SE gale. We got under way at once and sailed through the somewhat tricky Violet Channel and along the south of Jersey to St Helier which we found on arrival was crowded. The gale duly developed in the night, but next morning the weather improved and we sailed round the Minquiers to St Malo where we met several good friends and had showers at the club.

Next day we passed through the locks into La Rance where we spent one night, experiencing a terrific current when the level of the water was suddenly reduced. Then we sailed westward visiting the shallow harbour of Ploumanach and the Sept Iles, some 4 miles to northward. The anchorage, which can be used only in suitable conditions, lies between the large Ile Bono (a bird sanctuary) and Ile aux Moines, a couple of miles SW of it, where there is a landing with a road up to the old fort, unoccupied since 1875, at the western end of the island. Continuing westward we sailed to Primel and the Ile de Batz, where Portz Kernoch was one of our favourite ports of call. After putting into L'Abervrach we crossed the English Channel bound for Falmouth, but in the early morning we had to anchor for a while in fog lying off the coast before proceeding to St Mawes. From there we coasted eastward calling at Fowey, Polperro, the Yealm, up the Dart to Dittisham and back to Hurst Roads.

The longest of our cruises was in 1972 with a friend of Charles named George Grimshaw, to the Morbihan, the always interesting inland sea first visited in the Bay of Biscay cruise which I have described earlier.

On our homeward passage we sailed to Ile de Molène, the little oval shaped rocky island lying about half-way between Ushant and Le Conquet on the French mainland. The houses above the harbour are clustered so close together that viewed from a distance they look more like a town than a village. When cruising in strong tidal areas among rocks the principal hazard is fog. After spending a night at Molène we were bound for Argenton about 12 miles distant on the mainland coast. Visibility was poor and becoming worse. When we made our landfall at Le Four lighthouse (at the southern end of the Porsall Inner Passage) the fog became absolutely dense with only 100 yards visibility. We had to cross almost blindfold in a tideway to come to the entrance of the cable wide approach to Argenton, which lies between the Melgorm rocks on the starboard hand which could not be seen, and a series of three red beacon towers on rocks to port which I relied on being visible. All went well and the look-out sighted the first beacon, for red shows up well in fog; after that there was no difficulty in piloting *Sequel* to temporary anchorage off Ile Dolven, to proceed to the village of Argenton when the fog had cleared and the tide served. After a day there with *Sequel* drying out on legs we sailed back to Lymington putting in at L'Abervrach, Ploumanach and St Peter Port.

On another occasion we had a spell of cruising on the South Coast of England, first to Plymouth sailing up to Cargreen and then to Falmouth spending a night at Mylor, before motoring on a lovely morning up river almost to Truro where we touched bottom even with the centreboard up before returning with a fair wind to Mylor. Then taking our departure from St Anthony lighthouse the same day at 1210 and sailing through the night across the channel, we arrived at L'Abervrach next morning at 0900. It was rather a tiring passage under engine with little wind coupled with swell and a cross sea. The following day provided real summer weather and we sailed through the Porsall Inner Passage (which is prickled with underwater rocks, where once I met visibility so bad that the leading marks could not be seen) passing again the channel leading to Argenton before rounding Le Four lighthouse and returning outside in open water to L'Aberbenoit. There we spent a lovely peaceful evening, with a red sunset reflected in the water and colouring the still boats lying at anchor in the river.

Continuing eastward we visited many interesting harbours including Port de Blos-con, Morlaix, Trébeurden and the anchorage off Ile Grande where, being neap tides, *Sequel* lay afloat anchored north-east of a red and white beacon tower bearing the imposing Breton name of 'Karrek ar Merk' and we went to the landing slip by dinghy. From the slip it is a pleasant $\frac{3}{4}$ mile walk to Kervolant, the village on Ile Grande, where there are small shops and restaurants. Next day we left by north-western approach passing very close to Ar Peulven, the conspicuous rock SW of Ile Losquet which is the key to approach or departure; the island is easy to identify as there is a radio mast on it. We then cruised home checking more harbours on the way.

The year 1974 was an eventful one for Mamie and me. In April we celebrated our golden wedding, giving a small dinner party for relations and old friends at the Royal Lymington Yacht Club. At that time Mamie's principal hobbies were painting in her studio and gardening; we had a very pretty one sheltered on two sides by an old brick wall.

The next event that year was of a different sort. For a time I had grumbling pains amidships and on a sunny, hot Whit Monday bank holiday, instead of sailing, I was rushed by ambulance to Southampton General Hospital where my appendix was operated on in the afternoon. By good fortune the surgeon was a friend of ours who lived at Bursledon, and to him I am deeply indebted, as the appendix had burst en route to the hospital and peritonitis had set in.

I was back sailing again with Charles the following year for a fortnight's cruise in the West Country and, after rounding the Lizard, we had lovely sunny weather and visited all the harbours and anchorages in Mount's Bay: Mullion, Porthleven, Penzance, Newlyn, Mousehole and the little drying harbour at St Michael's Mount, which is well worth seeing.

My last cruise with Charles, before swallowing the anchor, was in 1976 when we made a ten day trip (a record one for fog) on our own to check over the new marinas, the Port de Hérel at Granville and the Port des Sablons at St Malo.

Starting from Lymington at 0600 on Tuesday June 8th, we made Cherbourg by RDF (at which Charles was a dab hand) in very poor visibility. Next day the fog was worse, and the crossing to Alderney required great care to avoid being set into the Race and the rocks off the north coast of Alderney, before entering Braye harbour by RDF on the air beacon. Visibility improved next day and, after passing through the Swinge, we made St Catherine Bay in Jersey and entered Granville Marina the day following. Next we sailed to St Malo where we entered the huge then half-completed Port des Sablons. This was interesting and in the evening we walked to Les Bas Sablons itself where we found two good but inexpensive little restaurants. We returned to Granville on Sunday to complete information on matters such as Customs, lock signals, times of openings, moorings in the basin, facilities, etc.; it was sunny weather and I took many photographs some of which appear in my book *Channel Harbours and Anchorages*.

The real 'fun and games' part of our cruise started next day on our return passage, bound back from Granville to St Catherine Bay. All went well until it became foggy east of the Boeuf tower. We were more than half way to St Catherine Bay, only some

12 miles distant, when the fog became denser and Charles had to navigate entirely by RDF. There was little risk of striking chance rocks until we approached the bay, but visibility was down to a quarter of a mile when we drew close to St Catherine and the fierce tides in its offing.

Suddenly something loomed ahead in the fog which was taken as the pierhead, but as *Sequel* drew nearer another object was dimly sighted on the starboard bow, and this time it really was the end of the pier with its lighthouse. Under such conditions Charles had made a miraculous landfall, and we were soon safely in the anchorage enjoying a sunny afternoon with ices at the café.

Next morning, Tuesday, we set off bound for St Peter Port, Guernsey. Conditions at sea remained much the same as on the previous day. Charles did the navigation entirely by RDF as before; indeed he was engaged on it all day. There was no difficulty in getting through the wide gap between Dirouilles and the Paternosters, but once in open water navigation was not so easy as we were sailing at the top of spring tides which set *Sequel* well to the eastward. However, although late we duly made a landfall on Guernsey and brought up in St Peter Port. The rest was easy and we were back at Lymington precisely on time at the conclusion of Charles's ten day holiday.

In addition to longer cruises Charles and I, sometimes with Betty, did many shorter ones in long week-ends to Poole Harbour, Swanage, Chapman's Pool and Lulworth. Some of the happiest were made on the Cherbourg peninsula, putting into all the little harbours from Barfleur in the east to Anse de St Martin and Goury in the west.

I write about cruising with Charles Sergel in *Sequel* with particular gratitude, for without him and his enthusiasm I might never have been able to bring my pilot books up to date. In writing of this now that my sailing years are over, I am reminded also of many friends who lent me a helping hand during my life; their names would fill a book.

And of all my good fortune the greatest is my wife, Mamie, who came on our sailing honeymoon in *Annette* with her big trunk 56 years ago.

INDEX